The

DICTIONARY OF
POPULAR YIDDISH WORDS,
PHRASES, AND PROVERBS

The
DICTIONARY OF
POPULAR
YIDDISH WORDS,
PHRASES, AND
PROVERBS

Fred Kogos

𝄐

Citadel Press
Kensington Publishing Corp.
www.kensingtonbooks.com

CITADEL PRESS books are published by

Kensington Publishing Corp.
850 Third Avenue
New York, NY 10022

A Dictionary of Yiddish Slang & Idioms © 1966, 1967, 1995 Kogos
Publications Co.
Instant Yiddish © 1967, 1995 Fred Kogos
1001 Yiddish Proverbs © 1970 Fred Kogos

All Kensington titles, imprints, and distributed lines are available at special
quantity discounts for bulk purchases for sales promotions premiums,
fund raising, educational, or institutional use. Special book excerpts or
customized printings can also be created to fit specific needs. For details,
write or phone the office of the Kensington special sales manager: Kensington
Publishing Corp., 850 Third Avenue, New York, NY 10022, attn: Special Sales
Department, phone 1-800-221-2647.

Kensington and the K logo Reg. U.S. Pat. & TM Office
Citadel Press is a trademark of Kensington Publishing Corp.

First printing 1997

10 9 8 7 6 5 4 3 2

Printed in the United States of America

ISBN 0–8065–1885–5

The Cataloging-in-Publication Data for this title may be obtained from the
Library of Congress.

CONTENTS

A Dictionary of Yiddish Slang & Idioms

Contents

YIDDISH-ENGLISH

A bisel   A little
A biseleh   A very little
A braireh hob ich?   Do I have a choice?
A braiteh daieh hoben   To do all the talking (Lit., To have the greatest say or authority)
A broch!   Oh hell! Damn it! A curse!
A broch tsu dir!   A curse on you!
A broch tsu mir!   Woe is me! I have been cursed! (Lit., A curse to me!)
A brocheh   A blessing
A choleryeh ahf dir!   A plague on you!
A chazer bleibt a chazer!   A pig remains a pig!
A chissoren, di kaleh iz tsu shain!   Too bad that the bride is too pretty (Said of a novel or unjustified complaint)
A dank   Thanks, thank you
A deigeh hob ich   I don't give a hang. I don't care. I should worry.
A deigeh hob ich?   Is it my worry?
A farshlepteh krenk   A chronic ailment; particularly a lingering one
A feier zol im trefen   He should burn up!
A gezunt ahf dein kop!   Good health to you (Lit., Good health on your head)
A gezunt dir in pupik!   Thanks for a small favor! (Lit., Good health to your belly button!)
A glick ahf dir!   Good luck to you (Sometimes used sarcastically about minor good fortunes) Big thing!
A glick hot dir getrofen!   Big deal! (Sarcastic; lit., A piece of luck happened to you!)
A klog iz mir!   Woe is me!
A klog tzu meineh sonim!   A curse on my enemies!
A lebedikeh velt   Happy-go-lucky people (Lit., A lively world)

A leben ahf dir! You should live! (And be well—and
have much more!)

A lek un a shmek A worker who does his job insufficiently
gives this; you get this when a hostess serves peanut-size
hors d'oeuvres—and too few of them; neither here nor
there (Lit., A taste and a smell)

A lung un leber oyf der noz Stop talking yourself into
illness! (Lit., Don't imagine a lung and a liver upon the
nose)

A magaifeh zol dich trefen! A plague on you!

A makeh unter yenem's orem iz nit shver tzu trogen
Another man's disease is not hard to endure (Lit.,
A boil under another's arm is not hard to bear)

A mentsh on glik is a toyter mensh An unlucky person
is a dead person (Lit., A man without luck is a dead
man)

A metsieh fun a ganef It's a steal (Lit., A bargain from
a thief)

A nar filt nit! A fool feels nothing!

A nar veist men nit kain halbeh arbet You don't show a
fool something half-finished

A nechtiker tog! Finished! Gone! Fait accompli!
Impossible! Nonsense (Lit., A yesterday's day)

A nishtikeit! A nobody!

A sach tsu reden, vainik tsu herren A lot to tell, little to
hear

A shaineh, raineh, kaporeh Serves him (her) right!
(Lit., A nice, pure sacrificial fowl)

A shainem dank dir in pupik! Thanks for nothing (Lit.,
Many thanks in your belly button)

A shandeh un a charpeh A shame and a disgrace

A shtik naches A great joy (Lit., A piece or slice of
pleasure)

A sof! A sof! Let's end it! End it!

A yor mit a mitvoch It will take a long, long time
(till Doomsday) (Lit., A year and a Wednesday)

Abi gezunt!   As long as you're healthy!
Abi tsu zein mit dir   As long as I can be with you
Achrahyes   Responsible
Aderabeh-ve'aderabeh   By all means
Ahf meineh sonim gezogt!   It should happen to my
   enemies!
Ahf mir gezogt!   I wish it could be said about me!
Ahf mir gezogt gevorn!   It should happen to me!
Ahf tsi 'lehaches; (ahf tsu loches)   In spite of everything
   you do, it still comes out wrong
Ahf tsores   In trouble
Ahfen goniff brent dos hittel   A guilty conscience; A
   guilty person is always sensitive (Lit., On the head of a
   thief, burns his hat)
Ahntoisht   Disappointed
Ahntoishung   Disappointment
Ahzes ponim   Impudent fellow
Aidel   Cultured
Aidel gepatshkit   Finicky, super-critical
Aidim   Son-in-law
Ain klainikeit   Big deal (Derisive; lit., A small matter,
   A mere bagatelle)
Aiver butel   Getting senile; absent-minded; mixed up
Alaichem sholom   To you be peace (The answer or
   response to the customary salutation, sholom alaichem,
   Peace be unto you)
Alef-bais   Alphabet; the first two letters of the Jewish
   alphabet; the beginning; common knowledge; ABC's
Aleh meiles hot zi!   She has all the virtues!
Aleh shusters gaien borves   All shoemakers go barefoot
Alevei!   It should happen to me (to you)! Would that it
   comes true!
Alteh moid   Spinster, old maid
Alter bocher   Bachelor
Alter Kucker (taboo)   A lecherous old man; a played-out
   person, even if young; a person unwilling to participate

(abbreviated to A.K.)

Altvarg Decrepit person or thing

Amho'orets Ignoramus, boor, peasant (also spelled "amorets)

An ain unaintsikeh A one and only, rarity

An alteh machashaifeh An old witch

An alter bakahnter An old acquaintance

An alter trombenick An old wreck, an old bum

Antshuldik mir. Excuse me.

Arbeh kanfess Sleeveless religious undershirt

Arein In, into; Come in!

Aribergechapt di mohs! Overdressed woman

Aroysgevorfeneh gelt Money thrown out; money wasted

Arumgeflickt! Milked! Plucked!

Arumgevolgert Wandered around; loafed

Arumloifer Street urchin; person who runs around

Az a yor ahf mir. I should have such good luck. (Lit., Such a year to me)

Az drei zogen meshugeh, darf der ferter zogen "Bim bom." The majority rules. (Lit., If three people say or do something screwy, the fourth has to go along.)

Az es klingt, iz misstomeh chogeh. When people talk about something, it is probably true. (Lit., when bells ring, it is usually a holiday.)

Az och un vai! Tough luck! Too bad! Misfortune!

Azoy? Really?

Azoy gait es! That's how it goes! So it goes!

Azoy gich? So soon?

Azoy iz es! That's how it is!

Azoy ret men tsu a taten? Is that how you talk to a father?

Azoy vert dos kichel tzekrochen! That's how the cookie crumbles!

Azoy zogstu! That's what you (pl.) say!

Ba'al gaiveh Conceited

Baba stories, bubba meisses Grandmother tales, fairy tales, inventions (See also bobbeh meisseh)

Badchan Jester, merry maker or master of ceremonies at a wedding; at the end of the meal he announces the presents, lifting them up and praising the giver and the gift in a humorous manner

Bagel Hard circular roll with a hole in the center (like a doughnut) and a glazed surface

Bagroben To bury; buried

Baitsim (taboo) Testicles; eggs (The proper word for eggs is aier)

Baizeh chei-eh Vicious animal (usually refers to an inhumane person)

Balagoleh Teamster, waggoner, coachman, driver; vulgar man, one without manners

Balebatish Fine, responsible, honorable

Balebatisheh yiden Respectable Jews, men of substance and good standing in the community

Balabatishkeit Household, property, substance

Balebos Owner, the big boss; an orderly person, householder, head of family

Balebosteh Housewife, hostess, capable homemaker (complimentary)

Balmelocheh Artisan, skilled worker, mechanic

Balnes Miracle-worker

Bal shem Term applied to a faith-healer, magic-worker, miracle performer

Bal Simcheh One who celebrates a happy occasion

Bal Toyreh Learned man, scholar

Bal tsedokeh Benefactor, philanthropits

Barabantshik Drummer in a band

Bareden yenem To gossip

Baren (taboo)   Fornicate; bother, annoy
Bareh mich nit   Don't bother me. Don't screw me around!
Bareh nit (taboo)   Don't fornicate around; don't fool around; don't annoy; don't bother (someone)
Barimer   Braggart, show-off
Bar-mitzvah   Boy who, upon the completion of his thirteenth year, accepts the responsibility of fulfilling the religious law; also the celebration of this event, of becoming a man (Lit., Son of commandment)
Baroygis   Angry, petulant
Bas   Daughter (Hebrew)
Bas-mitzvah   Girl who has reached the age when she is required to fulfill certain mitzvos (commands, obligations); the coming of age; a woman
Bashert   Fated
Bashert zein   To be destined
Basherter   Beloved; the fated one, the destined one
Bas-malkeh   Princess (Lit., Daughter of a queen)
Batlen   Egghead (Talmudic)
Baveibter   Married man (veib means wife)
Beblech   Beans
Behaimeh   Animal, cow (when referring to human being, means dull-witted or a fool)
Bei mir poilst du   It's O.K. with me
Ben   Son (Hebrew); zun, Yiddish
Ben toyreh   Learned man, scholar (Lit., Son of the Torah)
Bentshen lecht   Recite benedictions over lit candles on Sabbath eve and holidays
Bentshing   Anglicization of Yiddish word bentshen, to say grace
Beryeh   Efficient, competent housewife
Bes medresh   Synagogue
Billik   Cheap, inexpensive
Billik vi borsht!   Cheap as beet soup! A real bargain! A real buy!
Bist ahf ain fus?   Are you in a hurry? (Lit., Are you

standing on one leg?)

Bist meshugeh?   Are you crazy?

Biteh   Please

Blaich vi di vant   Pale as a sheet (wall)

Blintses   Cheese or jellied pancakes rolled in dough and fried in fat (The French call it crêpe suzette)

Blondjen   To wander; be lost, as in the woods or on strange roads

Blozen fun zich   Puffed with haughty pride; shows off

Bobbeh meisseh   Grandmother story (Figuratively, a fairy tale, an unbelievable story, a tall story)

Bobkes   Small things, triflings, peanuts, nothing, worthless (Lit., Excreta of sheep, goats)

Bocher   Bachelor, unmarried man, young man

Bohmer   Bum (masc., Americanism)

Bohmerkeh   Bum (fem., Americanism)

Boitshick   Little boy; affectionate term for boy or man (Americanism)

Bordel   Brothel, whorehouse

Borsht   Beet or cabbage soup

Borsht circuit   Hotels in the Catskill Mountain, New York, with an almost entirely Jewish clientele, who are fond of borsht (beet and potato soup); term is used by entertainers

Boruchu (Hebrew)   Bless ye

Boruch hashem (Hebrew)   Bless God!

Borves   Barefoot

Botshvineh   Spinach soup

Boych vaitik   Stomach ache

Brahv   Brave

Braiter vi lainger   He's so happy! (Lit., Wider than longer, as with a big wide smile)

Brech a fus!   Break a leg!

Bris   Circumcision; the ceremony of circumcision

Bris Mieleh   Circumcision

Bristen   Breasts, teats

Broch   Fracture, break (Figuratively, a curse)
Broitgeber   Head of family
Bronfen   Whiskey
Brust   Breast
B'suleh   Virgin
B'suleh-shaft   Virginity
B'sulim   Hymen
Bubbee (booh-bee)   Friendly term for anybody you like
Bubeleh   Endearing term for anybody you like, young or old
Bubkes   Beans; a mere bagatelle; (Slang, see Bobkes)
Bubu   Insignificant mistake
Bulvan   Man built like an ox; boorish, coarse, rude person
Burtchet   Growled

Cancer-shmancer, abi gezunt Cancer-shmancer, as long as you're healthy! (Americanism)

Chaleshen To faint

Challah Sabbath twists of white bread (Made in a variety of forms for the various holidays of the year)

Chaloshes Weakness, nausea, faintness, unconsciousness

Chamoyer du ainer! You blockhead! You dope! You donkey! You ass!

Chanifeh Over-praise

Chap a gang! Beat it! (Lit., Catch a way, catch a road)

Chap nit! Take it easy! Not so fast! (Lit., Don't grab)

Chas v'cholileh! God forbid! Not really at all!

Chaver (pl., Chavairim) Friend, Mr., comrade, colleague

Chaverteh Friend (fem.), Mrs. Miss, companion

Chazen Cantor

Chazenteh Wife of chazen

Chazzer Pig, a piggish person

Chazzerei Swill; pig's feed; anything bad, unpalatable, rotten

Chei Eighteen; life; word formed by the combination of Hebrew letters meaning eighteen and life

Chei(im) Life; (Le'cheiim (to life) is used as a toast equal to Here's to you, Skol, Down the hatch, etc. Chei-im is also a favorite name among Jews, becoming Hyman, later Henry, Herbert and other variations)

Chei kuck (taboo) Nothing, infinitesimal, worthless, unimportant (Lit., human dung)

Chevreh Company, society, associates

Chmalyeh! Bang, punch; Slam! Wallop!

Chochem Wise man; (slang) a wise guy

Chochem attick A wise guy

Chochmeh Wisdom, bright saying, witticism (often sarcastically)

Cholileh!   God forbid! Perish the thought!

Choleryeh   Cholera; a curse, plague

Choshever mentsh   Man of worth and dignity; elite person; respected person

Chosid   Rabid fan

Chossen   Bridegroom

Chossen-kalleh   Bride and groom; engaged couple

Chosser daieh   Feeble-minded

Choyzik machen   Make fun of, ridicule

Chropen   Snore

Chupeh   Bridal canopy (Its four poles signify the four corners of the world, and support a blue cloth, symbolic of the heavens); the marriage ceremony itself

Chutzpeh   Brazenness, gall, cheek

Chutzpenik   Impudent fellow

Cristiyah   Enema

Cristiyer   Enema

Danken Got! Thank God!

Davenen Pray

Davening mincheh Recite the afternoon or mincheh prayers, which consist of selections from psalms plus the Sh'moneh Esrei (Eighteen Benedictions) (Note English suffix "ing." The verb is davenen.)

Deigeh nisht! Don't worry!

Den Adverb used with questions to connote about (for example: "vo den?" for what else? "vi den" for how else?); then

Der oybershter in himmel God (Lit., The One above in heaven)

Derech erets Respect

Derniderriken Berate, to humble somebody

Dershtikt zolstu veren! You should choke on it!

Di emmeseh schoireh! The real article!

Dingen Bargain, hire, engage, lease, rent

Dos gefelt mir This pleases me

Dos gelt iz tserunen gevoren! My money went down the drain!

Dos hartz hot mir gezogt My heart told me. I predicted it.

Dos iz alts That's all

Dos iz geven a mechei-eh This was a pleasure!

Dos zelbeh Likewise.

Drai mir nit kain kop! Don't bother me! (Lit., Don't twist my head)

Drai zich! Keep moving!

Draikop Scatterbrain; one who tends to confuse you; one who connives and twists the facts to serve his own purpose (Lit., turn-head)

Drek (taboo) Human dung, feces, manure or excrement; inferior merchandise or work; insincere talk or excessive flattery

29

Drek ahf a shpendel (taboo)   As unimportant as dung on
a piece of wood

Du fangst shoyn on?   Are you starting up again?

Dumkop   Dumbbell, dunce (Lit., Dumb head)

Dybbuk   Soul condemned to wander for a time in this
world because of its sins. (To escape the perpetual tor-
ments inflicted upon it by evil spirits, the dybbuk seeks
refuge in the body of some pious man or woman over
whom the demons have no power. The dybbuk is a
Cabalistic conception)

Ech   A groan, a disparaging exclamation
Efsher   Maybe, could be
Ehe!   Nothing of importance (exclamation)
Ei! Ei!   Yiddish exclamation equivalent to the English "Oh!"
Ei, gut!   Great! Just great!
Eilt zich!   Get a move on! Hurry up! Rush!
Eingeshpahrt   Stubborn
Eingetunken   Dipped, dunked
Einhoreh   Evil eye
Eizel   Fool, dope
Ek velt   End of the world
Ekeldiker parshoya   Disgusting fellow
El, eleh   Suffixes denoting diminutive or affection
Emes   Truth; on the level, on the square
Er bolbet narishkeiten   He talks nonsense
Er drait zich vi a fortz in rossel! (taboo)   Is he bewildered! Is he in a fog! (Lit., he squirms like a fart in a foggy soup)
Er est vi noch a krenk.   He eats as if he just recovered from a sickness.
Er farkocht a kasheh   He makes a mess.
Er frest vi a ferd.   He eats like a horse.
Er hot a farshtopten kop.   He's thick headed.
Er hot a farshtopteh nonyeh.   He has a cold. He has a stuffed nose.
Er hot a makeh.   He has nothing at all (Lit., He has a boil or a minor hurt.)
Er hot kadoches.   He has nothing. (Lit., Malaria fever (ague) is all that he gets!)
Er hot modneh drochim.   He has odd ways.
Er hot nit kain daieh.   He has no say (authority).
Er hot nit kain zorg.   He hasn't got a worry.

31

Er iz a niderrechtiker kerl! He's a low down good-for-nothing.

Er iz shoyn du, der nudnik! The nuisance is here already!

Er kert iber di velt! He turns the world upside down!

Er kricht in di hoyecheh fenster. He aspires to high places (beyond his reach); a social climber (Lit., He creeps on high windows.)

Er kricht oyf di gleicheh vent. Trouble-maker; a man who criticizes things that don't exist or that are uncriticizable (Lit., He climbs up straight walls.)

Er kricht vi a vantz. He's slow as molasses. (Lit., He creeps like a bedbug.)

Er kukt vi a hun in a B'nai Odom. He doesn't know what he's looking at.

Er macht a tel fun dem. He ruins it.

Er macht mir a shvartzeh chasseneh! He makes a lot of trouble for me! (Lit., He makes my wedding black.)

Er molt gemolen mel. He repeats himself. He re-hashes things over and over again. (Lit., He grinds ground flour.)

Er redt in der velt arein! He talks nonsense! (Lit., He talks into the world.)

Er redt zich ein a krenk! He talks himself into a sickness!

Er zitst oyf shpilkes. He's restless. (Lit., He sits on pins and needles.)

Er toyg ahf kapores. He's worthless. (Lit., He's good only for a fowl sacrifice.)

Er zol einemen a mieseh meshuneh! He should go to hell! (Lit., He should meet with a strange death.)

Er zol vaksen vi a tsibeleh, mit dem kop in drerd! He should grow like an onion, with his head in the ground!

Eretz Yisroel. Land of Israel.

Es brent mir ahfen hartz. I have a heartburn.

Es cholemt zich mir . . . I am dreaming that . . .

Es gait nit! It doesn't work!It isn't running smoothly!

Es gefelt mir. I like it. (Lit., It pleases me.)

Es hot zich oysgelohzen a boydem! Nothing came of it! (Lit., There's nothing up there but a small attic.)

Es iz a shandeh far di kinder! It's a shame for the children!

Es iz bloteh. That's nothing. That's worthless. It's nothing. (Lit., It is mud.)

Es iz mir eingefalen a plan. A plan occurred to me.

Es iz nit geshtoigen un nit gefloigen! It never happened! It doesn't make sense! (Lit., It was never standing and never flying.)

Es iz noch do There still is

Es iz (tsu) shpet. It is (too) late.

Es iz vert a zets in drerd! It is as futile as stomping on the earth! (Lit., It's [not even] worth a knock on the earth.)

Es iz zaier teier (billik). It is very expensive (cheap).

Es ken gemolt zein. It is conceivable. It is imaginable.

Es kein zein. It could be.

Es ligt im (ir) in zinnen. It's on his (her) mind.

Es ligt im nit in zinnen. He doesn't give a damn. (Lit., It's not on his mind.)

Es macht mir nit oys. It doesn't matter to me.

Es macht nit oys. It makes no difference. It doesn't matter. It isn't important.

Es past nit. It is not becoming. It is not fitting.

Es past zich vi a patsh tsu gut shabbes! It's bad manners. It's not to the point. (Lit., It fits like a slap in the face in response to the greeting: Good Sabbath.)

Es tut mir a groisseh hanoeh! It gives me great pleasure! (often said sarcaastically)

Es tut mir bahng. I'm sorry. (Lit., It sorrows me)

Es tut mir laid. I'm sorry.

Es tut mir vai. It hurts me.

Es veist zich mir oys It appears to me

Es vert mir finster in di oygen. I am fainting! (Lit., It's getting dark in my eyes.)

Es vet gornit helfen!   Nothing will help!

Es vet helfen vi a toiten bahnkes!   It won't help (any)!
(Lit., It will help like blood-cupping on a dead body.)

Es vet kleken.   This will do. It will suffice.

Es vet zich alles oyspressen.   It will all work out.

Es vet zich oys-hailen far der chasseneh.   It will heal in
time for the wedding. (Told even to a child when it gets
hurt. The implication is that marriage is a cure-all.)

Es zhumit mir in kop.   There's a buzzing in my head.

Ess gezunterhait!   Eat in good health!

Essen mitik   Dine

Essen teg   Yeshiva students would arrange to be fed by
various householders on a daily basis in different houses.
(Lit., Eat days)

Faigeleh Little bird. Also, a pervert, fairy, homosexual, fag

Fang shoyn on! You may start now! Come on, get going!

Fangst shoyn on? Are you beginning again? Are you starting something?

Farantvortlech Responsible

Fantazyor Man who builds castles in the air

Farbissener Embittered; bitter person

Farblondzhet Lost, bewildered, confused

Farblujet Bending your ear

Farbrenter Rabid fan, ardent participant

Fardart Dried

Fardeiget Distressed, worried, full of care, anxiety

Fardinen a mitzveh Earn a blessing or a merit(by doing a good deed)

Fardrai zich dem kop! Go drive yourself crazy!

Fardrai zich dein eigenem kop vestu mainen s'iz meiner! Go drive yourself crazy, then you'll know how I feel! (Lit., Turn your own head around, and you'll think it's mine)

Fardross Disappointment, sorrow

Farein Society

Farfel Noodle dough, grated or chopped into barley-sized grains

Farfolen Lost

Farfoylt Mildewed, rotten, decayed

Farfroyren Frozen

Fargenigen Pleasure

Farglust Have a yen for

Farkuckt (taboo) Dungy, shitty

Farmach dos moyl! Shut up! Quiet. (Lit., Shut your mouth.)

Farmatert Tired

Farmish nit di yoytzres!   Don't mix things up!
(Lit., don't mix up the holiday prayers.)
Farmisht   Mixed up emotionally; befuddled
Farmutshet   Worn out, fatigued, exhausted
Farnem zich fun danen!   Beat it!
Farshlepteh krenk   Fruitless, endless matter
(Lit., A sickness that hangs on)
Farshmeieter   Highly excitable person; always on the go
Farshnoshket   Loaded, drunk
Farshtaist?   You understand?
Farshtopt   Stuffed up, cluttered
Farshtunken   Smells bad, stinky
Farshvitst   Sweaty
Fartrasket   Decorated (beautified)
Far-tshadikt   Confused, bewildered, befuddled, as if by
fumes, gas
Farzorger   Head of family
Feckuckteh (taboo)   Dungy, shitty
Feh!   Fooey!
Feinkochen   Omelet, scrambled eggs
Feinshmeker   Person with fine taste; elite, hi-falutin'
Ferd   Horse, (slang) a fool
Fet   Fat, obese
Filantrop   Philanthropist
Filen zich opgenart   Disappointed
Finf   A $5 bill; five; a fiver
Finferel $5 bill
Finster un glitshik   Miserable (Lit., Dark and slippery)
(A) Finsteren sof   Horrible ending (Lit., A dark ending)
(A) Finster yor!   A curse! (Lit., A dark year)
(A) Finsternish   Plague; a curse (Lit., Darkness, gloom)
Fisfinger   Toes
Flaishik, (Flaishidik)   Meat or meat ingredients (must not
Flaishik, (Flaishidik)   Meat or meat ingredients (must
not be eaten at the same meal with dairy, milechik,
foods)

Focha   Fan
Foigel   Smart guy
Foiler   Lazy man
Folg mich!   Obey me!
Folg mich a gang!   Quite a distance! Quite a job!
   Why should I do it? It's hardly worth the trouble!
   (Lit., Follow me on an errand.)
Folg mich a gang un gai in drerd!   Do me a favor and
   drop dead!
Fonfen   Speak through the nose. Unclear. To double talk.
(Er) fonfet unter   He bluffs his way out
Fonfevateh   Talking through the nose
For gezunterhait!   Bon voyage! Travel in good health!
Forshpeiz   Appetizer
Fortz (taboo)   Fart, wind-passing, flatulence, eructation
Fortzen (taboo)   Pass or break wind, flatulate, eructate
Frageh   Question
Frailech   Happy
Frassk   Slap in the face
Freg mich becherim!   Ask me another! How should I
   know? Who knows? (Lit., even if you excommunicate
   me, I cannot give you the answer.)
Freilein   Miss, young lady
Freint   Friend, Mr.
Fremder   Stranger
Fressen   Eat like a pig, devour
Fresser   Big eater, gourmand
Fressing   Gourmandizing (By adding the English suffix
   "ing" to the Yiddish word "fress," a new English word
   in the vocabulary of American Jews has been created.)
Froy   Woman, Mrs.
Frum, (frimer)   Pious, religious, devout
Fun eier moyl in Got's oyeren!   God should hear you and
   do as you say! (Lit., from your mouth to God's ears)
Funfeh   Speaker's fluff, error
Funfen   Speak through the nose; unclear; to double-talk

G

Gai avek!   Go away!

Gai bareh di vantsen!   Go bother the bedbugs!

Gai fardrai zich dein aigenem kop!   Go drive yourself crazy! Go mix yourself up, not me! (Lit., Go twist your own head.)

Gai feifen ahfen yam!   Go peddle your fish elsewhere! (Lit., Go whistle on the ocean)

Gai gezunterhait!   Bon voyage! Good-bye. (Lit., go in good health.)

Gai in drerd arein!   Go to hell! (Lit., Go down into the earthly grave.)

Gai kabenyeh mattereh!   Go to hell (Slavism)

Gai klap zich kop in vant!   It's useless (Lit., Go bang your head against the wall.)

Gai kucken ahfen yam! (taboo)   Don't bother me! Get lost! (Lit., Go defecate on the ocean.)

Gai plats!   Go split your guts!

Gai shlog zich mit Got arum!   Go fight City Hall! (Lit., Go fight with God.)

Gai shoyn, gai.   Scram! also, Don't be silly!

Gai strasheh di gens!   You don't frighten me! (Lit., Go threaten the geese)

Gai tren zich. (taboo)   Go frig yourself!

Gaien tsu kind   Going into labor to give birth.

Gait, gait!   Come now!

Gait es nit!   It doesn't work!

Galitsianer   Jewish native of Galicia

Gam atem   The same to you. (Hebrew)

Ganaiden   Garden of Eden; Paradise

Ganef   Crook, thief, burglar, swindler, racketeer

Gants gut   Quite well

Gantseh megilleh   Big deal! (derisive)

Gantser k'nacker!   Big shot!

Gantser mentsh Manly, a whole man, a complete man; an adult; a fellow who assumes airs

Gatkes Long winter underwear.

Gazlen Robber; criminal, racketeer, murderer

Geben shoychad To bribe

Gebentsht mit kinder Blessed with children

Gebrenteh tsores Utter misery

Gebrochener english Fractured English

Gechropet Snored

Gedainkst? Remember?

Gedarteh Dried

(Es) Gefelt mir I like it. It pleases me.

Geferlech Dangerous

Gifilteh fish Stuffed fish (Usually made of chopped fish, onions and seasoning, and cooked in salt water)

Gefilteh helsel Stuffed chicken-neck skin

Gefilteh kishkeh Stuffed derma (intestines)

Gehakteh english Fractured English

Gehakter hering Chopped herring

Gehakteh leber Chopped liver

Gehakteh tsores Utter misery (Lit., Chopped-up troubles.)

Geharget zolstu veren! Drop dead! (Lit., You should get killed.)

Gelaimter Person who drops whatever he touches

Gelibteh Beloved

Gelt Money

Gelt gait tzu gelt. Money goes to money.

Gembeh! Big mouth!

Gemitlich Slowly, unhurried, gently

Genaivisheh shtiklech Tricky, sharp, crooked actions or doings

Genug iz genug. Enough is enough!

Gesheft Business

Geshmak Tasty, delicious

Geshtank A stink, foul odor

Geshtroft   Cursed, accursed; punished

Geshvollen   Swollen, puffed up (Also applied to person with haughty pride)

Get   Divorce

Gevaldikeh zach!   A terrible thing! (often ironically)

Gevalt!   See G'vald

(A) Gezunteh moid!   Brunhilde, a big healthy dame

Gezunt vi a ferd   Strong as a horse

Gezunterhait   In good health

Gezunt-heit!   Good health! (Use when someone sneezes or as a toast!)

Gib mir nit kain einoreh!   Don't give me a canary! (Americanism, Lit., Don't give me an evil eye)

Gib zich a shockel.   Get a move on.

Gib zich a traisel   Get a move on

Gleichtseitik   Likewise, simultaneously

Gleichvertel   Wisecrack, pun, saying, proverb, bon mot, witticism

Gleichvort   Proverb

Glezel tai   Glass of tea

Glezeleh varems   Tea (Lit., A glass of warmth)

Glick   Luck, piece of luck

Gloib mir!   Believe me!

Glusten tsu   To have a yen for

G'nossen tsum emess!   The sneeze confirmed the truth!

Goilem   Dull person; clumsy and sluggish; mechanical man, robot

Goldeneh chasseneh   Fiftieth wedding anniversary

Goldeneh medineh   Golden country (meaning the United States)

Goniff   Thief, same as ganef

Gornisht   Nothing

Gornit   Nothing

Got di neshomeh shuldik   Innocent (Lit., All he owes is his soul to God)

Got hit op di naronim   God watches out for or protects

the fools

Got in himmel!   God in heaven! (said in anguish, despair, fear or frustration)

Got tsu danken   Thank God

Got vaist   God knows

Got vet shtrofen   God will punish

Got zol ophiten!   God forbid!

Gotteniu!   Oh God! (anguished cry)

Goy   Gentile; non-observant Jew; a Jew unfamiliar with Judaism

Goyeh   Gentile woman

Goyisher kop   Used in Eastern Europe to imply slow-wittedness

Greps   Belch; a burp if it's a mild one

Gribbenes (grivvenes, greeven)   Small crisp pieces left from rendered poultry fat or skin, fried and eaten as a delicacy or combined with kasha groats or rice; cracklings

Grizhen mit di tsain   To grind one's teeth

Grizhidiker   Gnawing, grinding person

Grob   Coarse, crude, gross, profane, rough, rude

Grober   Coarse, uncouth, crude; blasphemous person

Grober finger   Thumb

(A) Grober yung   (See Gruber yung)

Grobyungish   Vulgar

Grois-halter   Show-off, conceited person

Grois vi a barg   As large as a mountain

Groisseh gedilleh!   Big deal! (said sarcastically)

Groisseh metsieh   Big bargain

Groisser fardiner!   Big breadwinner! (sarcastically said. of person who isn't) (Lit., big earner)

Groisser gornisht   Big good-for-nothing

Groisser k'nacker!   Big shot! Big wheel!

Groisser potz! (taboo)   Big penis! Big prick! Big fool! Big shot! (Deragatory or sarcastic)

Groisser shisser   Big shot, big wheel

Gruber yung Uncouth, rude, boorish young man
Gut far him! Serves him right!
Gut Shabbes Good Sabbath
Gut Yontev Good Holiday
Guten tog Good day; good-bye
Guts, (gits) Good things—food, dollars, news, etc.
G'vald! Cry of distress for help; wail of sorrow
  (Lit., Force, violence)
G'vir Rich man

Hadassah Jewish women's organization which devotes iself to the maintenance of medical services in Israel (Hadassah means myrtle, a tree highly regarded by Israel of old; Haddassah became a favorite name for girls. Esther's name, as told in the Bible, was originally Hadassah. The women's organization bearing her name was founded on the Purim holiday of 1912)

Hagadah Book of services for the first two nights of Passover

Haimish ponem Friendly face, familiar face (from home)

Haiseh vanneh Hot bath

Haken a tsheinik Boring, long-winded and annoying conversation; talking for the sake of talking
(Lit., To bang on the tea-kettle)

Hak flaish Chopped meat

Hak mir nit in kop! Stop bending my ear (Lit., Stop banging on my head)

Hak mir nit kain tsheinik Don't bother me (Lit., Don't bang on the tea-kettle)

Haldz-shvenkechts Gargle solution

Halevei! Would that it came true!

Hamotzi lechem min ho'orets Blessing over bread (Hebrew) (Lit., Who bringeth forth bread from the earth)

Hamoyn Common people

Handlen To bargain; to do business

Hartsvaitik Heart ache

Hartseniu! Sweetheart, my heart's love

Heizel Brothel

Hekdish Decrepit place, a slumhouse, poorhouse; a mess

Heldish Brave

Hert zich ein! Listen here!

Hetsken zich Shake and dance with joy

Hikevater Stammerer

Hinten Rear, rear parts, backside, buttocks; in the rear
Hit zich! Look out!
Hit zich vi fun a feier! Watch yourself as if a fire
  threatened!
Hitsik Hothead
Hitskop Excitable person
Hob derech erets Have respect
Hob nit kain deiges Don't worry
Hoben chaishek tsu To have a yen for
Hoben tsu zingen un tsu zogen Have no end of trouble
  (Lit., To have to sing and to talk)
Hoizer gaier Beggar
Hoi-echer drong Long lean person
Hoizirer Peddler (from house to house)
Holebshess Stuffed cabbage
Holishkes Stuffed cabbage
Holubtshes Stuffed cabbage
Host du bei mir an avleh! So I made a mistake. So what!
Hultei Debauchee, person of loose morals
Hulyen Raise Cain, to carouse

Ich bin ahntoisht I am disapointed

Ich bin dich nit mekaneh I don't envy you

Ich darf es ahf kapores It's good for nothing! I have no use for it. (Lit., I need it for a [useless] fowl sacrifice)

Ich darf es vi a lung un leber ahfen noz I need it like a wart on my nose (Lit., . . . like a lung and liver on my nose)

Ich darf es vi a loch in kop! I need it like a hole in the head!

Ich eil zich (nit) I am (not) in a hurry

Ich feif oif dir! I despise you! Go to the devil! (Lit., I whistle on you!)

Ich fil zich opgenart I am disappointed. (Lit., I feel cheated.)

Ich hob dir! Go flap your ears! Drop dead! Scram! (Lit., I have you . . . !) (Americanism!)

Ich hob dich in bod! I despise you! (Lit., I have you in the bath house!)

Ich hob dich in drerd! I have you in hell! Go to hell! (Lit., I have you in the earth)

Ich hob es in drerd! To hell with it!

Ich hob im feint I hate him

Ich hob im in bod! Forget him! The hell with him! (Lit., I have him in the bath house)

Ich hob im in toches (taboo) "I have him in my buttocks." Usually said about someone you don't care for, or are angry with.

Ich vais. I know.

Ich vais nit. I don't know.

Ich vel dir geben kadoches! I'll give you nothing! (Lit., I'll give you malaria or a fever.)

Ich yog zich nit. I'm not in a hurry.

Ich zol azoy vissen fun tsores. I should know as little

45

about trouble (as I know about what you are asking me).

Iker Substance; people of substance

Ikevater Stammerer

In a noveneh For a change; once in a blue moon

In di alteh guteh tseiten! In the good old days!

In drerd mein gelt! My money went down the drain!
(Lit., My money went to burial in the earth, to hell.)

In miten drinen In the middle of; suddenly

Inten (hinten) Behind, fanny, buttocks (slang)

Ipish Bad odor, stink

Ir gefelt mir zaier. You please me a great deal.

Iz brent mir ahfen hartz. I have a heartburn.

Kaas (in kaas oyf) Angry (with)

Kabaret forshtelung Floorshow

Kabtzen, kaptsen Pauper

Kabtzen in ziben poless A very poor man (Lit., a pauper in seven edges)

Kaddish Mourner's prayer, in praise of and submission to the will of God

Kaddishel Baby son; endearing term for a boy or man (Derived from word "kaddish," which is a prayer for the dead that only males may recite)

Kadoches Fever, malaria (Also means, ironically, less than nothing)

Kadoches mit koshereh fodem! Absolutely nothing! (Lit., fever with kosher thread.)

Kaftan Long coat worn by religious Jews

Kain ein horeh. No evil eye! (Some say "don't give me a canary"; Lit., May no evil befall.)

Kakapitshi Conglomeration

Kalamutneh Dreary, gloomy, troubled

Kalleh moid Girl of marriageable age

Kallehniu Little bride

Kalyekeh Cripple; misfit; also, anybody not good at their craft or sport

Kalyeh Bad, wrong, spoiled

Kam derlebt Narrowly achieved (Lit., hardly lived to see)

Kam* mit tsores! Barely made it! (Lit., with some troubles)

*The word "Kam," also is pronounced "Kom" or "Koim" depending on the region people come from.

Kam vos er kricht Barely able to creep; Mr. Slowpoke

Kam vos er lebt He's hardly (barely) alive.

47

Kamtsoness   To be miserly

Kaneh   enema

Kaporeh, (kapores)   Atonement sacrifice; forgiveness; (slang) good for nothing

Karabelnick   Country peddler

Karger   Miser, tightwad

Kasheh   Groats, mush cereal, buckwheat, porridge; a mess, mix-up, confusion

Kasheh varnishkes   Cooked groats and broad noodles

Kashress   Kosher condition; Jewish religious dietary law

Kasnik, (keisenik)   Angry person; excitable person, hot head

Kasokeh   Cross-eyed

Katshkehdik (Americanism)   Ducky, swell, pleasant

Katzisher kop   Forgetful (Lit., Cat head)

Kazatskeh   Lively Russian dance

Kemfer   Fighter (usually for a cause)

Ken zein   Maybe, could be

(To) Kibbitz   To offer unsolicited advice as a spectator

Kibbitzer   Meddlesome spectator

Kiddish (Borai pri hagofen)   Blessing over wine or bread on the eve of the Sabbath or Festivals

Kimpet-tzettel   Childbirth amulet or charm (from the German "kind-bet-tzettel" meaning childbirth label containing Psalm 121, names of angels, patriarchs

Kimpetoren   Woman in labor or immediately after the delivery

Kind un kait   Young and old

Kinderlech   Diminutive, affectionate term for children

Kishef macher   Magic-worker

Kishkeh   Stuffed derma (Sausage shaped, stuffed with a mixture of flour, onions, salt, pepper and fat to keep it together, it is boiled, roasted and sliced)

(A) Kitsel   Tickle

Klainer gornisht   Little prig (Lit., A little nothing)

Klemt beim hartz   Clutches at my heartstrings

Klaperkeh Talkative woman

Klipeh Gabby woman, shrew, a female demon

Klogmuter Complainer, chronic complainer

(A) Klog iz mir! Woe is me!

Klop Bang, a real hard punch or wallop

Klotz Ungraceful, awkward, clumsy person; bungler

Klotz kasheh Foolish question; fruitless question

Kloymersht Not in reality, pretended (Lit., as if it were)

K'nacker Big shot; show-off; wise guy (Be sure to pronounce the first k)

K'naidel (pl., k'naidlech) Round dumplings usually made of matzoh meal and cooked in soup

K'nippel Button, knot; hymen, virginity; money tied in a knot in the corner of handkerchief

K'nish (taboo) Vagina

K'nishes Baker dumplings filled with potato, meat, liver or barley

Kochalain Summer boarding house with cooking privileges (Lit., cook by yourself)

Kochedik Petulant, excitable

Kochleffel One who stirs up trouble; gadabout, busy-body (Lit., a cooking ladle)

Kolboynik Rascally know-it-all

(A) Kop oif di plaitses! Good, common sense! (Lit., A head on the shoulders!)

Kopvaitik Headache

Kosher Food that meets rules of Jewish dietary laws; (slang) right, perfect, clean, proper

Kosher v'yosher! It's perfect! (Lit., It's legitimate.)

Kosokeh Cross-eyed

Koved Respect, honor, reverence, esteem

Krank Sick

Krank-heit Sickness

Krassavitseh Beauty, a doll, beautiful woman

Krechts Groan, moan

Krechtser Blues singer, a moaner

Krenk Sickness, disease

Kreplach Small pockets of dough filled with chopped meat or cheese which look like ravioli, or won ton soup, and are eaten in soup; (slang) nothing, valueless

Kroivim Relatives

Kuck im on (taboo) Defecate on him! The hell with him!

Kuck zich oys! (taboo) Go take a shit for yourself!

Kucken (taboo) To defecate

Kucker (taboo) Defecator, shit-head

Kuckteppel (taboo) Pot to defecate in

Kugel Noodle or bread suet pudding, frequently cooked with raisins

Kuk im on! Look at him!

Kum ich nit heint, kum ich morgen. Mañana! Procrastinating (Lit., If I don't come today, I'll come tomorrow.)

Kumen tsu gast To visit

Kuntzen Tricks

Kuntzen macher Magic worker, trickster

Kunyehlemel Naive, clumsy, awkward person; nincompoop; Casper Milquetoast

Kurveh Whore, prostitute

Kush in toches arein! (taboo) Kiss my behind! (said to somebody who is annoying you)

Kush mich in toches! (taboo) Kiss my behind! Stop annoying me.

Kushinyerkeh Cheapskate; woman who comes to a store and asks for five cents' worth of vinegar in her own bottle

K'vatsh Boneless person, one lacking character; a whiner, weakling

K'velen Glow with pride and happiness, beam; be delighted

K'vetsh Whine, complain; whiner, a complainer

K'vitsh Shriek, scream, screech

Lachen mit yash-tsherkes Forced or false laugh; laugh with anguish

Laidik-gaier Idler, loafer

Laks See "lox"

Lamden Scholar, erudite person, learned man

Lang leben zolt ir! Long may you live!

Langeh dronitzeh Long lean girl (Lit., a long pole)

Langer drong Lean male

Lantsman (pl., lantsleit) Countryman, neighbor, fellow townsman from the old country

Lapeh Big hand

Lax Smoked salmon (see Lox)

(A) Lebedikeh velt! A lively world!

(A) Lebediker Lively person

(A) Leben ahf dein kop! Words of praise like: Well said! Well done! (Lit., A long life upon your head.)

Lebst a chazerishen tog! Living high off the hog!

L'chei-im, le'chayim! To life! (the traditional Jewish toast); To your health, Down the hatch, Skol

Leibtzudekel Sleeveless shirt (like bib) with fringes, worn by orthodox Jews

Leiden To suffer

Lemeshkeh Caspar Milquetoast bungler

Leveiyeh Funeral

Lig in drerd! Get lost! Drop dead! (Lit., Bury yourself!)

Ligner Liar

Litvak Lithuanian; Often used to connote shrewdness and also skepticism, because the Lithuanian Jews are inclined to doubt the magic powers of the Hasidic leaders; Also, a person who speaks with the Northeastern Yiddish accent.

Loch Hole; vagina (taboo)

Loch in kop Hole in the head

Loi alaichem! (Hebrew) It shouldn't happen to you! (Lit., May it not come upon you!)

Lokshen Noodles; also Italians, because they love spaghetti! (Americanism)

Loz mich tzu ru! Leave me alone! (Lit., Let me be in peace!)

Lox Smoked salmon (pronounced lahks)

Lishonoh tovoh tikosevu. (Hebrew) May you be inscribed for a good year (traditional greeting during the season of the High Holy Days).

Luftmentsh Person who has no business, trade, calling, nor income and is forced to live by improvisation, drawing his livelihood "from the air" as it were (Lit., air man); builds castles in the air; never achieves anything; a man who starves by his wits.

Mach es kailechdik up shpitzik. Come to the point!
  (Lit., Make it round and pointy.)
Mach es shnel. Do it fast! Make it snappy! Hurry up!
Mach nit kain tsimmes fun dem! Don't make a big deal
  out of it!
Machareikeh Gimmick, contraption
Machashaifeh Witch
Machen a g'vald Make an outcry; shout for help
Machen a leben Make a living
Machen a tel fun dir. Make a nothing out of you; ruin you
Macher Agent with access to the authorities who procures
  favors for his clients for a fee, big shot; man with
  contacts.
Macht zich nit visendik Pretends to be ignorant
(A) Magaifeh zol dich trefen! A plague on you!
  (Lit., A plague should come to you!)
Mah nishtano? (Hebrew) What is the difference? (first
  words in the opening "Four Questions" of the Passover
  Hagadah, traditionally asked by the youngest child in
  the household at the Passover Seder service)
Maidel Unmarried girl; teen-ager
Maideleh Little girl (affectionate term)
Maivin Expert, connoisseur, authority; sarcastically,
  a know-it-all who really doesn't know it all
Makeh Plague, wound, boil, curse
Malech-hamovess Angel of death
Malech-hamovesteh Female angel of death; bad wife
Mamoshes Substance; people of substance
Mamzer Bastard (literally), disliked person, a trickster,
  an untrustworthy person; a superlatively clever fellow
Manyeren Tact
Mashgiach Inspector, overseer or supervisor of Kashruth
  (Jewish dietary observance) in restaurants and hotels

who makes sure everything is kosher

Matriach zein   Take pains; to take the trouble; to be so good as; please

Mazel tov!   Good luck. Loads of luck. Congratulations.

Mazuma, mezuma, mezumen   Money; ready cash

Me darf nit zein shain; me darf hoben chain.   You don't have to be pretty if you have charm.

Me hot alain ungekocht.   It's your own fault (Lit., You cooked it up yourself)

Me ken brechen!   You can vomit from this!

Me ken lecken di finger!   It's delicious! (Lit., [it is so good] one can lick his fingers!)

Me ken meshugeh veren!   You can go crazy!

Me ken nit puter veren!   You can't get rid of it (him, her)!

Me ken nit tantzen ahf tsvai chassenes mit ain mol.   Take it easy. Do one thing at a time. (Lit., you can't dance at two weddings at the same time!)

Me ken tzizetst veren!   You can burst!

Me ken zich baleken!   It's delicious

Me lacht mit yashtsherklis   False or forced laugh. (Lit., Laugh with lizard's laughter)

Me lost nit leben!   They don't let you live!

Me redt, me redt un me shushkit zich.   They talk and talk and say nothing.

Me redt zich oys dos hartz!   Talk your heart out!

Me zogt   They say; it is said.

Mechalel shabbes   Jew who works on or violates the Sabbath

Mecheieh   A great pleasure; something delicious, ultra delicious, life-giving, wonderful, superb, super-joy

Mechei-ehdik   Delicious tasting

Mechuten (pl., mechutonim)   Relatives through marriage, In-laws. Relationship of fathers of bride and groom.

Mechutonesteh   Mother of bride or groom—relationship to each other.

Megillah   Scroll or the Book of Esther; in slang, it means the whole works, the complete details, a long meaningless rigamarole.

Mehlech sobyetskis yoren Good old days (Lit., the years of King Sobyetski)

Meichel Delicacy, gourmet's delight; treat

Meileh Merit, asset, advantage, virtue

Mein bobbeh's ta'am! Bad taste! Old fashioned taste! (Lit., My grandmother's taste.)

Mein cheies gait oys! I'm dying for it! (Lit., my soul expires.)

Meineh sonim zolen azoy leben! My enemies should live so!

Mekler Go-between; broker, stockbroker

Meklerkeh Female broker, go-between

Melamed (pl., melamedim) Old style orthodox Hebrew teacher in "cheder"—one room school; a wise man

Melamedkeh Wife of a melamed

Men ken es in moil nit nemen Unpalatable (Lit., You can not put it in your mouth)

Menner vash tsimmer Men's room

Menorah Traditional Jewish seven-branched candlestick; also called menoyreh

Mentsh A special man or person. This word involves a whole philosophy of life. "Mentsh" means a human being in the moral and ethical sense; not merely a person, but a person with worth and dignity, one who can be respected.

Meshugass Crazy antics; craze; madness, insanity

Meshugeh Crazy

Meshugeh ahf toit! Crazy as a loon. Really crazy! Insane (Lit., dead crazy)

Meshugeneh Mad, crazy, insane woman; an eccentric female

Meshugeneh gens, meshugeneh gribbenes Goofy parents, goofy children (Lit., crazy fowl, bad cracklings or chitterlings)

(A) Meshugeneh velt! A crazy world!

Meshugener Mad, crazy, insane man; an eccentric male

Meshugener mamzer! Crazy bastard!

Metsiyeh Bargain, a find, a favorable purchase

Meyuches Elite, cultured

Mezuma, mezumen Money; ready cash

Mezuzah Tiny box affixed to the right side of the doorway of Jewish homes containing a small portion of Deuteronomy (vi. 4-9 and xi 13-2') in twenty-two lines, handwritten on parchment.

Mich shrekt men nit! You don't frighten me! They don't frighten me! It doesn't frighten me!

Mies Ugly

Mies un mos Tedious, abnoxious

Mieskeit Ugly thing or person

Miesseh meshuneh To wish lots of trouble on someone (Lit., a strange death or a tragic end)

Miesser nefesh Cheap person

Mikveh Indoor bath or pool required for Jewish **ritual purification,** particularly during and after menstruation; A bride-to-be always goes to the mikveh before the wedding.

Milchikeh Jewish religious dietary laws distinguishes between two chief types of food: the milchikeh (dairy) and the flaishikeh (meat) which may not be eaten together; also, cutlery, dishes and utensils have to be kept separately

Milchiks All dairy foods and cutlery, dishes and cooking utensils used exclusively for dairy foods according to Jewish ritual regulations. Also pronounced Milechiks. Comes from the word "milch"—milk.

Minyan Quorum of ten men necessary for holding public worship (Young boys can also be included, provided they are over thirteen)

Mir bamien zich shtarker! We try harder!

Mir velen bentshen. We shall say grace.

Mir velen im bagroben! We'll bury him!

Mir zolen zich bagegenen ahf simches. May we meet on happy occasions.

Mirtsishem (Hebrew) God willing (Contraction of Im Yirtseh Hashem)

Mirtsishem bei mir! It should happen to me, God willing!

Mishebairach (Hebrew) A blessing (Lit., He who blessed [beginning words of invoking a benediction])

Mishmash Mixture, mess, confusion, hodge podge, jumble

Mishpocheh Family, relatives

Mishpocheh-zachen Family affairs

Mittelmessiker Average man; person who is neither smart nor dumb; hoi polloi

Mitten derinnen All at once, suddenly

Mitsveh Commandment, mostly always used to mean a good deed, as helping the poor or visiting the sick; according to orthodox Jewish belief, there are 613 mitsves which Moses handed down; 365 of them were prohibitions and 248 were positive commands or mitsves.

Mizinikil Last or youngest child in family

Mizrach East; eastern; the eastern wall; front row in the synagogue, row of pews where the foremost members of the congregation sit

Mogen Dovid David's shield, a Jewish emblem; Star of David

Mohel The religious functionary who performs circumcisions

Moid Unmarried girl; a buxom girl; an old maiden; spinster. (Usually you would say "Alteh moid"—old maid.)

Moil-shvenkechts Mouthwash

Moisheh kapoyer Mr. Upside-Down! A person who does everything wrong or in reverse

Molodyets Clever fellow; jolly good fellow

Mordeven zich To work hard

Mosser Squealer
Mumcheh Expert
Mutek Brave
Mutik heldish Brave
Mutshen zich To sweat out a job
Muttelmessig Meddlesome person, kibbitzer

Na! Here! (in giving) Take it. Here you are. There you have it

Naches Joy; Gratification, especially from children.

Nacht falt tsu. Night is falling; twilight

Nadan Dowry

Nadven (Hebrew) Philanthropist, benefactor

Nafkeh Prostitute

Nafkeh bay-is Whorehouse

Naidlechech Rare thing

Nar Fool

Nar ainer! You fool, you!

Narish Foolish

Narishkeit Foolishness

Nash Snack, sweet, treat (between meals)

Nasher A continual eater of delicacies; person with a sweet tooth; nibbler, especially between meals

Neb . Contraction of nebbish

Nebach. It's a pity. May it not happen to you. Also a noun meaning an unlucky, pitiable person. A ne'er-do-well.

Nebbish Nobody; pitiable person, simpleton, weakling; shy, drab, awkward person

Nebechel Nothing, a pitiful person; or playing role of being one

(A) Nechtiker tog! He's (it's) gone! Forget it! Nonsense! (Lit., a yesterday's day)

Nekaiveh Female; derogatively, connotes prostitute

Nem zich a vaneh! Go take a bath! Go jump in the lake!

Neshomeh Soul, spirit; divine element in man; also refers to a child

Neshomeleh Sweetheart, darling, sweet soul (Lit., Little soul)

Nifter-shmifter, a leben macht er? What difference does it make as long as he makes a living? (Lit., nifter means deceased.)

Nishkosheh Not so bad, satisfactory. (This has nothing to do with the word "kosher," but comes from the Hebrew and means "hard, heavy," thus "not bad." The French equivalent—pas mal.

Nisht do gedacht! It shouldn't happen! God forbid! (Lit., May we be saved from it! [sad event])

Nishtgedeiget Don't worry; doesn't worry

Nisht gefonfit! Don't hedge. Don't fool around. Don't double-talk.

Nisht geshtoigen, nisht gefloigen. It's not true whatsoever. You're not making sense! (Lit., Didn't stand, didn't fly.)

Nisht getrofen! So I guessed wrong!

Nisht gut Not good, lousy

Nisht naitik Not necessary

Nishtgutnick No-good person

Nishtikeit! A nobody!

Nishtu gedacht! It shouldn't happen! God forbid! (Lit., May we be saved from it [re: a sad event])

Nit kain farshloffener A lively person

Nit ahin, nit aher Neither here nor there.

Nit gidacht! It shouldn't happen! (Same as nishtu gedacht)

Nit gidacht gevorn. It shouldn't come to pass.

Nit kosher Impure food. Also, slang, anything not good

Nit heint, nit morgen! Not today, not tomorrow!

Nit oif undz gedacht! It shouldn't happen to us!

Nit shatten tzum shiddech. It won't hurt (him or her) in making a (nuptial) match.

Nito There is not

Nito farvos! You're welcome! (Lit., nothing to be thankful for)

—Niu Suffix denoting endearment

Noc hneileh! Too late! (Lit., Arriving after the closing prayers of the Day of Atonement. The last prayer on "Yim Kippur" is called "Ne-ileh," after which God has sealed the fate of a human being.)

Noch nisht Not yet

Nochshlepper Hanger-on, unwanted follower

Nor Got vaist. Only God knows.

Nu? So? Well?

Nu, shoyn! Move, already! Hurry up! Let's go! Aren't you finished? (this has infinite meanings. Lit., So, already)

Nudnik Pesty nagger, nuisance, a bore, obnoxious person

Nudje Annoying person, badgerer (Americanism)

Nudjen Badger, annoy persistently

Ober yetzt?   So now? (Yetzt is also spelled itzt)
Obtshepen   Get rid of
Och!   Exclamation of surprise, dismay or disapproval
Och un vai!   Alas and alack; woe be to it!
Oder a klop, oder a fortz (taboo)   Either too much or not enough (Lit., either a wallop or a fart)
Ohmain   Amen
Oi!!   Yiddish exclamation to denote disgust, pain, astonishment or rapture
Oi, a shkandal, (oy, a skandal!)   Oh, what a scandal!
Oi, gevald!   Cry of anguish, suffering, frustration or for help
Oi, vai!   Dear me! Expression of dismay or hurt Vai means woe)
Oi vai iz mir!   Woe is me!
Oisgeshtrobelt!   Overdressed woman.
Oisgeshtrozelt   Decorated (beautified)
Oisgetzatzket!   Overdressed woman.
Ois-shteler   Braggart
Oiver botel   Absentminded; getting senile
Okuratner mentsh   Orderly person
Oleho Hasholem (Hebrew)   May she rest in peace
Olov Hasholem (Hebrew)   May he rest in peace. Peace unto him!
Olreitnik!   Nouveau riche! Parvenu! (Americanism.)
On langeh hakdomes!   Cut it short! (Lit., without long introductions.)
Ongeblozzen   Conceited; peevish, sulky, pouting
Ongeblozzener   Stuffed shirt. (Lit., Puffed up)
Ongematert   Tired out
Ongepatshket   Cluttered, disordered, scribbled, sloppy, littered, confusing, muddled; overly-done picture or work

Ongeshtopt   Very wealthy (Lit., Stuffed up or with)

Ongeshtopt mit gelt   Very wealthy; (Lit., stuffed with money)

Ongetrunken   Drunk

Ongetshepter   Bothersome hanger-on

Ongevarfen   Cluttered, disordered

Onshikenish   Hanger-on

Onshikenish   Pesty nagger

Onzaltsen   Giving you the business; bribe; soft-soap; sweet-talk (Lit., to salt)

Opgeflickt!   Done in! Suckered! Milked! (Lit., Plucked out like a chicken)

Opgehitener   Pious person

Opgekrochen   Shoddy

Opgekrocheneh schoireh   Shoddy merchandise

Opgelozen(er)   Careless dresser

Opgenart   Cheated, fooled

Opnarer   Trickster, shady operator

Opnarerei   Deception

Orehman   Poor man, without means

Oremkeit   Poverty

Oybershter   God (Lit., The One above)

Oybershter in himmel   God in heaven (Lit., The One above in heaven)

Oych a bashefenish   Also a V.I.P.! A big person! (said derogatorily, sarcastically, or in pity)

Oych mir a leben!   This too is a living! This you call living?

Oyfen himmel a yarid!   Much ado about nothing! Impossible! (Lit., In heaven there's a big fair!)

Oyfgekumener   Come upper, upstart

Oyfgekumener g'vir   Parvenu, nouveau riche

Oys shiddech.   The marriage is off!

Oysgedart   Skinny, emaciated

Oysgehorevet   Exhausted

Oysgematert   Tired out, worn out

Oysgemutshet   Worked to death, tired out
Oysgeputst   Dressed up, overdressed; overdecorated
Oysgetsert   Emaciated
Oysvurf   Outcast, bad person
Oyver butel   Senile, absent-minded, mixed up

Paigeren zol er!   He should drop dead!
Pamelech   Slow, slowly
Parech   Low-life, a bad man (Lit., having scabs on head)
Parechavatter   Low-life, bad man
Parnosseh   Livelihood
Parshiveh   Mean, cheap
Parshoin   He-man
Partatshnek   Inferior merchandise or work
Parveh   Neutral food, neither milchidik (dairy) nor
   flaishidik (meat)
Paskudnik, paskudnyak   Ugly, revolting, disgusting
   fellow; mean, evil person; nasty fellow; punk
Past nit.   It isn't proper.
Patsh   Slap, smack on the cheek
Patsher.   A person who carries on work or sport in a
   slipshod, unbusinesslike, half-assed manner.
Patshken   Mess around, to soldier on job, to work or play
   half-heartedly; futz around, doing things in a
   time-wasting manner without adequate results
Patshkies around   Anglicized characterization of one
   engaged in patshken
Patteren tseit   To lounge around; waste time
Pavolyeh   Slow, slowly
Peeric (taboo)   Vagina
Petseleh   Little penis (affectionately applied to infant boy)
Phooey! fooey, pfui   Designates disbelief, distaste,
   contempt
Pipek.   Navel, belly button, gizzard; same as "pupik"
Pirgeh (taboo)   Vagina
Pishechtz (taboo)   Urine
Pishen (taboo)   Urinate, piss
Pisher (taboo)   Male infant; a nobody; a little squirt.
   (Lit., a urinator)

Pisherkeh (taboo) Female infant (affectionate term); a nobody! (derogative term when applied to adult females; Lit., little urinator)

Pishteppel Pee pot

Pisk Slang, for mouth (moyl); insultingly, it means big mouth, loudmouth; a mouthpiece.

Pisk-Malocheh Big talker—little doer! (man who talks a good line but accomplishes nothing; Lit., work by mouth)

Pitshetsh Coquette, chronic complainer

Pitsel Wee, tiny

Pitsvinik Little nothing

Plagen Work hard, sweat out a job, suffer

Plagen zich To suffer

Plaplen Chatter

Plats! Burst! Bust your guts out! Split your guts!

Platsen To burst, bust

Plyotkenitzeh A gossip

Pooh! Exclamation of disdain

Potz (taboo) Penis (insulting when you call a man that)

Poyer Peasant, rustic, farmer, boor, dullard

Preplen To mutter, mumble

Prietzteh Princess; finicky girl; (having airs, giving airs; being snooty) prima donna!

Prost Coarse, common, vulgar

Prostaches Low class people

Prostak Ignorant boor, coarse person, vulgar man

Prosteh leit Simple people, common people; vulgar, ignorant, "low class" people

Proster mentsh Vulgar man, common man

Proster oilem Common people

Pupik Navel, belly button, gizzard, chicken stomach; (also a term of teasing endearment)

Pupiklech Dish of chicken gizzards

Pushkeh Poor box (In every traditional Jewish home, odd coins are put in this, particularly on Friday afternoon, before the Sabbath begins; money is used for the support of philanthropic and educational institutions)

Pustunpasnik Loafer, idler

Putskeh Something decorative, from "putsen," to decorate.

Pyesseh A play, drama

Rachmones   Compassions, mercy, pity

Rav   Rabbi, religious leader of the community

Reb   Mr., Rabbi; title given to a learned and respected man

Rebiniu   "Rabbi dear!" Term of endearment for a rabbi

Rebitsin   Literally, the rabbi's wife (often sarcastically applied to a woman who gives herself airs, or acts excessively pious); pompous woman

Rechielesnitseh   Dowdy, gossipy woman

Reden on a moss   To chatter without end

Redn tzu der vant   Talk in vain or to talk and receive no answer (Lit., talk to the wall for all the good it will do you)

Redt zich ein a krenk!   Imaginary sickness

Reich   Rich, wealthy

Reisen di hoit   Skin someone alive (Lit., to tear the skin)

Ribi-fish, gelt oyfen tish!   Don't ask for credit! Pay in cash in advance! Cash on the barrel-head! Money on the table!

Riboynoy-shel-oylom! (Hebrew)   God in heaven, Master of the Universe.

Richtiker chaifetz   The real article! The real McCoy!

Rirevdiker   A lively person

Rolleh   Acting a role in a play

Rosheh   Mean, evil person

(A) Ruach in dein taten's taten arein!   Go to the devil! (Lit., A devil [curse] should enter your father's father!)

Ruf mich k'nak-nissel!   I did wrong? So call me a nut!

Ruktish   Portable table

Saichel Common sense, good sense; tact, diplomacy

Sara . . . ! What a . . . ! What kind of a . . . !

S'art eich? What does it matter to you? Does it matter to you?

S'art mich vi di vant! I don't give a care!

Se brent nit! Don't get excited! (Lit., It's not on fire!)

Se hert zich a raiech! It stinks! It gives off a bad odor.

Se shtinkt! It stinks!

Se tsegait zich in moy...! Yummy-yummy! (It melts in your mouth!)

Se zol dir grihmen in boych! You should get a stomach cramp!

Sha! (gently said) Please keep quiet.
(shouted) Quiet! Shut up!

Shabbes goy Someone doing the dirty work for others (Lit., gentile doing work for a Jew on Sabbath)

Shadchen Matchmaker or marriage broker; (There is the professional type who derives his living from it, but many Jewish women used to engage in matchmaking without compensation only from religious motives)

Shaigetz Non-Jewish boy; wild Jewish boy

Shaigetz ainer! Berating term for irreligious Jewish boy, especially one who blatantly flouts Jewish law; fellow of great audacity

Shain vi di zibben velten Beautiful as the seven worlds

Shaineh literatur Belles lettres

Shaineh maidel Pretty girl

Shainer gelechter Hearty laugh (sarcastically, Some laughter!)

Shainkeit Beauty

Shaitel, (sheitel) Wig (at the wedding the ultra-orthodox bride has her hair cut off and she wears a shaitel ever after)

Shalach mohnes Customary gifts exchanged on Purim, usually goodies

Shalom Peace (a watchword and a greeting) Shalom Alaichem—peace unto you; hello; also, Good-bye, So long; also spelled sholom

Shammes Sexton, beadle of the synagogue, also, the lighter taper used to light other candles on a menorah, a policeman (slang)

Shandhoiz Brothel, whorehouse

Shat, shat! Hust! Quiet! Don't get excited!

Shatnes Proscription against wearing clothes that are mixed of wool and linen

Shema (Hebrew) Hear Ye! (the first word in the confession of the Jewish faith: "Hear O Israel: the Lord our God, the Lord is One!" It consists of the following passages: Deut. 6:4-9; 11:13-21 and Num. 15:37-41

Shemen zich in dein veiten haldz! You ought to be ashamed of yourself (Lit., You should be ashamed down to the bottom of your throat)

Shemevdik Bashful, shy

Shenereh laigt men in drerd. Prettier ones they bury! (implying the girl is ugly)

Shepen naches Enjoy; gather pleasure, draw pleasure, especially from children

Shidech (pl., shiduchim) Match, marriage, betrothal·

Shihi-pihi Mere nothings

Shik-yingel Messenger

Shikker Drunkard

Shikseh Non-Jewish girl (also used to imply an impious or wild Jewish girl)

Shinden di hoit Skin someone

Shiva Mourning period of seven days observed by family and friends of deceased

Shkapeh. A hag, a mare; worthless

Shkotz Berating term for mischivous Jewish boy

Shlak Apoplexy; a wretch, a miserable person; shoddy;

shoddy merchandise

Shlak joint Store that sells cheap, inferior merchandise, second-hand or cut-rate goods, where bargaining over prices is important (Americanism)

Shlang Snake, serpent; a troublesome wife; penis (taboo)

Shlanger (taboo) Long or big penis

Shlatten shammes Communal busybody, tale bearer; messenger

Shlecht Bad

Shlecht veib Shrew (Lit., a bad wife)

Shlemiel Clumsy bungler, an inept person, butter-fingered; dopey person, fool, simpleton

Shlep Drag, carry or haul, particularly unnecessary things, parcels or baggage; to go somewhere unwillingly or unwantedly

Shleppen To drag, pull, carry, haul

Shlepper Sponger, panhanddler, hanger-on; dowdy, gossipy woman; stupid person, dolt; a free-loader, one who expects something for nothing

Shlimazel Luckless person. Unlucky person; incompetent person; one who has perpetual bad luck (Everything bad happens to him; it is said that the shlemiel spills the soup on the shlimazel!)

Shlog zich kop in vant. Go break your own head! (Lit., bang your head against the wall)

Shlog zich mit Got arum! Go fight City Hall! (Lit., Go fight with God.)

Shlogen To beat up

Shlok A curse; apoplexy

Shlosser Mechanic

Shlub A jerk; a foolish, stupid or unknowing person, same as shlump; second rate, inferior.

Shlump Careless dresser, untidy person, foolish, dumb person; a jerk; as a verb, to idle or lounge around

Shlumper Same as shlump

Shlumperdik Unkempt, sloppy

Shlumpf   Sucker, patsy, fall guy, second rater
Shlumpy   Sweaty, unkempt
Shmaltz   Grease or fat; (slang) flattery; to sweet talk, overly praise; gooey (food)
Shmaltzy   Sentimental, corny
Shmatteh   Rag, anything worthless
Shmeis   Bang, wallop
Shmek   A smell
Shmek tabik   Nothing of value (Lit., a pinch of snuff)
Shmeer   The business; the whole works; to bribe, to coat like butter, to be excessively kind for selfish gain
Shmegegi   Buffoon, idiot, fool. See shmendrik
Shmeichel   To butter up
Shmeikel   To swindle, con, fast-talk.
Shmendrik   Fool; nincompoop; an inept or indifferent person (or one to whom you are indifferent); a dope, shlemiel, simpleton
Shmirt zich oys di shich!   You're welcome (in my home) (Lit., Wipe your shoes clean)
Shmo(e)   Naive person, easy to deceive; a goof (Americanism)
Shmock (taboo)   Self-made fool; obscene for penis; derisive term for a man
Shmohawk   Anglicized variant for "shmock" (penis)
Shmontses   Trifles, folly
Shmooz; (shmuess)   Chat, talk
Shmoozen, (shmuessen)   To discuss or converse idly or pleasantly
Shmulky!   A sad sack!
Shmuts   Dirt, slime
Shmutzik   Dirty, soiled
Shnapps   Whiskey, same as bronfen
Shnecken   Little fruit and nut coffee rolls
Shneider   Tailor; in gin rummy card game, to win game without opponent scoring
Shnell   Quick, quickly

Shnook A patsy, a dolt, a sucker, a sap, a meek person easy to impose on; Casper Milquetoast; easy-going, gullible

Shnorrer A beggar who makes pretensions to respectability; sponger, chisler, moocher; a parasite, but always with brass and resourcefulness in getting money from others as though it were his right

Shnur Daughter-in-law

Schochet A ritual slaughterer of animals and fowl

Sholem alaichem Hebrew-Yiddish salutation, Peace be to you (The person greeted responds in reverse, Aleichem sholem, To you be peace. Equivalent to hello. How are you? How do you do? Good-bye)

Shoymer Watchman; historically refers also to the armed Jewish watchman in the early agricultural settlements in the Holy Land

Shoymer mitzves Pious person

Shoyn ainmol a' metsei-eh! Really a bargain

Shoyn fargessen? You have already forgotten?

Shoyn genug! That's enough!

Shoyn opgetrent? (taboo) Have you finished the dirty work? (Lit., Have you finished fornicating?)

Shpilkes Pins and needles

Shpitsfinger Toes

Shpitz bekitzur! Cut it short!

Shpogel nei Brand-new

Shreklecheh zach A terrible thing

Shprichvort (pl., shprichverter) Proverb, saying

Shtain reich Very rich (Lit., Stone rich)

Shtark, shtarker Strong, brave

Shtark gehert Smelled bad (used only in reference to food; Lit., strongly heard)

Shtark vi a ferd Strong as a horse

(A) Shtarker Tough guy, a roughneck, a strong-arm character; a bully

(A) Shtarker charakter A strong character

Shav   Cold spinach soup, sorrel grass soup, sour leaves soup

Shtik   Piece, bit, lump; a special bit of acting

Shtik drek (taboo)   Piece of shit; shit-head

Shtik goy   Idiomatic expression for one inclined to heretical views, or to ignorance of Jewish religious values

Shtik holtz   Dumb like a piece of wood (Lit., Piece of wood)

Shtik naches   Grandchild, child, or relative who gives you pleasure or satisfaction; a great joy (Lit., A piece of pleasure)

Shtik nar   A big fool! Some fool!

Shtikel   Small bit or piece; a morsel

Shtiklech   Tricks; small pieces

Shtilinkerait   Quietly

Shtinken   To stink

Shtoltz   Pride; unreasonably and stubbornly proud, excessive self-esteem

Shtrudel   Sweet cake made of paper-thin dough rolled up with various fillings—usually fruit and nuts—and baked

(A) Shtunk   A guy who doesn't smell too good, also also applicable to a female; a stink (bad odor); a lousy human

Shtup   Push, shove; vulgarism for sexual intercourse (taboo)

Shtup es in toches! (taboo)   Shove (or stick) it up your rectum!

Shul   Colloquial Yiddish for synagogue; said to have stemmed from Germans who, seeing Jews studying in the synagogue, mistook the synagogue for a shul or school; according to another opinion, from the Latin term, a schola', used by Italian Jews as meaning community

Shule   School

Shush!   Quiet!

Shushkeh A whisper; an aside
Shushken zich To whisper, to gossip
Shutfim Associates
Shvachkeit Weakness
(A) Shvartz yor! A black year!
Shvebeleh Highly excitable person. (Lit., a match)
Shvegerin Sister-in-law
Shveig! Quiet! Stop talking!
Shvengern Be pregnant
Shver Father-in-law; heavy, hard, difficult
Shver tsu machen a leben It's tough to make a living!
Shviger Mother-in-law
Shvindel Fraud, deception, swindle
Shvindeldik Dizzy, unsteady
Shvindilt in di oygen Blinding the eyes; feeling dizzy
Shvitser "A big producer" (who doesn't produce); a braggart
Shvitz bod Steam bath
Shvoger Brother-in-law
Shvontz (taboo) Man who behaves stupidly, ungallantly, obscenely, or idiotically (Lit., tail); penis (uncomplimentary)
Sidder Jewish prayer book for weekdays and Saturday
Simcheh Joy; also refers to a joyous occasion, such as a birth, bar-mitzvah, engagement, marriage, etc.
Sitzfleish Patience that can endure sitting (Lit., sitting flesh)
S'iz mir gut! It's great!
S'iz oys. It's over. It's gone!
Skotsel kumt A caustic greeting used principally in reference to women
S'macht nit oys. It doesn't matter.
Smetteneh Sour cream; Cream
Sof kol sof Finally
S'teitsh! Listen! Hold on! How is that? How is that possible? How come?

Strasheh mich nit!   Don't threaten me!
Szhlob Moron
Szhlok Nincompoop; ne'er-do-well

T.O.T.   (See Toches ahfen tish)

Ta'am   Taste, flavor; good taste

Tahkeh   Really! Is that so? Certainly!

Tahkeh a metsieh   Really a bargain! (usually said with sarcasm)

Taiglech   Small pieces of baked dough or little cakes dipped in honey

Tallis   Rectangular prayer-shawl to whose four corners fringes (tzitzis) are attached (used by male Jews during morning prayers)

Talis koten   Religious fringed garment

Talmud   The complete treasury of Jewish law interpreting the Torah (Five Books of Moses) into livable law

Talmud Torah   The commandment to study the Law; an educational institution for orphans and poor children, supported by the community; in the United States, a Hebrew school for children

Tamavateh   Naive, simple-minded, feeble-minded

Tandaitneh   Inferior

Tararam   Big noise, big deal

Tashlich   Ceremony of the casting off of sins on the Jewish New Year (crumbs of bread symbolizing one's sins are cast away into a stream of water in the afternoon of the Jewish New Year, Rosh Hashoneh

Tateh, tatteh, tatteh, tatteleh, tatinka, tatteniu   Father, papa, daddy, pop

Tateh-mameh, papa-mama   Parents

Tateniu   Father dear (The suffix 'niu" in Yiddish is added for endearing intimacy; also, God is addressed this way by the pious; Tateniu-Foter means God, our Father

Tateniu-Foter   God, our Father

Tefillin (phylacteries)   (Leather cubes containing scriptural texts inscribed on parchment; they are a sign

77

of the covenant between God and Israel. They are worn
by males over thirteen years old; see Bar-mitzvah)

Teier Dear, costly, expensive

Tei-yerinkeh! Sweetheart, dearest

Telerel fun himel Something unattainable; the moon on
a plate (Lit., A plate from heaven)

Temp Dolt

Temper kop Dullard

Tinif Worthless! (Lit., excreta)

T'noim Bethrothal, engagement

Toches Buttocks, behind, fanny

Toches ahfen tish! (taboo) Put up or shut up! Let's
conclude this! Come clean, buddy! (Lit., Buttocks on
the table!)

Toches-lecker (taboo) Person who will do anything to
gain favor; brown-noser, apple-polisher, ass-kisser
(Lit., Buttock-licker)

Togshul Day school

Tog-teglech Day-to-day, daily

Toig ahf kapores! Good for nothing! It's worth nothing!

Toit hungerik Starved, dead hungry

Tokus, (tokis, tuckus) (taboo) Posterior, rectum,
buttocks, ass, behind (variant of "toches")

Toonked (tunked) Dunked, dipped

Traif Forbidden food, impure, contrary to the Jewish
dietary laws, or not prepared according to regulations
(applied also to forbidden literature and other
non-kosher matters)

Traifener bain Jew who does not abide by Jewish law
(derisive, scornful expression; Lit., non-kosher bone)

Traifeneh bicher Forbidden literature

Traifnyak Despicable person; one who eats non-kosher
food

Tranteh Rag; (used sarcastically) decrepit, useless,
worn out

Tren zich (taboo) Frig you! Go fornicate yourself!

Trenen To tear, rip, rape

Tripper Gonorrhea

Trogedik Pregnant

Trog gezunterhait! Wear it in good health!

Trombenik A bum, no-good person, ne'er-do-well; a faker

Tsaddik Pious, righteous person

Tsap mir nit mein blut! Don't bleed me!

Tsatskeh Doll, plaything; something cute (like a girl);
   an overdressed woman; a sexually attractive girl

Tsatskeleh der mamehs! Mother's favorite! Mother's pet!

Tsebrech a fus! Break a leg!

Tsedokeh Spirit of philanthropy; charity, benevolence

Tsedrait Nutty, crazy, screwy

Tsedraiter kop Bungler

Tsedrumshket Confused

Tsedrumshki Befuddled

Tsekocht Excited

Tsemisht Confused, befuddled, mixed-up

Tshatshki Toy, doo-dad; pretty girl (see tsatskeh)

Tshav Cold spinach soup, sorrel grass soup, sour leaves
   soup (usually pronounced "shav")

Tshepeh zich nit tsu mir! Don't bother me!
   (Lit., Don't attach yourself to me!)

Tshepeh zich op fun mir! Get away from me! Leave me
   alone!

Tshepen To annoy, irk, plague, bother, attack
   unwantedly

Tsevishen-shtotisheh telefonistkeh Long distance
   operator

Tsegait zich in moyl It melts in the mouth, delicious,
   yummy-yummy

Tsemishnich Confusion

Tsetrogen Absent-minded

Tsevildeter Wild person

Tsiklen zich The cantor's ecstatic repetition of a musical
   phrase

Tsimmes   Sweet carrot compote; (slang) a major issue made out of a minor event; a fuss over nothing

Tsitskeh   Breast, teat, udder

Tsnueh   Chaste

Tsores   Troubles, misery

Tsu kumen oifen zinen   To come to mind

Tsu shand un tsu shpot   In disgrace and humiliation

Tsutsheppenish   Hanger-on; unwanted companion; pest; nuisance

Tsum glik, tsum shlimazel   For better, for worse

Tu mir a toiveh.   Do me a favor.

Tu mir nit kain toives.   Don't do me any favors.

Tu mir tsulib.   Do me a favor. Do it for my sake.

Tuckus   (See Toches)

Tumel   Confusion, noise, uproar

Tumler   A noise-maker (person); an agitator, boisterer, roisterer

Tush   Buttock (refers only to an infant's)

Tut mir hanoeh   It gives me pleasure (also used sarcastically)

Tut vai dos harts   Heartbroken

Tzatzkeh   Ornament, toy; a dingus, doo-dad; a living doll, a sexually attractive girl; an overdressed woman; a playgirl (same as "tsatskeh")

Tzitzis   Fringes attached to the four corners of the tallis; the prayer shawl

Tzufil!   Too much! Too dear! Too costly!

Tzu tei-er   Too costly

Tzures   Troubles (same as tsores)

Um-be-rufen Unqualified, uncalled for; God forbid; (A deprecation to ward off evil)

Um-be-shrien God forbid! It shouldn't happen! (A deprecation to ward off evil)

Umgeduldik Petulant

Ummeglich! Impossible!

Umglick A misfortune, tragedy; when it refers to a man, it means a born loser; an unlucky one

Umshteller Braggart

Umzist For nothing

Un langeh hakdomes! Cut it short! (Lit., Without a long introduction)

Unterkoifen To bribe

Untershmeichlen To butter up

Untervelt mentsh Racketeer

Utz To goad, to needle

Vai!   Woe, pain; usually appears as "oi vai!"

Vai iz mir!   Woe is me!

Vais ich vos   Stuff and nonsense! So you say! (Lit., Know from what)

Vaitik   An ache

Valgeren zich   Wander around aimlessly

Valgerer   Homeless wanderer

Vaneh   Bath, bathtub, tub

Vantz   Bedbug; (slang) a nobody

Varenikehs   Pastry made of rounds of noodle dough filled with jelly, fruit, or meat, and fried

Varfen an oyg   To watch out; to guard; to mind; (Lit., To throw an eye at)

Varnishkes   Kasha with noodles; stuffed potato cakes

Vart!   Wait! Hold on!

Vash-tsimmer   Bathroom, washroom

Vash-tsimmer far froyen   Ladies' room

Vash-tsimmer far menner   Men's room

Vechter   Watchman

Veibernik   Debauchee

Veibersheh shtik   Female tricks

Veis vi kalech!   Pale as a sheet!

Vek-zaiger   Alarm clock

Vemen barestu? (taboo)   Whom are you kidding? Whom are you fooling? (Lit., Whom are you screwing?)

Vemen narstu?   Whom are you fooling?

Ven ich ess, hob ich zai alleh in drerd   When I eat, they can all go to hell!

Ver derharget!   Get killed! Drop dead! (Also "ver geharget")

Ver dershtikt!   Choke yourself!

Ver farblondjet!   Get lost! Go away!

Ver vaist?   Who knows?

Ver volt dos geglaibt? Who would have believed it?

Veren a tel To be ruined

Vi a barg Large as a mountain

Vi der ruach zogt gut morgen Where the devil says good morning! (has many meanings; usually appended to another phrase)

Vi gait dos gesheft? How's business?

Vi gait es eich? How goes it with you?

Vi gaits? How goes it? How are things? How's tricks?

Vi haistu? What's your name?

Vi ruft men . . . ? What is the name of . . . ?

Vi ruft men eich? What is your name?

Viazoy? How come?

Vifil? How much?

Vilder mentsh A wild one; a wild person

Vilstu . . . Do you want . . .

Voglen To wander around aimlessly

Voiler yung! Roughneck (sarcastic expression)

Vo den? What else?

Vortshpiel Pun, witticism

Vos art es (mich)? What does it matter (to me)? What do I care?

Vos barist du? (taboo) What are you screwing around for? What are you fooling around for?

Vos bei a nichteren oyfen lung, is bei a shikkeren oyfen tsung. What a sober man has on his lung (mind), a drunk has on his tongue.

Vos draistu mir a kop? What are you bothering me for? (Lit., Why are you twisting my head?)

Vos failt zai? What are they lacking?

Vos gicher, alts besser The faster, the better

Vos hakst du mir in kop? What are you talking my head off for?

Vos hert zich? What do you hear around? What's up?

Vos hert zich epes nei-es? What's new?

Vos hob ich dos gedarft? What did I need it for?

Vos-in-der-kort   Capable of doing anything bad (applied to bad person; Lit., everything in the cards)

Vos iz?   What's the matter?

Vos iz ahfen kop, iz ahfen tsung!   What's on his mind is on his tongue!

Vos iz der chil'lek?   What difference does it make?

Vos iz der tachlis?   What's the purpose? Where does it lead to?

Vos iz di chochmeh?   What is the trick?

Vos iz di untershteh shureh?   What's the point? What's the outcome? (Lit., What's on the bottom line?)

Vos iz mit dir?   What's wrong with you?

Vos kocht zich in teppel?   What's cooking?

Vos macht dos oys?   What difference does it make?

Vos macht es mir oys?   What difference does it make to me?

Vos macht ir?   How are you? (pl.); How do you do?

Vos machstu?   How are you? (sing.)

Vos maint es?   What does it mean?

Vos noch?   What else? What then?

Vos ret ir epes?   What are you talking about?

Vos tut zich?   What's going on? What's cooking?

Vos vet zein (Que sera?)   What will be?

Vos vet zein, vet zein!   What will be, will be!

Vos zogt ir?   What are you saying?

Vu tut dir vai?   Where does it hurt you?

Vuhin gaistu?   Where are you going?

Vund   Wound

Vursht   Bologna

Vyzoso   Idiot (named after youngest son of Haman, archenemy of Jews in Book of Esther); also, penis

Yachneh A course, loud-mouthed woman; a gossip; a slattern

Yachsen Man of distinguished lineage, highly connected person; privileged character

Yarmelkeh Traditional Jewish skull cap, worn usually during prayers; worn at all times by observant Orthodox Jews, to indicate that someone (God) is above them; also worn by Catholic prelates

Yatebedam A man who threatens; one who thinks he's a big shot; a blusterer

Yeder mentsh hot zeineh aigeneh meshugahss. Every person has his own idiosyncrasies.

Yedies News; cablegrams; announcements

Yefayfiyeh Beauty; woman of great beauty

Yenems Someone else's; the other's (the brand of cigarettes moochers smoke!)

Yeneh velt The other world; the world to come

Yenteh Gaggy, talkative woman; female blabbermouth

Yentzen (taboo) To fornicate, to whore

Yentzer (taboo) Fornicator, whoremaster

Yeshiveh Jewish traditional higher school, talmudical academy

Yeshiveh bocher Student of talmudic academy

Yeshuvnik Farmer, rustic

Yichus Pedigree, ancestry, family background, nobility

Yiddisher kop Jewish head

Yingeh tsats-keh! A young doll! A living doll!

Yisgadal, vyiskadash (Hebrew) First two words of mourner's prayer honoring the dead

Yiskor Prayer in commemoration of the dead (Lit., May God remember.)

Yold! Dope, boor, chump, hick

Yontefdik Festive, holiday-ish; sharp (referring to

clothes)

Yontiff Any Jewish holiday (also spelled yomtov and yontev from the Hebrew—"yom tov"—a good day.)

Yortseit Anniversary of the day of death of parents or other relatives; yearly remembrance of the dead

Yoysher Justice, fairness, integrity

Yukel Buffoon

(A) Yung mit bainer! A powerhouse! Strongly built person (Lit., A boy with sturdy bones)

Yung un alt Young and old

Yungatsh Street-urchin, scamp, young rogue

Yungermantshik A young, vigorous lad; a newlywed

Zaft Juice
Zaftik Pleasantly plump and pretty (woman); well-stacked; sensuous looking (Lit., juicy)
Zaftikeh moid! Sexually attractive girl
Zaideh Grandfather
Zaier gut O.K. (Lit., very good)
Zaier shain gezogt! Well said! (Lit., Very beautifully said!)
Zeh nor, zeh nor! Look here, look here!
Zei (t) gezunt Be well! Good-bye! Farewell
Zei mir frailich! Be happy!
Zei mir gezunt! Be well!
Zei mir matriach Be at pains to . . . Please; make an effort.
Zei nit a nar! Don't be a fool!
Zei nit kain goylem! Don't be a fool! Don't be a robot!
Zei nit kain vyzoso! Don't be a damn fool! Don't be an idiot! also, don't be a penis! (taboo)
Zeit azoy gut Please (Lit., Be so good)
Zeit ir doch ahfen ferd! You're all set! (Lit., You're on the horse!)
Zeit (mir) moychel Excuse me! Be so good as . . . Forgive me!
Zelig Blessed (used mostly among German Jews in recalling a beloved deceased—mama zelig)
Zeltenkeit Rare thing
Zetz Punch, bang! Pow! Also slang for a sexual experience (taboo)
Zhaleven To be sparing, miserly
Zhlob A jerk; foolish, stupid, uncouth
Zhulik Faker
Zhumerei Whirring noise
Zhumet Makes a whirring noise
Zi farmacht nit dos moyl She doesn't stop talking

(Lit., She doesn't close her mouth)

Zindik nit   Don't complain. Don't sin. Don't tempt the Gods.

Ziseh neshomeh   Sweet soul

Ziseh raidelech   Sweet talk

Ziskeit   Sweet thing, sweetness (Also endearing term for child)

Zitsen ahf shpilkes   Sitting on pins and needles; being fidgety

Zitsen shiveh   Sit in mourning (Shiveh means seven, the number of days in the mourning period)

Zitsflaish   Patience (Lit., Sitting meat)

Zog a por verter!   Say a few words!

Zogen a ligen   Tell a lie.

Zogerkeh   Woman who leads the prayers in the women's section in the synagogue

Zoineh   Prostitute

Zol dich chapen beim boych.   You should get a stomach cramp!

Zol dir klappen in kop!   It should bang in your head (as it's annoying me!)

Zol er tsebrechen a fus!   May he break a leg! He should break a leg!

Zol es brennen!   The hell with it. (Lit. let it burn!)

Zol Got mir helfen!   May God help me!

Zol Got ophiten!   May God prevent!

Zol ich azoy vissen fun tsores!   I haven't got the faintest idea! (Lit., I should so know from trouble as I know about this!)

Zol vaksen tzibbelis fun pipek!   Onions should grow from your navel!

Zol zein!   Let it be! That's it!

Zol zein azoy!   O.K.! Let it be so!

Zol zein gezunt!   Be well! It (you, etc.) should be well!

Zol zein mit glik!   Good luck!

Zol zein shah!   Be quiet!

Zol zein shtil!   Silence! Be quiet! Let's have some quiet!

Zolstu azoy laiben!   You should live so!

Zolst geshvollen veren vi a barg!   You should swell up like a mountain!

Zolst leben un zein gezunt!   You should live and be well!

Zolst ligen in drerd!   Drop dead! (Lit., You should lie in the earth!)

Zolst nit vissen fun kain shlechts.   You shouldn't know from bad (evil).

Zolst es shtipin in toches! (taboo)   Shove it up your (anus) rectum!

Zorg zich nit!   Don't worry!

Zshlob   Slob

Zuninkeh!   Dear son! Darling son!

ENGLISH-YIDDISH

ABC's Alef-bais

A.K. Alter Kucker (taboo)

A bad person (capable of doing anything bad or evil!) Vos-in-der-kort

A big, good-for-nothing A groisser gornisht

A big healthy dame A gezunteh moid

A blessing Mi shebairach (sarcastically means a curse)

A blessing on your head A leben ahf dein kop; a brocheh ahf dein kop (used to mean "Well said!" "Well done!")

A curse on my enemies A klog tzu meineh sonim

A curse on you! A broch tsu dir! A choleryeh ahf dir! A finster yor ahf dir!

A fool feels nothing A nar filt nit

A great joy A shtik naches

A Hebrew school Talmud Torah

A little A bisel

A little nothing Shmendrik, nishtikeit, gornit

A lot to tell, little to hear A sach tsu reden, vainik tsu herren

A lucky thing happened to you! A glick hot dich getrofen!

A one and only An ain un aintsikeh

A person who drops whatever he touches Gelaimter

A pig remains a pig A chazer bleibt a chazer

A plague! A magaifeh! A finsternish!

A plague on you! A choleryeh ahf dir!

A shame and disgrace A shandeh un a charpeh

A smell and a taste (what you get when a hostess serves peanut-size hors d'oeuvres—and too few of them) A lek un a shmek

A strong character A shtarker charakter

Absent-minded Tsetrogen; oiver botel

Absolutely nothing! Kadoches mit koshereh fodem!

Accursed   Geshtroft
(An) Ache   Vaiťik
Acting bit   Shtik
Advantage   Meileh
**Agent with access to the authorities who procures favors
  for his clients for a fee**   Macher
Agitator   Tumler (at a resort)
Alarm clock   Vek-zaiger
Alas and alack!   Och un vai!
All at once   Mitten derinnen
All shoemakers go barefoot.   Aleh shusters gaien borves.
Alphabet   Alef-bais (the first two letters of the
  Hebrew-Yiddish alphabet)
Also a V.I.P.!   Oych a bashefenish!
Amen   Ohmain
Ancestry   Yichus
Anecdote   Meiseleh
Angel of death (male)   Malech-hamovess (sarcastically,
  bad husband)
  (female)   Malech-hamovesteh (sarcastically, bad wife)
Angry (with)   Kaas (in kaas oyf), baroygis
Angry person   Kaasnick, kaasen, farbrenter
Animal (cow)   Behaimeh (when referring to human being,
  means dull-witted)
Animal (wild)   Chei-eh, vildeh chei-eh
Anniversary of the death of a person   Yortseit
Announcements   Yedies
(To) Annoy   Tshepen zich, tsutshepen
Annoy persistently   Nudjen, tshepen zich
Annoying person   Nudje, nudnik
Another man's disease is not hard to endure.   A makeh
  unter yenems orem iz nit shver tzu trogen.
Antique   Tranteh (refers to rag; sarcastically, worn out
  or useless)
Any Jewish holiday   Yontiff, also spelled yomtov and
  yontev

Anybody no good at their job Kalyekeh
Anything bad to eat or own Chazzerei
Anything worthless Shmatteh (Lit., rag)
Anxious Fardeiget
Apoplexy Shlak
Appetizer Forshpeiz
Apple-polisher Toches-lecker (taboo)
Are you beginning again? Fangst shoin on? Haibst shoin on?
Are you crazy? Bistu meshugeh?
Are you in a hurry? Bist ahf ain fus?
Are you starting up again? Du fangst shoyn on?
Aren't you finished? Nu, shoyn?
Artisan Balmelocheh
As futile as stomping on the earth Es iz vert a zets in drerd
As long as I can be with you Abi tsu zein mit dir
As long as you're healthy Abi gezunt
As unimportant as dung on a piece of wood Drek ahf a shpendel (taboo)
(An) Aside Shushkeh
Ask me another! (To show indifference or ignorance)
Ass Chamoyer, ezel, eizel
   Freg mich becherim
Asset Meileh
Ass-licker (taboo) Toches-lecker
Ass-kisser (taboo) Toches-lecker
Associates Chevreh, chaverim, shutfim
Assuredly Tahkeh
Astonishment (exclamation) Oi!
Atonement Kaporeh
Attractive girl Tsatskeh
(An) Authority Maivin
Average man Mittelmessiker
Aw, hell! A broch!
Awful! Geferlech!
Awkward person Klotz, kunyehlemmel; nebbish, nebach

Baby son   Kaddishel (endearing term)
Bachelor, unmarried man   Bocher, nit baveibter, alter bocher
Back-handed slap   Frassk
Backside   Hinten
Bad   Shlecht, kalyeh
Bad odor   Ippish
(A) Bad man   Parech, parechavatter, oisvurf
Bad person   Oisvurf, vos-in-der-kort
Bad taste   Main bobbeh's ta'am (Lit., My grandmother's taste)
(To) Badger   Nudjen
(A) Badgerer   Nudje, nudnik
(A mere) Bagatelle   Bubkes, bobkes; ain klainikeit!
Baked dumplings (filled with potato, meat, liver or barley)   K'nishes (pronounce the K!)
(A) Bang   Chmalyeh, klop, zetz, k'nack
Bang your head against the wall!   Klop zich kop in vant!
Barefoot   Borves
Barely able to creep   Kam vos er kricht
Barely alive!   Kam vos er lebt!
Barely made it!   Kam mit tsores!
Bargain   Metsieh
(To) Bargain   Dingen zich, handlen
Bashful   Shemevdik
Bastard   Mamzer
Bath   Vaneh, bod
Bath-ritual   Mikveh
Bat at pains to, (please)   Zeit zich matriach
Be happy!   Zeit frailich!
Be so good, (please)   Zeit azoy gut!
Be so good as   Zeit moychel; zeit zich matriach
Be quiet!   Zol zein shtil! Zol zein sha!

(To) Be ruined Veren a tel
Be well! Zei(t) gezunt
Beadle of the synagogue Shammes
(To) Beam Kvelen
(To) Beam with delight and pride K'velen fun naches
Beans Bubkes, beblech
Beast Behaimeh; (sarcastically, fool)
Beat it! Chap a gang! Farnem zich fun danen! Gai avek!
(To) Beat up Shlogen
Beautiful as the seven worlds Shain vi di zibben velten
Beautiful woman Krassavitseh
(A) Beauty Krassavitseh, shainkeit, yefayfiyeh
Bedbug Vantz
Beet soup Borsht
Befuddled Farmisht, tsemisht, tsedrumshki, tsetumelt, fartshadikt
Beggar Shnorrer, hoizer, gaier, betler
Behind (buttocks) Toches, inten, hinten
Belch Greps
Believe me! Gloib mir!
Belles lettres Shaineh literatur
Belly-button Pipek, pupik
Beloved Basherter (fated); gelibteh
Bending your ear Farblujet
Benefactor Bal-tsedokeh, nadven
Benevolence Tsedokeh
(To) Berate Derniderriken
Betrothal T'no'im, shidech
Bewildered Farmisht, tsemisht, tsetumelt, farblondjet
Big bargain Groisseh metsieh
Big boss! Balebos
Big breadwinner! (Sarcastically said of a person who isn't) Groisser fardiner! Parnosseh gebber!
Big deal! Ain klainikeit! (derisive expression, a small matter); gantseh megillah, groisseh gedillah, tararam; (sarcastically, about someone else) A glich hot dich

getrofen!
Big eater   Fresser
Big healthy damsel   Gezinteh moid!
Big hand   Lapeh
Big mouth (sarcastic)   Pisk, gembeh
Big noise   Tararam
Big prick!   Groisser potz! (taboo)
Big producer! (who doesn't produce)   Shvitser!
Big shot (who thinks he's a big shot)   Yatebedam;
  groisser gornisht; groisser potz (derogatory and taboo)
Big shot (big wheel)   K'nacker; gantser k'nacker;
  groisser shisser; macher
Big talker, little doer!   Pisk-malocheh!
Big thing!   A glick ahf dir! (sarcastically used for little
  good fortunes that occur)
Bit   Shtik, shtikel
Bit of acting   A shtik
Bitter person   Farbissener
Blabbermouth (female)   Yenteh
(A) Black year!   A shvartz yor!
Blasphemous person   Grober yung, grobyon, grubyon
Bless ye!   Boruchu! (Hebrew)
Blessed   Zelig
Blessed be God!   Boruch hashem (Hebrew)
Blessed with children   Gebentsht mit kinder
Blessing over bread   Hamoitzeh. The full blessing is:
  Boruch ato adonoi elo-hainu melech oilom hamotzi
  lechem min ho'orets.
Blessing over wine   Kiddish. The full blessing is: Boruch
  ato adonoi elo-hainu melech oilom borai pri hagofen.
Blinding the eyes!   Shvindilt in di oygen!
Blockhead! (Ass!)   Chamoyer, du ainer!
Blues singer   Krechtser
Blundering   Farblondjet
(A) Blusterer   Yatebedam
Boarding house with cooking privileges   Kochalain

Boil Makeh
Boisterer Tumler; shaigets, shkotz
Bologna Vursht
Bon mot Gleichvertel
Bon voyage For gezunterhait! Gai gezunterhait!
(The) Book of services for the first two nights of Passover Hagadah
Boor Yold, amo'orets, amorets, poyer
Boorish young man Gruber yung
Boorish or coarse person Bulvan
Bore Nudnik
Born loser Shlimazel; umglicklecher
Borsht circuit The Catskill mountains where there are so many Jewish hotels (see Yiddish-English section)
Boss Balhabos (pl., balalbatim); balebos
(To) Bother Tshepen, bareh
Bothersome hanger-on Ontshepenish, tsutshepenish
Boy (affectionate) Boitshik, boitshikel (**Americanism**); yingel
Boy (becoming a man) Bar-mitzvah
Braggart Barimer, shvitser, ois'shteler, umshteller
Brand-new Shpogel nei.
Brave Mutik heldish; brahv; shtark
Brazenness Chutzpeh
Break a leg! Brech a fus!
Break wind Fortz, fortzen (taboo)
Breast Tsitskeh (taboo), brist, brust
(To) Bribe (slang) Shmeer, unterkoifen, geben shoychad
Bridal canopy Chupeh
Bride Kalleh
Bride and groom Chossen-kalleh
Bridegroom Chossen
Bright saying Chochmeh
Broker Mekler (fem., meklerkeh)
Brothel Bordel, shandhoiz, heizel
Brother-in-law Shvoger

Brown-noser Tocheslecker (taboo)
(A) Brunhilde Gezunteh moid
Buckwheat Kasheh
Buffoon Shmegegi, yold, shmendrik, yukel
Bum Trombenik
Bum (he) Bohmer ((Americanism)
   (she) Bohmerkeh (Americanism)
Bungler Klotz, shlemiel, shlimazel, tsedaiter kop
Burst! Plats!
Burglar Ganef, goniff
Burp Grepts
Burst with frustration Platsen
(To) Bury Bagroben
Business Geshefts
(The) Business (as, giving you . . .) Shmeeren, onzaltzen
Bust! Plats!
Bust your guts out! Plats!
(To) Bust Platsen
(A) Busy-body Kochleffel
Butter-fingered Shlemiel
(To) Butter up Untershmeichlen, shmeichel
Buttocks Toches, hinten, inten; tush (only applied to
   infant)
Button K'neppel, k'nop
Buxom girl Moid; gezunteh moid; zaftikeh moid
By all means! Aderabeh-ve'aderabeh

Cancer-shmancer, as long as you're healthy
Cancer-shmancer, abi gezunt
Candlestick (seven-branched)   Menorah, menoireh
Cantor   Chazen
Cantor's singing   Tsiklen zich
Capable housewife and homemaker (complimentary term)   Balebosteh, beryeh
Careless dresser   Shlump, opgelozen(er)
Carrot compote   Tsimmes
(To) Carouse   Hulyen
(To) Carry   Shlepen
(To) Carry or pull an extra object or person   Shlep, shlepen
Cash   Mezuma, mezumen
Cash only! Don't ask for credit!   Ribi-fish, gelt ah-fen tish!
Cash on the barrel-head!   Ribi-fish, gelt ah-fen tish!
Casper Milquetoast   Kunyehlemel, shnook, lemeshkeh
Casting off sins on the New Year   Tashlich
Caustic greeting (used in reference to women)   Skotsel kumt!
Ceremony of the casting off of sins on the New Year   Tashlich
Certainly!   Tahkeh!
Charity   Tsdokeh
Chaste (applied to a female)   Frum, opgehit, tsnueh
Chat   Shmu'es
(To) Chat   Shmuessen
(To) Chatter   Plaplen
Chattering   Reden on a moss; Yatatata
Cheap (price)   Billik
(person)   Parshiveh, parech, mieser nefesh, karger
Cheap as soup   Billik vi borsht (a real bargain!)
Cheap skate (female)   Kushinyerkeh, mark-yiddeneh

Cheap skate (male) Karger, mieser oisvorf
(To) Cheat Yentzen, opnaren
(A) Cheater Yentzer, shvindler, oisvorf
Cheated Opgenart, opgeyentzt
Cheek (impudence) Chutzpeh
Cheese or jellied pancakes rolled in dough and fried in fat
  Blintses
Chicken gizzards Pupiklech
Child Shtik naches (Lit., Piece of joy); kind
Child (youngest in family) Mizinikil
Childbirth amulet (or charm) Kimpet-tzettel
Children Kinder
Children (affectionate term) Kinderlech
Chiseler Shnorrer
Choke yourself! Ver dershtikt!
Cholera Chalerya, choleryeh
Chopped herring Gehakteh hering
Chopped liver Gehakteh leber
Chopped meat Hak flaish
Chronic ailment Farshlepteh krenk
Chronic complainer Pitshetsh, klogmuter (masc. and
  fem.)
Chump Yold
Circumcision, (the ceremony of circumcision) Bris, bris
  mieleh
Circumciser (man who performs ritual of circumcision)
  Mohel
Clever fellow Molodyets
Clumsy bungler Shlemiel, kunyeh-lemel, lemeshkeh,
  shlimazel
Clumsy, sluggish person (robot-type) Golem, goilem
Clumsy person Klotz, kunyehlemel, shlemiel, shmendrek,
  shlimazel, lemeshkeh
Clutched at my heartstrings Klemt mir beim hartz
Cluttered Ongepatschket, ongervarfen
Coachman Balagoleh

Coarse Grob, prost

(A) Coarse person Grober yung, bulvan, grober, prostak, grubyan

Coarse, loud-mouthed woman Yachneh, yenteh

Coat like butter (bribe) Shmeer

Coat (long) worn by ultra religious Jews Kaftan

Coffee cake (like Danish pastry) Shnecken

Cold spinach soup Tshav

Colleague Chaver (pl., chavairim)

Come in! Arein! Kumt arein!

Come now! Gait, gait!

(To) Come to mind Tsu kumen oifen zinen

Come to the point! Mach es kalechdik un shpitzik! Nit gandjet!

Come-upper Oyfgekumener; olreitnik (Americanism)

Commandment Mitzveh, di (-s)

Commandment to study the Law Talmud torah

Commemoration service of the dead Yiskor

Common Prost

Common man Proster mentsh

Common people Prosteh leit, proster oilem, hamoyn

Common sense; good sense Saichel; mit a kop oif the plaitses

Communal busybody Shlatten-shammes

Company (of people) Chevreh

Compassion Rachmones

Competent housewife Balebosteh, beryeh

Complain K'vetsh, klogen

Complainer K'vetsher, klogmuter (male and fem.)

Complaint (of a novel sort) A chissoren, di kaleh is tsu shain

Complete details Gantseh megilleh (slang)

Compulsive eater Fresser

Comrade Chaver (pl., chavairim)

(To) Con Shmeikel

Conceited Ongeblozzen, grois-halter, ba'al gaiveh

Confused　Tsemisht, tsetumelt, tsedrumshket
Confusing (work)　Ongepatshket
Confusion (noise)　Tumel, tsemishnich
Confusion (mix-up) (slang)　Kasheh, mishmash
Conglomeration　Kakapitshi
Congratulations!　Mazel-tov!
Conniver　Draikop
Connoisseur　Maivin
Continuous eater of delicacies　Nasher
Conversation　Shmu'es
Cooked groats and broad noodles　Kasheh varnishkes
Coquette　Pitshetsheh, koketkeh
Corny　Shmaltzy
Costly　Teier
Could be!　Ken zein! Efsher!
Countryman　Lantsman, landsman (a fellow townsman
　from the old country)
Country peddler　Karabelnick, hoizirer
Cow　Behaimeh (sarcastically, dull-witted person)
Cracklings　Gribbenes (or grivvenes, greeven)
Craze　Meshugahss
Crazy　Meshugeh, tsedrait
Crazy antics　Meshugahss
Crazy as a loon!　Meshugeh ahf toi't!
Crazy bastard!　Meshugener mamzer!
Crazy man　Meshugener
Crazy woman　Meshugeneh
(A) Crazy world　A meshugeneh velt!
Crepe suzettes　Blintses
Criminal, murderer, racketeer (depending on your point of
　view)　Gazlen untervelt mentsh
Cripple　Kalyekeh
**Critic who criticizes things that don't exist or that are
　uncriticizable**　Er kricht oyf di gleicheh vent!
Crook　Ganef
Crooked actions　Genaivisheh shtiklech

Cross-eyed　Kasokeh, kosokeh
Crude　Grob
Crude person　Grober yung, grobyan, grubyan
Cry for help　Oi g'vald! or just plain "G'vald!!!!"
Cry of anguish　Oi, g'vald!
Cry of distress for help (Lit., force, violence)　G'vald!!
Cry of suffering, or frustration　Oi, g'vald!
Curse　Choleryah, makeh, shlok; a broch! A finster yor!
　An umglik! A finsternish!
Cursed, accursed　Geshtroft
Curses!　A broch! A klog!
Customary gifts exchanged on Purim (usually goodies)
　Shalach mohnes
Cut it short!　Un langeh hakdomes! Shpitz bekitzur!
Cut-rate store　Shlak joint (Americanism)
Cute (like a girl)　Tsatskeh

Daddy   Tateh, tatteh, tatteleh, tatinkeh, tatteniu
Daily   Tog-teglech
Daily prayer book   Sidder
Dairy dietary law   Milchiks (milk product foods must not be eaten at same meal with meat (flaishik) foods); (adj.) Milchikeh or milichdik
Dairy foods   Milchiks (of milk base content); milechiks
Damn it!   A broch!
Danger   Sakoneh
Dangerous   Geferlech, sakoneh
Darling   Neshomeleh, teiers
Darling son   Zuninkeh
Daughter   Bas (Hebrew); tochter (Yiddish)
Daughter-in-law   Shnur
David's shield   Mogen David
Day-to-day   Tog-teglech
Dead hungry   Toit hungerik
Dear   Teier
Dear me!   Oi vai!
Dear son   Zunin-keh
Debauchee   Hultei, veibernik
Decayed   Forfoilt, tsefoilt
Deception   Shvindel, opnarerei
Decorated (beautified)   Oysgeputst, fartrasket, oisgeshtrozelt
Decorative (something)   Putskeh
Decrepit person or thing   Tranteh, altvarg, noiteh lomus
Deep sorrow or hurt   Fardross
(To) Defecate   Kucken (taboo)
Defecate on him!   Kuck im on (taboo)
Defecator   Kucker (taboo)
Delicacy   Meichel
Delicious   Tsegait zich in moyl

Delicious tasting Geshmak, mecheieh, mecheiehdik
Delight Naches, hanoeh, fraid, fargenigen
(To be) Delighted K'velen
(To be) Destined Bashert zein
Devout Frum (frimer)
Dietary laws Kashress
Diminutive suffixes El, eleh
Diminutive, affectionate term for children Kinderlech
(To) Dine Essen mitek
Dingus Tsatskeh
Diplomacy Saichel, diplomatyeh
Dipped Toonked, tunked, eingetunken
Dirt Shmuts
Dirty Shmutsik
Disappointment Ahntoisht, zich filen opgenart
Disappointment Ahntoishung, fardross
Disbelief, distaste, contempt Phooey! Fuie! Fu zol es veren!
Disdain (exclamation) Pooh!
(In) Disgrace and humiliation. Tsu shand un tsu shpot
Disgust (exclamation) Oi! (Please say this in a disgusting way—with a grunt-like sound coming deep from the throat!)
Disgusting fellow Paskudnik, paskudnyak, ekeldiker parshoyn
Dismay Oi vai!
Disordered Ongepatshket, ongevarfen
Distressed Fardeiget
Divorce Get
Dizzy Shvindeldik
(Feeling) Dizzy Shvindilt in di oygen
(To) Do all the talking A braiteh daieh hoben
Do it fast! Maches shnel!
Do it for my sake. Tu mir tsulib.
Do me a favor. Tu mir a toiveh. Tu mir tsulib.
Do me a favor and drop dead! Folg mich a gang un gai

in dr'erd!
(To) Do things in time-wasting manner   Patshken
Do you want?   Vilstu?
Does it matter to you?   S'art eich?
Doesn't worry.   Nishgedeiget
Doll   Tsatskeh, krassavitseh, yefayfiyeh
Dolt   Shnook, shlepper, temp
Done in!   Opgeflickt
Donkey, you!   Chamoyer du ainer!
Don't annoy me!   Bareh mich nit!
Don't ask for credit!   Ribi-fish, gelt ahfen tish!
Don't be a damn fool!   Zei nit kain vyzosoh!
Don't be a fool!   Zei nit a nar! Zei nit kain goylem!
Don't be an idiot!   Zei nit kain vyzosoh!
Don't be silly!   Gai shoyn, gai! Zei nit kain nar!
Don't bleed me!   Tsap mir nit dos blut!
Don't bother me!   Drai mir nit kain kop! Hak mir nit kain
   tsheinik! Tshpeh zich nit tsu mir! Tshepeh zich op fun
   mir!
Don't bother me!   Gai kucken ahfen yam! (taboo)
   (Lit., go defecate on the ocean!)
Don't complain.   Zindik nit. Baklog zich nit.
Don't do me any favors.   Tu mir nit kain toives.
Don't double talk.   Nisht gefonfet. Fonfeh nit.
Don't fool around.   Nisht gefonfet; bareh nit! (taboo)
Don't fornicate around.   Bareh nit! (taboo)
Don't get excited!   Shat, shat. Se brent nit!
Don't give me a canary; (don't give me an evil eye).   Gib
   mir nit kain einhoreh
Don't hedge.   Nisht gefonfet.
Don't make a big deal out of it!   Mach nit kain tsimmes
   fun dem!
Don't mix things up!   Farmisht nit di yoytzres!
Don't screw me around.   Bareh mich nit.
Don't sin!   Zindik nit!
Don't tempt fate.   Zindink nit

Don't threaten me!   Strasheh mich nit!
Don't twist my head!   Drai mir nit kain kop!
Don't worry!   Deigeh nisht! Hob nit kain deiges!
   Nishtgedeiget! Zorg zich nit!
Dope   Shmendrik, yold, chamoyer, eizel, nar
Dopey, clumsy person   Shlemiel
Doo-dad   Tshatshki, tsatskeh
(To) Double-talk.   Funfen, fonfen
Dowdy, gossipy woman   Shlepperkeh, rechielesnitseh
Down the hatch!   Le'chayim, l'chei-im
Dowry   Nadan
Drab   Nebbish, nebach
(To) Drag, carry or haul (particularly unnecessary things
   or parcels) Shlepen
Dreary   Kalamutneh
Dressed up (to the hilt!)   Oysgeputst
Dried   Gedarteh, dareh
Driver   Balagoleh
Drop dead!   Geharget zolstu veren! Ver derharget! Ver
   geharget! Zolst ligen in drerd! Lig in drerd! Ich hob
   dich! (mildest)
Drummer in a band   Barabantshik
Drunk   Shikker
Drunkard   Shikker
Drunken, inebriated   Shikker, farshnoshket
Ducky (swell, pleasant)   Katshkedik
Dull person, clumsy and sluggish   Goilem
Dull-witted   Behaimeh, poyer
Dullard   Temper kop, poyer
Dumb like a piece of wood!   Shtik holtz!
Dumbbell!   Dumkop!
Dumplings (round and cooked)   K'naidlech
   (flat, filled and baked)   K'nishes
Dunce   Dumkop
Dung   Drek (taboo)
Dungy   Farkakteh, fekuckteh
Dunked   Tunked, toonked, eingetunken

(To) Earn a blessing (by doing a good deed)   Fardinen a
   mitzveh
East   Mizrach
Eastern   Mizrach
Eastern wall in synagogue   Mizrach vant
Eat in good health!   Ess gezunterhait!
(To) Eat like a pig!   Fressen vi a chazzer!
Eccentric (man)   Meshuggener, tsedreiter
   (woman)   Meshuggeneh, tsedreiteh
Egghead (Talmudic)   Batlen
Eggs   Baitsim (taboo), aier
Either too much or not enough.   Oder a klop, oder a fortz
   (taboo)
Elite   Feinshmeker, meyuches, choshever mentsh
Emaciated   Oysgedart, oysgetsert
Embittered   Farbissener
End of the world!   Ek velt!
Endearing suffix   -Niu; el, eleh
Endearing term (for anybody you like, young or old)
   Bubeleh, bubbee, tsatskeleh
Enema   Kaneh, cristiyer, cristiyah
(To) Engage (hire)   Dingen
Engaged couple   Chossen-kalleh
Enjoy   Shepen naches
Enough is enough!   Genug is genug!
Erudite person   Lamden
Esteem   Koved, derech erets
Every person has his own idiosyncrasies.   Yeder mentsh
   hot zeineh aigener meshugahssen.
Evil eye   Einhoreh
Excited   Tsekocht
Excitable person   Kasnik, keisnik, hitskop, farbrenter
Exclamation of disgust, pain, astonishmen or rapture   Oi!!

110

Exclamation of surprise, dismay or disapproval   Och! Oh!
Exclamation of disdain   Pooh!
Excrement (human)   Drek (taboo)
Excuse me.   Zeit (mir) moychel. Antshuldik mir.
Exhausted   Oysgehorevet, farmutshet.
Expensive   Teier
Expert   Maivin, mumcheh
Expression of dismay   Oy, vai! (vai means pain)
Expressman   Balagoleh
Extreme pleasure   Grois fargenigen

Fag Faigeleh (taboo)
(To) Faint Chaleshen
Fainted Gechahlesht
Faintness Chaloshes
Fairness Yoysher
Fairy tale Bobbeh meisseh
Fait accompli! A nechtiker tog! Farfallen!
Faith-healer Bal Shem
Faker Trombenik, zhulyik
Fall guy Shlumpf; seir l'azozel (Hebrew for scapegoat)
False or forced laugh Lachen mit yash-tsherkis
Family Mishpocheh
Family affairs Mishpocheh-zachen
Fan Focher, fochah
Fanny (buttocks) Inten, hinten, toches (taboo)
Farewell! Zei(t) gezunt!
Farmer Yishuvnik, poyer
Fart (taboo) Fortz (taboo)
(To) Fast-talk Shmeikel
Fat Shmaltz (grease or oil compounds)
Fat Fet (robust, plump)
Fated Bashert
(The) Fated one; the destined one Basherter
Father Tateh, tatteh, tatteleh, tatinka, tatteniu, foter
Father-in-law Shver
Fatigued Farmutshet
Feces (Dung) Drek (taboo)
Feeble-minded Tam chosser daieh; tamavateh
Feeding rabinnical students Essen teg
Feeling dizzy Shvindilt in di oygen
Fellow (young) who assumes airs Gantser mentsh
Female Nekaiveh (also means tart or whore)

112

Female Angel of Death Malech-hamovesteh
Female blabbermouth Yenteh
Female broker Meklerkeh
Female demon Klipeh
Female infant (affectionate term) Pisherkeh (taboo;
Lit., Little urinator)
Female tricks Veiberisheh shtik
Festive Yontenfdik
Fever Kadoches, feeber, hitz
Fidgety Zitsen ahf shpilkes
Fiftieth Wedding Anniversary Goldeneh chasseneh
Fighter (usually for a cause) Kemfer
Filthy rich Ongeshtopt mit gelt
Finally Sof-kol-sof
(A) Find (bargain) Metsieh
Fine (upstanding) Balebatish
Finicky Aidel gepatshket; prietskeh (refers only to a girl)
Finished! A nechtiker tog!
First two words of mourner's prayer for the dead
Yisgadal, vyiskadash
Five dolar bill Finef, finferl
Flattery Shmaltz (slang); drek (taboo)
(To) Flatulate Fortzen (taboo)
Flatulence Fortz (taboo)
Flavor Ta'am
(To) Fleece Yentz, opnaren
Floorshow Kabaret forshtelung
Folly Shmontses
Food forbidden under Jewish dietary laws Traif, traifeh
Food that meets rules of Jewish dietary laws Kosher
Fool Nar; slang—shlemiel, shmendrik, shmegegi,
behaimeh, ferd, yold
Fool (self-made) Shmok (taboo)
Fooled Opgenart
Foolish Narish
(A) foolish, dumb person Shlump, shlub, zhlub

Foolish (fruitless) question　Klotz kasheh
Foolishness　Narishkeit
Fooey!　Feh!
For a change!　In a noveneh!
For better, for worse　Tsum glik, tsum shlimazel
For nothing　Umzist
For the sake of　Vegen
Forbidden food　Traif
Forbidden literature　Traifeneh bicher, traifeneh literatur
Forget him!　Ich hob im in bod!
Forget it!　A nechtiker tog! (idiom) Fargess es! (Lit.)
Forgetful　Katzisher kop, katz-in-kop
Forgive me　Zeit (mir) moychel
(To) Fornicate　Baren, trenen, yentzen (all taboo)
Fornicator (taboo)　Yentzer
Fracture　Broch
Fractured English　Gebrochener english; gehakteh english
Fraud　Shvindel
(A) free-loader　Shlepper, shnorrer
Free-thinking Jew　Apikoiress ,goy
Free-thinking Jewish girl　Apikoiresteh, goyeh
Fried chicken skin or fat　Gribbenes, grivvenes, greeven
Friend (male)　Chaver (pl., chavairim)
　　　(fem.)　Chaverteh
Friendly face　Haimish ponim
Friendly term for anybody you like　Bubbee (booh-bee)
Frig you! (taboo)　Tren zich! (taboo)
Fringed garment　Tsitseh-kanfes, talis koten
Fringed sleeveless shirt　Leibtsudekel
**Fringes attached to the four corners of the tallis (prayer
　shawl)**　Tsitsis, tzitz
From your mouth to God's ear!　Fun dein moyl in Gots
　oyern!
Front row in the synagogue　Mizrach-vant
Frozen　Farfroyren
Fruit and nut coffee rolls　Shnecken

Fruitless, endless matter Farshlepteh krenk
Full of care, anxiety Fardeiget
Funeral Levei-yah
(To) Futz around Patshken
(A) Fuss over nothing Machen a tsimmes

Gabby, talkative, shrewish woman   Yenteh, klipeh

Gadabout   Kochleffel

Gall (impudence)   Chutzpeh

Garden of eden, paradise   Ganaiden

Gargle solution   Haldz-shvenkechts

Gather pleasure   Shepen naches

Gentile   Goy

Gentile boy   Shaigetz (pl., shkotzim)

Gentile woman   Goyeh

Gentle   Gemitlich

Get a move on!   Gib zich a shockel! Gib zich a traisel! Eilt zich!

Get away from me!   Tshepeh zich op fun mir!

Get killed!   Ver derharget! Ver geharget!

Get lost! Go away!   Ver farblondjet! Trog zich op!

Get lost!   Gai kucken ahf dem yam (taboo; Lit., Go defecate in the ocean)

(To) Get rid of   Obtshepen zich

Getting senile   Aiver butel, veren oiver botel

Gimmick   Machareikeh

Girl of marriageable age   Kalleh moid

Gizzard   Pipek, pupik

Glass of tea   Glezel tai

Gloomy   Kalamutneh, kalemutneh

(To) Glow with pride and happiness   K'velen

(A) Gnawing, grinding person   Grizhidiker

Go away!   Gai avek!

Go away, get lost!   Ver farblondjet!

Go bang your head against the wall!   Gai klop zich kop in vant!

Go-between (male)   Mekler

  (fem.)   Meklerkeh

Go bother the bedbugs!   Gai bareh di vantsen!

116

Go break a leg!   Gai tsebrech a fus!

Go break your own head!   Shlog zich kop in vant!

Go drive yourself crazy!   Gai fardrai zich dein (aigenem) kop!

Go drive yourself crazy, then you'll know how I feel.   Fardrai zich dein kop, vest du mainen s'iz meiner!

Go fight City Hall!   Shlog zich mit Got arum! Gai shlog zich mit Got arum!

Go fight heaven!   Gai shlog zich mit Got!

Go flap your ears!   Ich hob dich!

Go frig yourself!   Gai tren zich (taboo)

Go jump in a lake!   Nem zich a vaneh!

Go mix yourself up, not me!   Gai fardrai zich dein aigenem kop!

Go peddle your fish elsewhere!   Gai feifen ahfen yam!

(To) Go somewhere unwillingly or unwantedly   Shlepen zich

Go split your guts!   Gai plats!

Go take a bath!   Nem zich a vaneh!

Go take a shit for yourself (taboo)   Kuck zich oys! (taboo)

Go to hell!   Gai in drerd arein! Ich hob dich in drerd! Gai kabenyah mattereh!

Go to the devil!   A ruach in dein taten's taten arein!

Goad   Utz

God   Oybershter; der Oybershter in himel; Got

God damn it!   A broch!

God forbid! (It shouldn't happen!)   Cholileh! Got zol ophiten! Nishtu gedacht! Chas v'cholileh Chas v'sholem! Umbeshrien! Umberufen!

God in Heaven, Master of the Universe!   Riboynoy-Shel Oylom! (Hebrew)

God in Heaven!   Got in himmel! (said in anguish, despair, fear or frustration); also, Oybershter in himmel!

God knows   Got vaist

God, our Father   Tateniu-Foter

God should hear you and favor you!   Fun eier moyl in

Gots oyeren!

God watches out for fools!   Got hit op di naronim

God will it!   Alivei! Halevai!

God will punish!   Got vet shtrofen!

God willing!   Mirtsishem (contraction of Im yirtseh Hashem)

Going into labor to give birth   Gaien tsu kind

Golden country   Goldeneh medineh (usually refers to the United States)

Gonorrhea   Tripper

Good-bye   Zei(t) gezunt. (A) Guten tog. Gai gezunterhait! A guten!

Good-day   (A) Guten tog

Good deed   Mitsveh

(A) Good-for-nothing   Groisser gornisht

Good for nothing!   Toig ahf kapores!

Good health!   Gezunt-heit!

Good health to you!   A gezunt ahf dein kop!

Good holiday!   Gut yontev!

Good Jew   Shainer Yid

Good luck!   Zol zein mit glick! Mazel tov!

Good luck to you!   A glick ahf dir!

Good Sabbath!   Gut Shabbes

Good taste   Ta'am

Good things (food, dollars, news, etc.)   Guts (gits)

Gooey food   Shmaltz, shmaltzik

(A) Goof   Shmoe (Americanism)

Goofy parents, goofy children   Meshugeneh gens, meshugeneh gribenes

(A) Gossip   Yachneh, yenteh; rechilesnutzeh; plyotkenitzeh

(To) Gossip   Shushken zich, bareden yenem

(A) Gourmand   Fresser

Gourmandizing   Fressing (Americanism)

Gourmet's delight   Meichel

Grace at meals   Bentshen; birchas hamozoin (Hebrew)

Grandchild Ainikel; shtik naches (fig.)
Grandfather Zaideh
Grondmother Bobbeh
Grandmother's story (figuratively, a fairy tale, an unbelievable story) Bobbeh meiseh, baba meiseh, bubbeh meiseh
Gratification (from children) Naches
Grease (fat) Shmaltz
Great! Ei, gut!
(A) Great pleasure (usually food) Mecheieh!
(A) Great pleasure (to meet you) A fargenigen (tzu eich bagaigenen)
Great satisfaction Mecheieh
Groan Ech! (of disgust); oy, vai! (of distress)
Groans Krechts
Groats Kasheh
Growl Burtshen
(To) Guard Varfen an oyg
(A) Guilty person is always sensitive Ahfen goniff brent dos hittel
Guy who desn't smell too good Shtunk, shtinker

(A) Hag (also worthless) Shkapeh
Hanger-on Shlepper, nuchshlepper, tsutsheppenish
Happiness Naches, frailechkeit
Happy Frailech
Happy-go-lucky people A lebedikeh velt
Happy Sabbath! Gut shabbos!
Hard Shver
Hard circular roll with hole in the center like a doughnut
 Bagel, baigel
Hard doughnut with glazed surface Bagel, baigel
Hard-luck guy Shlimazel
Hard-luck sucker Shlimazel
Hard-working, efficient housewife Beryeh
(To) Haul Shlepen
(To) Have a yen for Farglist, farglust, glusten tsu,
 hoben chaishek tsu
(To) Have no end of brouble Hoben tsu zingen un tsu
 zogen
Have respect! Hob derech erets!
Have you finished the dirty work? Shoyn opgetrent?
 (taboo) (Lit., Have you finished fornicating?)
Having a ball! Laibt a tog! Leben a guten tog!
He aspires to higher places (beyond his reach) Er kricht
 in di hoyecheh fenster
He doesn't give a damn! Es ligt im nit in zinnen. Er hot
 es in drerd.
He doesn't know what he's looking at! Er kukt vi a hun
 in a B'nai Odom!
He eats like a horse. Er frest vi a ferd.
He eats as if just recovered from a sickness. Er est vi noch
 a krenk.
He has a cold. Er hot a farshtopteh nonyeh. Er iz farkilt.
He has odd ways. Er hot modneh drochim Er pravhet

meshugeneh shtik.

He has no say (authority).　Er hot nit kain daieh!

He has nothing!　Er hot kadoches!

He has nothing at all.　Er hot a makeh (boil)!

He hasn't got a worry!　Er hot nit kain zorg!

He makes a lot of trouble for me.　Er macht mir a shvartzeh chasseneh! Er tut mir on tsores.

He makes a mess.　Er farkocht a kasheh.

He-man　Mentsh, parshoin

He repeats himself; (he re-hashes things over and over again)　Er molt gemolen mel.

He ruins it.　Er macht a tel fun dem.

He should burn up!　A feier zol im trefen! Brenen zol er!

He should drop dead!　Paigeren zol er!

He should go to hell!　Er zol einemen a miesseh meshuneh! A gehenem oif ihm!

He should grow like an onion, with his head in the ground.　Er zol vaksen vi a tsibeleh, mit dem kop in drerd.

He should have lots of trouble!　A miesseh meshuneh! Alleh tzores oif zein kop!

He talks himself into a sickness!　Er redt zich ein a krenk!

He talks nonsense!　Er redt in der velt arein. Er bolbet narishkeiten.

He turns the world upside down!　Er kert iber di velt!

Head of a family　Balhabos, balebos, broitgeber, farzorger

Headache　Kop vaitik

Healthy as a horse　Gezunt vi a ferd

Hear ye!　Shema (Hebrew)

Heart ache　Harts vaitik

Heartbroken　Tsebrochen harts

Hearty laugh　Hartsik, shaineh gelechter

Heavy　Shver

Hebrew school for children　Talmud Torah

(The) Hell with him!　Kuck im on! (taboo)

Hello　Sholem aleichem, shalom!

Help!　G'vald!

Here, take it (in giving)   Na!
Here's to you! (toast)   L'chei-im!
He's a low down, good-for-nothing!   Er iz a niderrechtiker
   kerl!
He's a nothing!   Shmegeggi!
He's (it's) gone! Forget it!   A nechtiker tog!
He's hardly (barely) alive   Kam vos er lebt
He's restless!   Er zitst oyf shpilkes
He's slow as molasses!   Er kricht vi a vantz!
He's so happy!   Braiter vi lainger! Er iz azoy frailech!
He's thick   Er hot a farshtopten kop
He's thick-headed   Er hot a farshtopteh kop
He's worthless   Er toyg ahf kapores
Hifalutin   Feinshmeker
Hick   Yold
Highly connected person   Yachsen
Highly excitable person   Farshmei-iter, shvebeleh
   (Lit., a match)
(To) Hire   Dingen
Hodgepodge   Mishmash, kasheh
Hoi polloi   Mittelmeissiker
Hold on! (wait)   Vart! S'teitsh!
Hole   Loch
Hole in the head   Loch in kop
Holiday   Yontev, yontiff, yomtov
Holiday-ish   Yontefdik
Homeless wandering   Valgeren zich
Homosexual   Faigeleh (taboo)
Honor   Koved
Honorable   Balebatish
Horrible ending   Finsteren sof
Horrible year   Finster yor
Horse   Ferd
Host   Balabos (pl., balaibatim)
Hot bath   Haiseh vanneh
Hot-head   Kasnik, keisenik, hitsik

Hostess who serves you meagerly, gives you A lek un a shmek

Householder Balabos (pl., balaibatım); balebos

Housewife (efficient and comptent) Beryeh, balebosteh

How are things? Vi gaits? Vos hert zich?

How are things (with you)? Vi gait es (eich)?

How are you? (sing.) Vos machstu?

    (pl.) Vos macht ir?

How come? Viazoy? S'teitsh!

How do you do? Sholem alaichem! Vos macht ir?

How else? Vi den?

How goes it? Vi gaits? Vos hert zich?

How goes it with you? Vi gait es eich?

How is that? S'teitsh?

How is that possible! S'teitsh?

How much? Vifil?

How should I know? Freg mir becherim!

How's business? Vi gait dos gesheft?

How's tricks? Vi gaits? Vos hert zich?

(To) Humble somebody Derniderriken

Hurry up! Eilt zich! Mach shnel! Nu, shoyn? Yogt zich unter!

Hush! Quiet! Shat, shat!

Hymen K'nippel (taboo): b'sulim

I am disappointed. Ich bin ahntoisht. Ich fil zich opgenart.

I'm dying for it! Mein cheiyes gait oys noch dem!

I am fainting! Es vert mir finster in di oygen. Ich gai chaleshen!

I am in a hurry. Ich eil zich.

I'm not in a hurry. Ich yog zich nit.

I'm sorry. Es tut mir bahng.

I defecate on him (usually said about someone you're angry with, disgusted with, or rejected) Ich kuck ahf im. (taboo)

I despise you! Ich hob dich in bod! Ich feif oif dir!

I did wrong? So call me a "nut." Ruf mich k'nak-nissel

I don't envy you Ich bin dich nit mekaneh

I don't give a care! A deigeh hob ich! S'art mich vi di vant!

I don't give a hang! A deigeh hob ich!

I don't know. Ich vais nit.

I dream of Es cholemt zich mir

I hate him. Ich hob im feint.

I have a choice? A braireh hob ich?

I have a heartburn. Iz brent mir ahfen hartz.

I have him in my buttocks! (usually said about someone you don't care for, or angry with) Ich hob im in toches! (taboo)

I have no use for it. Ich darf es ahf kapores.

I haven't the faintest idea! Zol ich azoy vissen fun tsores! Ich zol azoy vissen fun baiz!

I have you in hell! Go to hell! Ich hob dich in drerd!

I know. Ich vais.

I like it. It pleases me. Es gefelt mir.

I need it like a hole in my head Ich darf es vi a loch in kop

I need it like a wart on my nose. Ich darf es vi a lung un leber oif der noz.

I predicted it (my heart told me) Dos hartz hot mir gezogt

I should have such a year! Az a yor ahf mir!

I should have such good luck! Az a glick ahf mir!

I should know from trouble (as little as I know about what you are asking me). Ich zol azoy vissen fun tsores.

I should worry. A deigeh hob ich.

I wish it could be said about me. Ahf mir gezogt.

(An) Idea occurred to me. Es iz mir eingefalen a plan.

Idiot Shmegegi, vyzoso (both slang); idiyot

(To) Idle Shlump (slang)

Idler Laidik-gaier; batlen (if he's a perpetual scholar); pustunpasnik

Ignoramus Am-ho'orets, amorets

Ignorant boor Prostak, poyer

Ignorant Jew Goy, shtik goy, grobber kop

Ignorant people Prosteh mentshen

I'll give you nothing! Ich vel dir geben kadoches!

I'm dying for it! Mein cheies gait oys!

I'm not in a hurry Ich yog zich nit. Ich eil zich nit.

I'm sorry Es tut mir bahng. Es tut mir laid.

Impossible! A nechtiker tog! Ummeglich!

Impudent fellow Chutzpenik, ahzes ponim

Impure food (contrary to dietary laws) Traif, nit kosher

In, into Arein

In disgrace and humiliation Tsu shand un tsu shpot

In good health Gezunterhait

In-law Mechuten

In-laws Mechutonim

In spite of everything you do, it still comes out wrong Aft tsi'lehaches, ahf tseloches

In the middle of In miten drinen

In a pig's eye! A nechtiker tog!

In the rear Fun hinten; in hinten

In trouble Ahf tsores

Incompetent person (who has perpetual bad luck) Shlimazel, loy yitslach
Inept person Shlemiel
Inexpensive Billik
Inferior Shlub, tandaitneh
Inferior merchandise or work. Drek (taboo); partatshnek
Innocent Got di neshomeh shuldik; nit shuldik
Insane Meshugeh ahf toyt; meshugeh tsum toyt
Insanity Meshugahas
Insignificant mistake Bubu
Insincere talk Falsheh raid. Drek (taboo)
Inspector or supervisor of Kashreth (Kashress) in restaurants or hotels who makes sure everything is kosher Mashgiach
Integrity Yoysher
Intercourse (sexual) Zetz, shtup (taboo)
(To) Irk Tshepen
Irreligious Jew Apikoires; shtik goy
Irrelegious Jewish boy. Shaigetz shkotz.
Irrelegious Jewish girl. Shikseh.
Is he bewildered! Er drait zich vi a fortz in rossel. (taboo)
Is he in a fog! Er drait zich vi a fortz in rossel. (taboo)
Is it? Tsi?
Is it my worry? A deigeh hob ich?
Is that how you talk to a father? Azoy ret men tsu a taten?
Is that so? Azoy zugstu? Takeh?
It appears to me Es veist zich mir oys
It could be! Es ken zein.
It doesn't make sense! Es iz nit geshtoigen un nit gefloigen.
It doesn't matter. S'macht nit oys.
It doesn't matter to me. Es macht mir nit oys.
It doesn't work! Es gait nit! Gaiet es nit! Se arbet nit!
It gives me a great pleasure! Es tut mir a groisseh hanoeh! Se git mir a groisseh ano-eh! (often said

sarcastically)

It gives me pleasure Es tut mir hanoeh. (often said sarcastically.) Es git mir a (groissen) fargenigen.

It hurts me. Es tut mir vai.

It is conceivable Es ken gemolt zein

It is imaginable Es ken gemolt zein

It is (too) late. Es iz (tsu) shpet.

It is not becoming Es past nit.

It is revealed Veist oys

It is said Me zogt

It is very expensive (cheap). Es is zaier teier (billik).

It isn't proper! Es past nit!

It isn't running smoothly! Es gait nit!

It looks like Veist oys

It makes no difference (it doesn't matter). Es mach nit oys.

It melts in your mouth! Tsegait zich in moyl.

It never happened! Es iz nit geshtoigen un nit gefloigen!

It pleases me. Es gefelt mir.

It should be well! Zol zein gut!

It should bang in your head (as it's annoying me)! Zol dir alain klapen in kop!

It should happen to me (to you)! Alevei! Ahf mir (dir) gezogt!

It should happen to me! Mirtsishem bei mir! Ahf mir gezogt gevoren!

It should happen to my enemies! Ahf maineh sonim gezogt!

It shouldn't come to pass! Nit do gidacht! Umberufen! Unbeshrien!

It shouldn't happen! Nishtu gedacht. Nit do gedacht!

It shouldn't happen to you! Nit far eich gedacht! Loi alaichem (Hebrew)

It sorrows me. Es tut mir bahng.

It stinks! Es gait a raiech! Se hert zich a raiech Se shtinkt!

It will all work out. Es vet zich alts oyspressen.
It will heal in time for the wedding. Es vet zich oys-hailen biz der chasseneh.
It will suffice. Es vet kleken.
It will take a long, long time (till Doomsday!). A yor mit a mitvoch.
It won't help (any)! Es vet helfen vi a toiten bahnkes!
It won't hurt in making a match. Es vet nit shatten tzum shiddech.
It's a pity Nebach; a rachmones
It's a shame for the children! Es iz a shandeh far di kinder!
It's a steal! A metzieh fun a ganef!
It's bad manners! Es past zich vi a patch tzu gut shabbes!
It's delicious! Me ken zich baleken! Me ken leken di finger fun dem!
It's gone! S'iz oys!
It's gone; forget it! A nechtiker tog!
It's good for nothing! Es toig ahf kapores!
It's great! S'iz mir gut!
It's hardly worth the trouble. Folg mich a gahng (scoffing statement)
It's not to the point! Es past zich vi a patsh tsu gut shabbes!
It's not true whatsoever. Nisht geshtoigen, nisht gefloigen.
It's O.K. with me! Bei mir poilst du!
It's on his (her) mind. Es ligt im (ir) in zinnen.
It's over. S'iz oys.
It's perfect! Kosher v'yosher!
It's tough to make a living! Shver tzu machen a leben!
It's useless! Gai klop zich kop in vant!
It's worth nothing Toig ahf kapores.
It's your own fault. Me hot alain ungekocht.

(A) Jerk Shlub, shlump
Jester at a wedding Badchan
Jew who works on Sabbath Mechalel shabbes, shabbes
 goy
Jewish head Yiddisher kop
Jewish holiday Yontiff, yomtov, yontev
Jewish law (book) Talmud
Jewish native of Galicia Galitsianer
Jewish parochial school Yeshivah togshul
Jewish prayer shawl Tallis
Joke Vitz, chochmeh
Joy (from children) Naches
Joyous occasion (birth, bar mitzvah, engagement,
 marriage, etc.) Simcheh
Juice Zaft
Jumble Mishmash
Just great! Ei, gut!
Just made it! Kam derlebt
Justice Yoysher

Kasha with noodles   Varnitshkes

Keep moving!   Drai zich!

Keep quiet!   Shveig!

Kiss my behind!   Kush mich in toches! (taboo); kush in toches arein (taboo)

Knock on wood! No evil eye! (some say "Don't give me a canary.")   Kain einhoreh (also, kain ain-einoreh).

Knot   K'nippel

Know-it-all, who really doesn't know it all (sarcastic) Macht zich far a gantsen kenner; far a ya-tebbeh-dahm; K'nacher

Kosher condition   Kashress

Ladies' room Vashtsimmer far froien

Land of Israel Eretz Yisroel

Large as a mountain Grois vi a barg

Last child in family Mizinikil

Lazy man Foiler, foilyak

Leader of the Jewish religious community Rav, rov

Learned man Lamden. Talmid chochem. Ben Toyreh; Reb (used as title)

(To) Lease Dingen

Leave me alone! Loz mir tzu ru! Tshepeh zich op fun mir!

Lecherous old man Alter kucker (taboo)

Less than nothing Kadoches

Let it be! Zol zein!

Let me be in peace! Loz mich tzu ru!

Let's conclude this! Toches ahfen tish.

Let's end it! A sof! A sof!

Let's go! Nu, shoyn!

Let's have some quiet! Zol zein shtil!

Liar Ligner

Life Chei (numerical value of two Hebrew letters, cheth and yood, read together as Chei). Chei also means 18.

Lighter taper Shammes

Likewise Dos zelbeh

Listen! Her nor!

Listen here! Hert zich ein!

Lithuanian Litvak

Littered Ongevorfen

Little Bisel

Little bird Faigeleh

Little boy Boitshick (Americanism)

Little bride Kallehniu

Little cakes dipped in honey Taiglech

Little girl (affectionate term)   Maideleh
Little infant (affectionate term)   Pisherkeh
Little nothing   Pitsvinik; klainer gornisht, banimenish
(A) Little of a fool   Narishehvateh. Shtik nar.
Little ones   Pitzelech
Little penis   Petseleh (used only to describe infant boy!)
Little prig   Klainer gornisht
Little squirt   Pisher
Livelihood   Parnosseh
(A) Lively person   Rirevdiker; nit kain farshloffener; lebediker
Lively Russian dance   Kazatskeh
(A) Lively world!   A lebedikeh velt!
Living by one's wits   Luftmentsh
(A) Living doll!   Yingeh tzahtzkeh (young one); lyalkeh; tzatzkehleh (a very pretty or capricious one); tzatzkeh (take your choice!)
Living high off the hog   Leben a chazershen tog
Loaded (drunk)   Farshnoshket; ongetrunken
Loads of luck!   Mazel tov!
Loafer   Laidik-gaier, pustunpasnik
Long coat worn by religious Jews   Kapoteh, kaftan
Long dist ance operator   Tsevishen-shtotisheh telefonistkeh
Long, lean girl   Langeh dronitzeh; hoieher drong
Long may you live!   Lang leben zolt ir!
Long winter underwear   Gatkes
Look at him!   Kuk im nor on!
Look here, look here!   Zeh nor, zeh nor!
Look out!   Hit zich!
Loquacious   Yatatata
Lost   Tsemisht (confused); farfalen (physical loss)
Lot of nonsense   Drek (shit; taboo)
Loudmouth   Pisk!
(To) Lounge around   Shlump; patterren tseit
Lousy   Nisht gut

Low-class people   Prosteh mentshen; prostaches
Luck   Glick
Luckless person   Shlimazel
Lump of sugar   Shtik tsuker

Madness Meshugahss
Magic-worker Kishef macher, kuntsen macher, Bal Shem (Hebrew)
Make a living Machen a leben
Make a major issue out of a minor event Tsimmes
(To) Make a nothing out of you. Machen a tel fun dir.
(To) Make fun of Choyzik machen
Make it snappy! Mach es shnel!
Making a livelihood Hoben parnosseh, machen a leben (Americanism)
Making an outcry Machen a g'vald
Malaria Kadoches
Male infant Pisher (taboo; Lit., a urinator); mentshal
Male person Mentsh; kaddishel (one who can say mourning prayers for his parents)
Malingering sickness A farshlepteh krenk (a sickness or matter that hangs on endlessly)
Man (derisive term) Shmok (taboo)
Man (with worth and dignity) Choshever mentsh
(A) Man built like an ox Bulvan
Man of distinguished lineage Yachsen
Man who assumes airs Bal ga'aveh; grois-halter
Man who behaves meanly, miserly, ungallantly, or vulgarly Rosheh
Man who builds castles in the air; never achieves anything Fantazyor; luftmentsh
Man who lives by his wits Luftmentsh
Man who threatens Yatebedam
A man with contacts Macher
Manana! Kum ich nit heint, ku mich morgen
Manly Gantser mentsh
Manure Drek (taboo)
(A) Mare (also worthless) Shkapeh

Marriage Chasseneh
Marriage broker Shadchen
Marriage ceremony Chupeh
Married man Baveibter
Master of ceremonies at weddings or banquets Badchan
Master of the Universe Riboynoy-shel-oylom
Match (marriage) Shidech, der (shiduchim, pl.)
Matchmaker Shadchan
May God help me! Zol Got mir helfen!
May God prevent! Zol Got op-hiten!
May he break a leg! Zol er tsebrechen a fus!
May he rest in peace. Olov hasholem.
May it be so! Alivei! Halevei!
May it not happen to you! Loi alaichem! (Hebrew); nebach
May it not happen to you! Loi aleichem! (Hebrew)
May no evil befall us! Kain einoreh! Kain ein horeh
May she rest in peace. Oleho hasholem.
May we meet on happy occasions. Mir zolen zich bagegenen ahf simches.
May you be inscribed for a good year. L'shono tova tikosevu.
May you live long. Lang leben zolt ir.
Maybe Efsher, ken zein
Mean Parshiveh
Mean, evil person Paskudnyak, parch, rosheh
Meat dietary law Flaishiks (Meat must not be eaten together with dairy (milichdik) foods).
Mechanic Shlosser, machinist
Mechanical man (robot) Goilem, golem
(To) Meddle (as a spectator) Kibbitzen
Meddlesome spectator Kibbitzer, muttelmessig
Meek person Shnok, lemeshkeh, kunye lemel
Memorial service Yiskor
Men's room Vashtsimmer far menner
Mercy Rachmones

Mere bagatelle!   Bobkes! Bubkes!
Mere messenger   Shlatten-shammes
Mere nothing   Shihi-pihi
Merit   Meileh
Merrymaker at a wedding   Badchan
(A) Mess (slang)   Kasheh, mishmash, hekdish
(To) Mess around   Patshkeh, patshken
Messenger   Shik-yingel; shlatten-shammes
(A) Middleman (also a person who is neither smart nor dumb)   Mittelmissiker
Mildew   Farfoylt
Milked!   Opgeflickt! Arumgeflickt!
(To) Mind something   Varfen an oyg; halten an oyg, bal moifess
Miracle-worker   Balnes
Miser   Karger
Miserable weather   Finster un glitshik
Miserable person   Shlak
(To be) Miserly   Zhaleven, kamtsoness
Misery   Tsores
Misfit   Kalyekeh
Misfortune   Umglick
(A) Misfortune! (wail)   Az och un vai!
Mistake (insignificant)   Bubu
Miss   Maidel, freilein, chaverteh
Mistress of a household   Balhabosteh, balebosteh
Mix-up (slang)   Kasheh, mishmash; kuckamaimie
Mixed up   Tsemisht, farmisht
Mixed up emotionally   Farmisht
(A) Mixture   Mishmash
(A) Moaner   Krechtser (also means a blues singer)
Moans   Krechtst (verb)
Money   Gelt
Money (ready cash)   Mezuma, mezumen
Money goes to money   Gelt gait tzu gelt.
Money on the table!   Ribi-fish, gelt ahfen tish!

Money thrown out   Aroysgevorfen gelt
Money tied in a knot in corner of a handkerchief
   K'nippel
Money wasted   Aroysgevorfen gelt
Moocher   Shnorrer
Moron   Szhlob
Morsel   Shtikel
Mortally insane!   Meshugeh ahf toyt!
Mother-in-law   Shviger
Mother's pet (favorite)   Tsatskeleh der mameh's
Mourner's prayer   Kaddish
Mourning period   Shiva, shiveh (seven days observed by
   family and friends of deceased)
Mouth (unflattering)   Pisk (moyl: mouth)
Mouthpiece   Pisk
Mouthwash   Moil-shvenkechts
Move, already!   Nu, shoyn! Gai shoyn!
Mr.   Reb., chaver, bruder; freint (salutation)
Mr. Slowpoke   Kam vos er kricht.
Mr. Upside Down! (person who does everything in reverse)
   Moisheh kapoyer
Mrs.   Chaverteh, froy; madame (salutation)
Much ado about nothing   Ahfen himmel a yarid
Muddled (slightly drunk)   Far-shnoshket
Muddled work, picture or situation   Ongepatshket,
   tsepatsket
(To) Mumble   Preplen
Mush cereal   Kasheh
My enemies should live so!   Meineh sonim zolen azoy
   leben!
My heart told me   Dos hartz hot mir gezogt
My money went down the drain.   In drerd mein gelt!
   Dos gelt iz tserunen gevoren!

Naive Tam, tamavateh
Naive person Kunyehlemel, shmo (Americanism)
Narrowly achieved Kam derlebt
Nasty fellow Paskudnyak
Nausea Chaloshes
Navel. Pipek, pupik
Ne'er-do-well Trombenik, nebechel, nebbish, nebach, shlak
Neighbor (from the old country) Lantsman
Neither here nor there Nit ahin, nit aher
Neutral food (neither milchdik nor flaishdik) **Parveh**
Newlywed (male) Yungermantshik
News Yedies; neies
Nibble between meals Nash, nashen
Nibbler, especially between meals Nasher
Night is falling. Nacht falt tsu.
Nincompoop Shmendrik, kunyehlemel, shlok
No evil eye Kain einoreh (also, kain ain-einoreh)
No good Kockamaimie (slang); nit gut; nisht gut
No-gooder Trombenik
No-good person Nishgutnick, trombenik
Nobility Yichus
(A) Nobody (male) Pisher (taboo); a gornisht; a nishtikeit
    (female) Pisherkeh (taboo); a gornisht; a nishtikeit
    (a pitiable person) Nebbish, nebach, nebechel
    (a little person) Vantz (bedbug); a gornisht; a nishtikeit
Noise Tumel
Non-Jewish boy Shaigetz, shkotz (colloquial)
Non-Jewish girl Shikseh (colloquial)
Non-kosher Traif, traifeh
Nonsenses! A nechtiker tog! Drek (taboo)

Noodle dough Farfel
Noodle or bread suet pudding (frequently cooked with raisins) Kugel
Noodles Lokshen
Noodle pudding Kugel
Not a word of truth in it! A nechtiker tog! Also, nit emes
Not good Nisht gut; nit gut
Not in reality; supposedly Kloymersht
Not making sense Nit geshtoigen, nit gefloigen
Not necessary Nisht naitik
Not really at all! Chas v'cholileh!
Not so bad Nishkosheh
Not so fast! Chap nit!
Not today, not tomorrow! Nit heint, nit morgen!
Not yet Noch nisht
Nothing Gornit, gornisht
Nothing (of small value) Kreplech (slang); bobkes (slang); chei kuck (taboo)
(A) Nothing, a pitiful person Nebechel, nebbish
Nothing came of it! Es hot zich oysgelohzen a boydem!
Nothing of importance! Eh!
Nothing of value Shmek tabik (bit of snuff)
Nothing will help you! Es vet dir gornit helfen!
Nouveau riche....Oyfgekumener g'vir; olreitnik (Americanism)
Nuisance Nudnik; tsutsheppenish
Nutty Tsedrait

O.K.   Zaier gut; oisgetsaichent
Obey me!   Folg mich!
Obnoxious person   Nudnik, paskudnik, paskudnyak
(To) Offer unsolicited advices as a spectator   Kibbitz, kibbitzen
Oh!   Ei! Ei!
Oh, God!   Gottenyu!
Oh, what a scandal!   Oi, a shkandal! Oy, a skandal
O.K.! Let it be so!   Zol zein azoy!
Old acquaintance   Alter bakahnter
Old-fashioned taste   Mein bobbeh's ta'am
(An) Old bum   An alter trombenik
(An) Old man   An alter kucker (taboo)
Old maid   Alteh moid
Old-style orthodox Hebrew teacher in a "cheder" (one-room-school)   Melamed (pl., melamdim)
Old witch   Alteh machashaifeh
Old wreck   Alteh trombenik
Omelet   Feinkochen, feinkuchen
On the level   Emmis, emmes, be'emes
On the square   Emmis, emmes, be'emes
Once in a blue moon!   In a noveneh!
One who stirs up things   Kochleffel
One who tends to confuse you   Draikop
Onions should grow from your navel!   Zol dir vaksen tzibbeles fun pupik!
Only God knows   Nor Got vaist
Orderly person   Balebos; okuratner mentsh
Ornament   Tzatzkeh
Orthodox Hebrew teacher   Melamed
(The) Other's   Yenems
Other world   Yeneh velt, oilom habbo (Hebrew)
Ouch!   Oi, vai!

Outcast Oysvurf
Overdressed Oysgeputst, oisgeshtrobelt, oisgetzatzket
Overdressed woman Oisgetzatzket; aribergechapt di mohs
Over-praise (slang) Shmaltz, chanifeh
Overseer Mashgiach
Owner Balabos (pl., palibatim); balebos

Pain   Vai! vaitik
Pain (exclamation)   Oi!
(Real) Pain (ouch!)   Oi, vai!
Pale as a sheet (wall)!   Blaich vi di vant! Veis vi kalech!
Palsy-walsy   Aderabeh-ve'aderabeh
Pancakes (jellied or with cheese)   Blintzes (and they must be rolled)
Panhandler   Shnorrer
Pansy (male)   Faigeleh
Papa   Tateh, tatteh, tatteleh, tatinka, tatinkeh, tatteniu
Paradise   Ganaiden (Garden of Eden)
Parasite   Shnorrer
Parents   Tateh-mameh
Parvenu   Oyfgekumener g'vir; olreitnik (Americanism)
(To) Pass wind   Fortzen (taboo)
Pastry   Varenikes (special type). Gebeks.
Patienece (that can edure sitting)   Zitzflaish
(A) Patsy   Shnook, shlumpf
Pauper   Kabsten, kapsten
Pauper in seven edges (a very poor man)   Kabtsen in ziben poless.
Peace   Sholem
Peace be to you!   Sholem alaichem!
Peanuts! (small things)   Bobkes, bubkes (If you're curious, the word for nuts, also peanuts, is "nislech."
Peasant   Poyer
Peddler   Hoizirer; pedler (Americanism)
Pedigree   Yichus
Pee pot   Pishteppel
Peeved   Ongeblozzen
Peevish (pouting)   Ongeblozzen
Penis   Potz, shmok, shlang, shvontz, vyzoso (all taboo)
Penis (derisive and derogatory term for a man)   Shmok.

142

potz (taboo)

    Shmohawk (Anglicized variant for "shmok")

    Petseleh (affectionately applied to infant boy)

Perfect Kosher (slang)

Perish the thought! Cholileh!

Person from Lithuania Litvak

Person of loose morals Hultei

Person who butts into everything Kochleffel

Person who carries on work or sport in a slipshod, unbusiness-like, half-assed manner Patsher

Person who does not abide by Jewish law Traifener bain! Traifenik! Traifnyok! Shaigetz!

Person who will do anything to gain favor Toches-lecker (Lit., ass-licker; taboo)

Person with a sweet tooth Nasher

Person with fine taste Feinshmeker

Pervert Faigeleh (taboo)

Pest Tsutsheppenish, nudnik

Pesty nagger Nudnik, onshikenish, tsutsheppenish

Petulant Baroyges, umgeduldik, kochedik

Philanthropist Baltsedokeh, filantrop; nadven (Hebrew)

Philanthropy (spirit of) Tsedokeh

Phylacteries Tefillen, tfillen (worn by observant Jews on head and left arm each weekday morning while praying)

Piece Shtik

Piece of luck Glick, mazel

(A) Piece of shit Shtik drek (taboo)

Pig Chazzer

Piggish person Chazzer (slang)

Pig's feed Chazzerei; also, slang for food unfit to eat or merchandise unworthy to buy or own

Pins and needles Shpilkes

Pious Frum (frimer)

Pious person Tsaddik, opgehitehner, shoimer mitzves

Piss (taboo) Pishechtz

(To) Piss (taboo) Pishen

(A) Pitiable person Nebach, nebechel, nebbish
Pity Rachmones
(A) Plague Makeh, finsternish, magaifeh
(To) Plague Tshepen, tshepen zich tsu
(A) Plague on you! A magaifeh zol dich trefen! A
  choleryeh ahf dir!
Play Shtik, drameh, pyesseh
**Played-out person, even if young; a person unwilling to
  participate** Alter kucker; oisgeputtert mentsh
Playgirl Tsatskeh, tsatskeleh
Plaything Tsatskeh, tsatskeleh (female)
Pleasantly plump and pretty (woman) Zaftik
Please Zeit zich matriach; zeit azoy gut; bitteh;
  zeit moichell
Please; I beg you. Ich bet eich.
Please forgive me. Zeit (mir) moychel.
Please keep quiet! Sha! (gently said)
(A) Pleasure! A fargenigen!
Pleasure (from children) Naches
Plump (woman) Zaftik
Policeman (slang) Shammes (actually a synagogue
  sexton)
Pompous woman Rebitsin (Lit., the Rabbi's wife)
Poor box Pushkeh (In every traditional Jewish home odd
  coins are put in this, particularly on Friday afternoon,
  before the Sabbath begins)
Poorhouse Hekdish
Poor man Orehman
Porridge Kasheh
Portable table Ruktish
(The) Posterior Toches! also tokus, tokis, tuckus,
  hinten (taboo)
Pot to defecate in Kuckteppel (taboo)
Pouting Ongeblozzen
Poverty Oremkeit
Powerhouse! A yung mit bainer!

(To) Pray Davenen
Prayer book daily in use Sidder
Prayer of mourner Kaddish
Prayer shawl Tallis
Pregnant Shvengert, trogedik
Pretend Kloymersht
Pretends to be ignorant of fact Macht zich nit visindik
Prettier ones they bury! (The girl is ugly!) Sheners laigt men in drerd arein.
Pretty girl Shaineh maidel; tshatshkeh (slang)
Pride (unreasonable and stubborn) Shtoltz, ga'aveh
Prima donna Prietskeh, pritseteh
Princess Bas-malkeh, printsesn
Privileged character Yachsen
Procrastinating! (Manana!) Kum ich nit heint, kuim ich morgen!
Profane Grob
Proper Kosher (slang)
Property Balebatishkeit
Proscription against wearing clothes that are mixed of wool and linen Shatnes
Prostitute Nafkeh, kurveh, nekaiveh, zoineh
Proverb Shprichvort (pl., sprichverter); gleichvort, gleichvertel
Puffed up (peeved) Ongeblozzen
Puffed up with haughty pride Geshvollen, ongeblozzen, blozen fun zich
(To) Pull Shlepen
Pun Vortshpiel
Punch Chmalyeh, klop, zetz, shmeiss, patsh, frask
(A) Punk Paskudnyak
Push Shtup (also used for sexual intercourse; taboo)
Put up or shut up! Toches ahfen tish!

Question   Frageh, sheileh
Quick, quickly   Shnell
Quiet, don't get excited!   Shat, shat! Hust!
Quiet! Stop talking!   Shveig! Shush!
Quiet! Shut up!   Sha! (shouted)
Quietly   Shtilinkerhait
Quite a job!   Folg mich a gahng!
Quite well   Gants gut, nishkosheh
Quorum of ten worshippers for praying   Minyan, minyen

Rabbi Rav, Rov, Rev
"Rabbi dear!" Rebiniu
Rabbi's wife Rebitsin
Rabid fan (also an ardent participant) Farbrenter; chosid
Racketeer Untervelt mentsh, gazlen (slang); ganef, goniff
Rag Shmatteh, tranteh
Raise cain Hulyen
(To) Rape Trenen (taboo)
Rare thing Naidlecheh zach; zeltenkeit
Rarity An ain un aintsikeh
Rascally know-it-all Kolboynik
Ravioli Kreplech
Ready cash Mezuma
Real article; the real McCoy! Richtiker chaifetz
Real bargain! Billik vi borsht! (Lit., Cheap as beet soup)
Real buy! Billik vi borsht! (Cheap as beet soup)
Real fine, honorable man Mentsh
Really a bargain Tahkeh a metsieh, shoin ainmol a
  metsieh
Really crazy Meshugeh ahf toyt
Really? Is that so? Takeh? Azoy?
Rear Hinten
Rear parts Hinten
Recite prayers over lit candles Bentsh lecht;
  bentshen licht
Recite the afternoon prayers Davenen mincheh
Rectum Toches(taboo)
Relative through marriage (in laws) Mechuten
  (pl., mechutonim)
Relatives Mishpocheh, kroivim
Religious Frum (frimer)
Religious dietary law Kashress
Religious functionary who performs the circumcision

Mohel
Remember? Gedainkst?
(To) Rent Dingen
Respect Koved, derech erets
Respectable Jews Balebatisheh yiden
Responsible Balebatish, achrahyes, farantvortlech
Reverence Koved, derech eretz
Rich Reich
Rich man G'vir
(To) ridicule Choyzik machen
Right Richtik; kosher (slang)
Righteous person Tsaddik
(To) Rip Trenen
Ritual bath (part of the orthodox bride's wedding preparation) Mikveh
Ritual slaughterer of animals and fowl Shochet
Robber Gazlen, ganef
Robot Goilem
Rogue Yungatsh
Roisterer Tumler
Rotten (decayed) Farfoylt
Rotten person Paskudnik, paskudnyak
Rough Grob
Roughneck Shtarker, yungatsh; (sarcastically, voiler yung)
Round dumpling (usualy made of matzoh meal, served with soup) K'naidel (pl., k'naidlech)
Row of pews at the eastern wall of the synagogue where the foremost members of the congregation sit Mizrach
Rude Grob
Rude, coarse person Bulvan, grober yung
Rude young man Grober yung
(To) Ruin you Machen a tel fun dir
(To be) Ruined Verren a tel
Rush! Eilt zich!
Rustic Yishuvnik

Sabbath (twists of white) bread   Challeh
Sacrifice of atonement   Kaporeh
Sad sack!   Shmulky!
Salmon (smoked)   Lax, lox
(The) Same to you!   Gam atem! (Hebrew)
(A) Sap   Shnook
Satisfactory   Nishkosheh
Savory   Varnitshkes
Say a few words   Zog a por verter
(A) Saying   Gleichvertel
Scamp   Yungatsh
Scatterbrain   Draikop
Scholar   Lamden, ben toyreh
School   Shule
Scram!   Trog zich up! Avek!
Scrambled eggs   Feinkuchen
Scream   K'vitsh
Screech   K'vitsh
Screwy   Tsedrait
Scroll or the Book of Esther   Megillah
Second rater   Shlumpf
Self-made fool   Shmok (taboo because it also means penis)
Senile   Aiver butel, oiver botel
Sensuous looking (girl)   Zaftik
Sentimental   Shmaltzy, sentimentahl
Serpent   Shlang (also big penis taboo)
Serves him right!   Gut oyf im! A shaineh, raineh, kaporeh!
Sexton of the synagogue   Shamas, shammes
Sexual experience   Zetz (taboo)
Sexual intercourse   Shtup (taboo)
Sexually attractive girl   Tzatzkeh, zaftik, zaftikeh moid
(To) Shake and dance with joy   Hetskentzich, tzitern fun
    fraid

Shame and disgrace Mies un mos; a shandeh un a charpeh

Sharp (referring to clothes) Yontevdik

Sharp practices Genaivisheh shtiklech

She doesn't stop talking Zi farmacht nit dos moyl

She has all the virtues Aleh meiles hot zi

She should rest in peace. Oleho hasholom.

Shit Drek (taboo)

(To) Shit Kucken (taboo)

Shit-head Kucker, shtik drek (both taboo)

Shitty Farkackt, fekuckteh (taboo)

Shmohawk Anglicized variant for shmok (penis)

Shoddy Opgekrochen, shlak

Shoddy merchandise Opgekrocheneh schoireh, shlak vareh

(To) Shout for help Machen a g'vald

Shove Shtup, shtuppen

(You should) Shove it up your rectum Zolst es shtupin in toches arein! (taboo)

Shove (or stick) it up your rectum! Shtup es in toches! (taboo)

(A) Show-off K'nacker, grois-halter, barimer, shvitser

Shrew Shlecht veib; klipeh, mirshaas

Shriek Kvitsh

Shut up! Sha! Shveig! Farmach dos moyl!

Shy Shemevdik

Shy person Nebbish, nebechel, shemevdiker

Sick Krank

Sickness Krenk, krank-heit, cholaas

Sickness that hangs on Farshlepteh krenk

Silence! Zol zein shtil!

Simple-minded Tamavateh

Simple people Prosteh leit, prosteh mentshen

Simpleton Nebbish, shlemiel, shmendrik, tam

Sister-in-law Shvegerin

Sit in mourning Zitsen shiveh (Shiveh means seven—

the number of days in the mourning period)
Sit on pins and needles   Zitsen ahf shpilkes.
Skilled worker   Balmelocheh
Skin someone alive   Reisen di hoit, shinden di hoit
Skinny   Oysgedarcht
Skol   Le'cha-yim, lechei-im, l'chei-im
Skull cap usually worn during prayers and worn at all times by extreme Orthodox Jews—also worn by Catholic prelates   Yarmelkeh
Slam   Chmalyeh
Slap (open hand)   Patsh
      (back of the hand)   Frassk
(To) Slap   Geben a patsh
Slattern   Yachneh
Sleeveless shirt (religious undershirt)   Leibtzudekel, tallis koton, arbeh kanfess
Slightly drunk   Farshnoshket
Slime   Shmuts
Slipshop worker or player (sports)   Patsher
Slob   Zhlob
Sloppy   Ongepatshket
Slow   Pamelech, pavolyeh, gemitlech
Slowly   Pamelech, pavolyeh, gemitlech
Slowpoke   Kam vos er kricht
Slow-wittedness   Goyisher kop; kunyehlemel
Slumhouse   Churveh
Small pieces   Shtiklech
Small pieces of baked dough   Taiglech
Small pockets of dough filled with chopped meat (like ravioli) or cheese   Kreplech
Smell   Shmek; also plural for shmok, penis (taboo)
Smelled bad (used only in reference to food)   Shtark gehert; ge'avert
(To) Smell bad   Farshtunken, shtinken
Smoked salmon   Lox (pronounced "lahks")
Snack (between meals)   Nash

Snake　Shlang, (also, big penis; taboo)
(The) Sneeze confirmed the truth.　G'nossen tsum emess;
　Genossen oifn emmes!
Snored　Gechropet
So? Well?　Nu?
So, so! (evasive reply to So?)　Nu, nu!
So I guessed wrong.　Nisht getrofen!
So I made a mistake, so what?　Host du bei mir an avleh!
So it goes.　Azoy gait es.
So now?　Ober yetzt? Ober itzt?
So soon?　Azoy gich?
So you say!　Vais ich vos!
So what!　Host du bei mir an avleh!
Social background　Yichus
Social climber　Er kricht in di hoyecheh fenster.
Society　Chevreh; farein
Soiled　Shmutsik
(To) Soldier on the job　Patshkeh
Someone else's　Yenems
Something decorative (like a woman)　Putskeh
Something delicious　Mecheiehdik
Something unattainable　Telerel fun himel
Son　Ben (Hebrew); zun (Yiddish)
Son-in-law　Aidim
Sorrel grass soup　Shtshav, tshav
Sorrow　Fardross
Soul　Neshomeh
**Soul condemned to wander for a time in this world because
　of its sins**　Dybbuk
Sour cream　Smetteneh
Sour leaves soup　Shtshav, tshav
(To be) Sparing　Zhaleven
(To) Speak through your nose (unclear)　Fonfen
(A) Speaker's fluff, an error　Ponf
Special bit of acting　Shpilen shtik, rolleh
Spinach soup　Shtshav, botshvineh

Spinster Alteh moid
Spirit Neshomeh
Spirit of philanthropy Tsedokeh
Spitefully Ahf tsi lehaches; ahf tsuloches
Split your guts! Plats!
Spoiled Kalyeh
Sponger (beggar) Shnorrer
    (a hanger-on) Shlepper, onshikenish, tsutshepenish
(A) Squealer Mosser
Squirt Pisher (taboo)
Stacked (referring to a girl) Zaftik
Stammerer Ikevater, hikevater
Star of David Mogen Dovid
Start! Fang shoyn on!
Starved Toit hungerik
Steam bath Shvitz bod
(A) Stink Ipish, geshtank
(To) Stink Shtinken
(It) Stinks! Se shtinkt!
Stinky Farshtunken (adj.), farshtunkener (noun)
Stockbroker Mekler
Stomach ache Boych vaitik
Stop annoying me. Drai mir nit kain kop!
    Kush mich in toches (taboo, Lit., Kiss my behind)
Stop bending my ear! Hak mir nit in kop!
Stop talking! Shveig!
Stop talking yourself into illness! A lung un leber ahf
    der noz!
**Store that sells cheap, inferior merchandise, second-hand
    or cut-rate goods where bargaining over prices is
    important** Shlak joint (Americanism)
(A) Strange death! A miesseh meshuneh!
    (Fig., It shouldn't happen to a dog!)
Stranger Fremder
Street urchin (street Arab) Yungatsh; arumloifer
Strong Kreftik, shtark

Strong as a horse Shtark vi a ferd
Strong-arm character Shtarker
Strong character Shtarker charakter
Strongly built person A yung mit bainer!
Stubborn Eingeshpart; akshen
Student of rabbinical academy Yeshivah bocher
Stuff and nonsense! Vais ich vos!
Stuffed cabbage Holishkes, holubtshes, holebshess
Stuffed chicken-neck skin Gefilteh helsel
Stuffed derma Kishkeh (looks like sausage)
Stuffed fish Gefilteh fish (usually made of chopped fish, onions and seasoning, and cooked in salt water)
Stuffed potato cakes Varnishkes, varnitshkes
Stuffed shirt Ongeblozzener
Stuffed up Farshtopt, ongeshtopt
Substance Balebatishkeit, iker, mamoshes
Sucker Shlumpf, shnook, yold
Suckered! Opgeflickt!
Suddenly In miten drinen; miten derinnen
(To) Suffer Plagen zich, leiden
Suffix to denote diminutive or affection El, eleh
Summer boarding house with cooking privileges Kochalain
Super-sensitive Aidel gepatshkit
Superb (in taste) Mecheiehdik
(To) Sweat out a job Plagen zich, mutshen zich
Sweaty Shlumpy (Americanism), farshvitst
Sweet cake Shtrudel
Sweet carrot compote Tsimmes
Sweet soul Ziseh neshomeh
Sweet talk Shmaltz, ziseh raidelech
Sweet thing Ziskeit
Sweetheart Neshomeleh! Tei-yerinkeh! Hartseniu!
Sweetness Ziskeit
Swill Chazzerei
(To) Swindle Shmeikel

Swindler Ganef, shvindler
Swollen up; puffed up (applied to person with haughty pride) Geshvollen
Synagogue Shul, bes medresh

T.O.T.   See Toches ahfen tish
Tact   Saichel, takt, manyeren
Tail   Shvontz (also refers to a man who behaves ungallantly or idiotically)
Tailor   Shneider
Take it!   Na!
Take it easy!   Chap nit! also, Me ken nit tantzen ahf tsvai chassenes mit ain mol!
(To) Take pains   Zich matriach zein
(To) Take trouble   Zich matriach zein
Tale bearer   Shalatten-shammes
(To) Talk (idly)   Shmoozen, shmuessen
Talk oneself into sickness   Zich einreden a krenk
Talk to the wall (to talk in vain or to talk and receive no answer)   Red tsu der vant
Talk your heart out   Me redt zich oys dos hartz
Talkative woman   Yenteh, klaperkeh
Talking for the sake of talking   Haken a tsheinik
Talking through the nose   Reden fonfevateh; fonfen
Talking yourself into illness!   Zich einreden a krenk; zich einreden a lung un lebber ahf der noz!
Tall story   Bobbeh meisseh; nit geshtoigen
Talmudic academy   Yeshiva
Taste   Ta'am
Tasty   Geshmak
Tea   Tai; glezel tai; glezeleh varems
Teacher   Melamed, lehrer
Teamaster   Balagoleh
(To) Tear   Trenen, reisen
Teats   Tsitskes (taboo); bristen
Teen-ager (female)   Maidel, maideleh
        (male)   Yingel; boytshik; boytshikel (Americanism)
(To) Tell a lie   Zogen a ligen

(A) Terrible thing Gevaldikeh zach, shreklecheh zach
Testicles Baitsim (taboo)
Thank God! Danken Got! Got tsu danken!
Thank you! A dank! A shainen dank!
Thanks for a small favor. A gezunt in dein pupik.
Thanks for nothing. A shainem dank in pupik.
That's all Dos iz alts
That's enough! Shoyn genug!
That's how it goes. Azoy gait es.
That's how it is. Azoy iz es.
That's how the cookie crumbles! Azoy vert dos kichel
 tzekrochen!
That's it! Dos iz es!
That's nothing. Ez iz bloteh.
That's what you say! Azoy zugstu! (sing.) Azoy zugt
 ir! (pl.)
That's worthless Es iz bloteh. Es iz drek. (taboo)
The business (slang) Shmeer
The devil with him! Zol er gaien tsu alleh ruaches!
The faster the better Vos gicher, alts besser
The good old days Mehlech sobieskis yoren (Lit., the
 years of King Sobieski); In di alteh guteh tseiten
The hell with him! A brand oif im! Kuck im on! (taboo)
The hell with it! Ich hob es in drerd! Zol es brennen!
The marriage is off! Oys shiddech!
The majority rules! Az drei zogen meshugeh, darf der
 ferter zogen "Bim bom." Az dos velt zogt shikker, laigt
 men zich shlofen.
The nuisance is here already! Er iz shoyn du, der nudnik!
The real article! Richtiker chaifetz! Di enmeseh schoireh!
The real McCoy! Richtiker chaifetz! Di emmeseh
 schoireh!
The sneeze confirmed the truth. G'nossen oyfen emess.
The whole works (slang) Shmeer, megillah
Then Den
There's a buzzing in my head! Es zhumit mir in kop!

There is not   Nito
There still is   Es iz noch do
They don't let you live.   Me lost nit leben.
They say   Me zogt
They talk and talk and say nothing.   Me redt, me redt
un me shushkit zich.
Thief   Goniff, ganef
This pleases me.   Dos gefelt mir.
This too is a living! (This you call a living?)   Oych mir a
leben!
This was a pleasure!   Dos is geven a mecheieh!
This will do.   Es vet kleken.
Thrown-out money   Aroysgevorfen gelt
Thumb   Grober finger
Tickle   Kitsel
Tightwad   Karger
Tiny   Pitsel, pitseleh
Tired   Farmatert
Tired out   Oysgematert, ongematert, farmatert
(To do all the) Talking   A braiteh daieh hoben
(To have no end of) Trouble   Hoben tsu zingen un tsu
zogen (Lit., To have to sing and to talk)
To life!   Le'chayim! Lechei-yim!
To your health!   Le'chayim! Lechei-yim!
Toes   Fisfinger, shpitsfinger
Too bad!   Az och un vai!
Too bad (novel complaint) that the bride is too pretty
A chissoren di kaleh iz tsu shain
Too costly   Tsufil, tsu tei'er
Too dear   Tsufil, tsu tei'er
Too late   Noch ne-ileh! Tsu shpait!
Too much   Tsufil
Tough guy   Shtarker; k'nacker
Tough luck!   Az och un vai!
Toy (doo-dad)   Tshatshki, tsatskeh
Traditional higher school   Yeshiva

Tragedy Umglick, tragedyeh
Travel in good health! For gezunterhait!
Treasury of Jewish law, interpreting the Torah (five books of Moses) into livable law Talmud
(A) Treat (food) Meichel, nash
Tremendous purchase (bargain) Metsieh
Tricks Shtiklech, kuntzen
Trickster Mamzer, draikop, opnarer
Tricky doings Gehnaivisheh shtiklech
Trifles Shmontses, bobkes, bubkes
Triflings Shmontses, bobkes, bubkes
Trouble-maker Er kricht oyf di gleicheh vent
Troubles Tsores (sing., tsoreh)
Troublesome wife Shlang (slang, also means penis— taboo); shlecht veib; shlok
Truth Emmis, emmes
Tub Vaneh

Ugly   Mies
Ugly thing or person   Mieskeit
Unattainable   Telerel fun himmel
Unconscious   Chaloshes
Uncouth person   Grober, grober mentsh, grobyan, grubyan
Uncouth young man   Grober yung
Underwear (long, winter)   Gatkes
(An) Unfortunate   Kalyekeh
Ungraceful person   Klotz
Unhurried   Gemitlich
Unkempt   Shlumpy, shlumperdik
Unlucky one   Shlimazel
(An) Unlucky person is a dead person   A mentsh on glik iz a toyter mentsh
Unlucky, pitiable person   Nebach, shlimazel, nebbishel, nebachel
Unmarried girl   Maidel (young one); moid (older one); b'suleh (virgin)
Unmarried man   Bocher
Unnecessary   Nisht, naitek
Unpalatable food   Chazzerei, men ken es in moil nit nemen
Unsteady   Shvindeldik, shokeldik
Untidy person   Shlump, shlumper
Untrustworthy person   Mamzer, draikop
Unwanted (companion or) follower   Noch-shlepper; tsutsheppenish; onshikenish
Uproar   Tumel
Upstart   Oyfgekumener
(To) Urinate   Pishen
Urinator   Pisher (taboo, derogatory term applied to adult; affectionately applied to infant)
Urine   Pishechtz (taboo)
Utter misery   Gehakteh tsores; gebrenteh tsores

Vagina   Loch, peeric, pirgeh, k'nish (all taboo)
Very little   A biseleh
(A) Very poor man   Kabtzen in ziben poless
Very wealthy (slang)   Ongeshtopt; ongeshtopt mit gelt
Vicious animal (usually refers to an inhuman person)
   Baizeh chei-eh
Virgin   B'suleh
Virginity   K'nippel, b'sulehshaft
Virtue   Meileh
(To) Visit   Kumen tsu gast; gaien tsu gast
Vulgar   Prost; grobyungish
Vulgar man (one without manners)   Balagoleh, prostak,
   proster mentsh
Vulgar people   Prosteh leit, prosteh mentshen, prostaches

Wail of sorrow G'vald!
Wait Vart
Walk on toes Gain oif di shpitsfinger
Wallop Klop, shmeis, zetz, chmalyeh
(To) Wander (to be lost) Blonjen
(To) Wander around aimlessly Valgeren zich, voglen
Wandered around Arumgevolgert; arumgevalgert
Washroom Vashtsimmer
Watch out (to mind) Varfen an oyg
Watch yourself as if a fire threatened! Hit zich vi fun a
   feier!
Watchman Shoymer, vechter
We shall say grace. Mir vellen bentshen.
We try harder! Mir bamien zich shtarker!
We'll bury him! Mir velen im bagroben!
Weakling Nebbish, nebachel, k'vatsh
Weakness Chaloshes (faintness); shvachkeit
Wealth Reich
(Very) Wealthy (slang) Ongeshtopt (overly stuffed)
Wear it in good health! Trog es gezunterhait!
Wee (very small) Pitsel, pitseleh
Well? Nu?
Well done! Well said! A leben ahf dein kop!
   (complimentary)
Well said! Zaier shain gezogt! Gut gezogt!
What a . . . ! Sara . . . !
**What a sober man has on his mind (lung), a drunkard has
   on his tongue.** Vos bei a nichteren oyfen lung, iz bei
   a shikkeren oyfen tsung.
What are they lacking? Vos felt zai?
What are you bothering me for? Vos draist mir dem kop?
What are you saying? Vos zogt ir?
What are you fooling around for? Vos barist du?

What are you screwing around for? Vos barist du? (taboo)

What are you talking about? Vos ret ir epes?

What are you talking my head off for? Vos hakst du mir in kop?

What did I need it for? Tsu vos hob ich dos gedarft?

What difference does it make? Vos macht dos oys? Vos iz der chil'lek?

What difference does it make as long as he makes a living? Nifter-shmifter, a leben macht er? (Lit., "nifter" means dead)

What difference does it make to me? Vos macht es mir oys?

What do I care? Vos art es mich?

What do you hear around? Vos hert zich?

What does it lead to? Vos iz der tachlis?

What does it matter (to me)? Vos art es (mich)? **(to you)?** Vos art eich? S'art eich?

What does it mean? Vos maint es?

What else? Vo den? Vos noch?

What is the name of . . . ? Vi ruft men . . . ? Vi haist es . . . ?

What is the trick? Vos iz di chochmeh?

What kind of a . . . ? Sara . . . ?

What matters it to you? S'art eich? Vos art es eich?

What then? Vo den? Vos noch?

What will be? (Que sera?) Vos vet zein

What's cooking? Vos tut zich? Vos kocht zich in teppel?

What's going on? Vos tut zich?

What's new? Vos hert zich epes neies?

What's on his mind is on his tongue Vos ahfen lung iz ahfen tsung

What's the matter? Vos iz?

What's the outcome? Vos iz di untershteh shureh?

What's the point? Vos iz di untershteh shureh?

What's the purpose? Vos iz der tachlis?

What's the trick?   Vos iz di chochmeh?
What's wrong with you?   Vos iz mit dir? Vos felt dir?
What's your name?   Vi haistu? Vi ruft men eich?
When I eat, they can all go to hell!   Ven ich ess, hob ich zai alleh in drerd.
When people talk about something, it is probably true.   Az es klingt, iz misstomeh chogeh.
Where are you going?   Vuhin gaistu? Vu gaistu?
Where does it hurt you?   Vu ut dir vai?
Where the devil says "good morning"   Vu der ruach zogt "gut morgen"
Whine   K'vetsh, klogen
(A) Whiner   A k'vetsher, a k'vatsh, a k'vetsh
Whirring noise   Zhumet, zhumerei
Whiskey   Bronfen, shnapps, mashkeh
(A) Whisper   Shushkeh
(To) Whisper   Shushken zich
Who knows!   Freg mir becherim! (slang); Ver vaist? (Lit.)
Who would have believed it?   Ver volt dos geglaibt?
Whom are you fooling?   Vemen baristu? Vemen narstu?
Whom are you kidding?   Vemen baristu?
Whore   Kurveh, nafkeh, nekaiveh
Whorehouse   Bordel, shandhoiz, nafkeh bayis
Whoremaster   Yentzer
Why should I do it?   Folg mich a gang! (sarcastically)! Farvos zol ich es tun? (Lit.)
Wider than longer   Braiter vi lainger
Wife of a chazen   Chazenteh
Wife of a melamed   Melamedkeh
Wife of a rabbi   Rebitsin
Wig   Shaitel, (sheitel)
Wild Jewish boy   Shaigetz, tsevildeveter
Wild Jewish girl   Shikseh, vildeh moid
(A) Wild man!   A vilder mentsh!
(A) Wild one!   A vilder mentsh!
(To) Win gin rummy game without opponent scoring

Shneider (Colloquial)
Wisdom Chochmeh
Wisecrack Gleichvertel
(A) Wise guy K'nacker, chochem, chochem attick
Wise man Chochem
(To) Wish lots of trouble on someone A miesseh meshuneh!
Witch Machashaifeh
Without means (poor) Orehman
Witticism Gleichvertel (also used sarcastically) chochmeh
Woe! Vai!
Woe be to it! Och un vai!
Woe is me! Oi! Vai is mir! A klug iz mir! A broch tsu mir!
Woman in labor Kimpetoren
Woman of great beauty Yefayfiyeh; shainkeit
Woman prayer leader Zogerkeh
(To) Work or play half-heartedly Patshkeh, patshken
(To) Work hard Plagen zich; mutshen zich; mordeven zich
Worked to death Oysgemutshet
(A) Worker who does a job insufficiently gives you A lek un a shmek
Working on Sabbath Mechalel Shabbes; shabbes goy.
World to come Yeneh velt; oilem habbo (Hebrew)
Worn out Oysgemahtert, farmutshet
Worried Fardeiget
Worthless Gornit vert; shkapeh, bobkes, tinif (all slang); chei kuck! (taboo)
Worthless clothing Shmatteh; tranteh
Would that it come true! Alevei! Halevai!
Wound Makeh, vund
Wretch Shlak, shlok
Wrong Kalyeh, shlecht

Yearly remembrance of the dead Yortzeit
You already forgot? Host shoyn fargessen?
You can burst? Me ken tsezetzt veren!
You can go crazy! Me ken meshugeh veren!
You can vomit from this! Me ken brechen fun dem!
You can't dance at two weddings simultaneously. Me ken
  nit tantzen ahf tsvai chassenes inainem.
You can't get rid of it. Me ken nit poter veren!
You don't frighten me! Gai shtrasheh di gens!
  Mich shrekt men nit!
You don't have to be pretty if you have charm. Me darf
  nit zein shain; me darf hoben chain.
You don't show a fool something half-finished. A nar
  veist men nit kain halbeh arbet.
You fool, you! Nar ainer!
You ought to be ashamed of yourself! Shemen zolstu
  zich in dein veiten haldz!
You please me a great deal. Ir gefelt mir zaier.
You should choke on it! Dershtikt zolstu veren!
You should get a stomach cramp! Se zol dich chapen
  beim boych! Se zol dir grihmen in boych!
You should live (and be well)! A leben ahf dir
  Zolst leben un zein gezunt!
You should live so! Zolstu azoy laiben!
You should swell up like a mountain! Zolst geshvollen
  veren vi a barg!
You shouldn't know from bad! Zolst nit vissen fun kain
  shlechts.
You understand? Farshtaist?
Young and old Kind un kait; yung un alt
Young doll Yingeh tsahtskeh; yefaiyfiyeh
(A) Young, vigorous lad Yungermantshik, chevrehman
Youngest child in family Mizinikil

You're all set!   Zeit ir doch ahfen ferd!

You're not making sense.   Nisht geshtoigen, nisht gefloigen.

You're welcome!   Nito farvos!

You're welcome (in my home).   Shmirt zich oys di shich.

Yummy-yummy!   Se tsegait zich in moyl!

INSTANT
Yiddish

CONTENTS

ONE _____

Words
and Phrases
Classified

Remember the pronunciations: A=ah; Ai=ay; E=eh; Ei=i; I=ee (or i as in it); O as in toss; U as in put; Ch as in Scottish "loch" or German "lach"; Oi and Oy, S and Z, Nit and Nisht, Oo and U, and Ahf and Oyf are used interchangeably

WHEN YOU MEET PEOPLE

Yes yoh

No nain

Good gut

Thank you. A dank.

Glad to meet you. Tsufriden eich tsu kenen.

You are welcome. Nit do far vos.

Excuse me. Zeit moichel; antshuldik mir.

It's all right. Es iz gants gut.

Please. Zeit azoy gut.

I would like ich volt velen

What? Vos?

This dos

Where vu

Here doh

When ven

Now   itzt

Later   shpeter

Who   ver

I   ich

You   du (sing.), ir (pl.)

He   er

She   zi

Your name?   Eier nomen? Vi haist ir?

My name is...   Ich hais...

Good morning.   Gut morgen.

Good evening.   Gutn ovent.

Good night.   A gute nacht.

Good-by.   A gutn. Shalom.

How are you?   Vos macht ir?

Very well, thank you, and you?   Zaier gut, a dank, un vos macht ir?

I do not understand. Please repeat.   Ich farshtai nit. Zeit azoy gut, chazert es iber.

So long.   Zeit gezunt.

See you again.   Me vet zich zen.

I'm sorry.   Es tut mir laid.

WHEN YOU NEED NUMBERS

Cardinal Numbers

One   ains
Two   tsvai
Three   drei
Four   fir
Five   finf
Six   zeks
Seven   ziben
Eight   acht
Nine   nein
Ten   tsen
Eleven   elef
Twelve   tsvelf

Thirteen dreitsen
Fourteen fertsen
Fifteen fuftsen
Sixteen zechtsen
Seventeen zibetsen
Eighteen achtsen
Nineteen neintsen
Twenty tsvontsik
Twenty-one ain-un tsvontsik
Thirty dreisik
Forty fertsik
Fifty fuftsik
Sixty zechtsik
Seventy zibetsik
Eighty achtsik
Ninety neintsik
One hundred hundert
Thousand toyzent
Million milyon

Ordinal Numbers

First ershte(r)
Second tsvaite(r)
Third dritte(r)
Fourth ferte(r)
Fifth finfte(r)
Sixth zekste(r)
Seventh zibete(r)
Eighth achte(r)
Ninth neinte(r)
Tenth tsente(r)
Eleventh elfte(r)
Twelfth tsvelfte(r)

WHEN YOU GO TO A HOTEL

Where is a good hotel? Vu iz a guter hotel?

I want a room. Ich vil a tsimmer.
    For one person. Oif ain mentsch.
    For two persons. Oif tsvai mentschen.
    With bath. Mit a vanneh.
    For two days. Far tsvai teg.
    For a week. Far a voch.

Till Monday. Biz montik.
   Tuesday. dinstik.
   Wednesday. mitvoch.
   Thursday. donershtik.
   Friday. freitik.
   Saturday. shabbes.
   Sunday. zuntik.

How much is it? Vifil kost es?

Here is my passport. Ot iz mein pass.

Here are my bags. Ot iz mein bagazh.

I like it. Es gefelt mir.

I don't like it. Es gefelt mir nit.

Show me another room. Veist mir an ander tsimmer.

Where is the toilet? Vu iz der klozet?

Where is the men's room? Vu iz dos vashtsimmer
  far menner?

Where is the ladies' room? Vu iz dos vashtsimmer
  far froien?

Hot water haiseh vasser

A towel a hantech

Soap zaif

Come in! Kumt arein!

Please, I want to have this washed. Zeit azoy gut, ich
  vil lozen dos oysvashen.
   Press, v. oyspressen
   Clean, v. oysrainiken

When will it be ready? Ven vet es zein fartig?

I need it for tonight. Ich darf es oyf heint ovnt.
  for tomorrow. Oyf morgen.

Put it there. Laig es dorten.

My key, please. Mein shlisel, zeit azoy gut.

Any mail for me? Iz doh far mir a briv?

Any packages? Zeinen doh packlech?

I want five airmail stamps for the United States. Ich vil
  finf luftpost markes far di farainikteh shtaten.

I want to send a telegram. Ich vil shiken a telegrameh.

Some postcards etlechch postkartlech

Call me at seven in the morning. Ruft mir ziben a zaiger in der fri.

Where is the telephone? Vu iz der telefon?

Hello! Haloh! Shalom!

Send breakfast to room 702, please. Shikt arein frishtik tsum tsimmer ziben hundert un tsvai, zeit azoy gut.

Orange juice marantsn-zaft

Rolls and coffee bulkes un kaveh

I am expecting someone. Ich dervart emetsen.

Tell him (her) to wait for me. Zog im (ir) tsu varten oyf mir.

If anyone calls me, I'll be back at six. Oyb emetser telefonirt mir, vel ich tsurik kumen seks a zaiger.

Tell me, please, where is there a drug store? Zogt mir, zeit azoy gut, vu iz doh an apteik?
    a barber shop? a sherer?
    a beauty parlor? a shainkeit salon?

What is the telephone number? Vos iz der telefon-numer?

What is the address? Vos iz der adres?

I want to change some money. Ich vil oysbeiten a bissel gelt.

What is the rate to the dollar? Vifil iz der kurs fun dolar?

My bill, please. Mein cheshben, zeit azoy gut.

WHEN YOU GO TO EAT

I am hungry. Ich bin hungerik.

I'm thirsty. Ich bin durshtik.

I want to eat. Ich vil essen.

Where is a good restaurant? Vu is doh a guter restoran?

A table for two, please. A tish far tsvai, zait azoy gut.

Waiter! Kelner!

Waitress! Kelneren!

The menu, please. Di shpaizkart, zeit azoy gut.

What is good today? Vos iz gut heint?

Is it ready? Es iz fartig?

How long will it take? Vi lang vet es nemen?

This, please. Dos, zeit azoy gut.

Bring some water. Brengt mir a bissel vasser.

A glass of beer a gloz bir

Milk milch

White wine veisser vein

Red wine royter vein

A cocktail a coktail

A whisky soda a viski mit sodeh

To your health! Down the hatch! L'cheiyim!

Soup zup, yoich

Fish fish

Meat flaish

Bread and butter broyt mit putter

A sandwich a sendvich

Roasted chicken gebroteneh hun

Veal cutlets kelberneh kotleten

Beef stew rinderner gulash

Salt and Pepper zalts un feffer

Steak ku-flaish, oksen-flaish

Rare nit derbroten

Well-done gut durchgebroten

I don't want any sauce. Ich vil nit kain gedempts.

With potatoes mit kartofles

Fried gepregelteh

Rice reiz

An omelet a feinkuchen

And what vegetables? Un vossereh grins?

Peas arbes

Carrots meren

Beans beblach, fasolyes

Onions tsibeles

Cauliflower kalafyor

Salads salaten

Lettuce salat

Tomatoes tomaten

Cucumber ugerkeh

Please bring me another fork. Zeit azoy gut, brengt mir an anderen gopel.

Knife messer

Spoon leffel

Glass gloz

Plate teller

What is there for desert? Vos hot ir far kompot?

Fruit frucht

Pastry gebeks

Strawberry trushkaveh

Ice cream eiz krem

Pie flodn

Cheese kez

Cheese cake kez-kuchen

Honey cake honik-lekech

Swiss cheese shvaitser kez

Black coffee, please. Shvartzeh kaveh, zeit azoy gut.

With or without sugar? Mit tzuker oder on tzuker?

Coffee with cream kaveh mit shmant

Tea with lemon tai mit limeneh

Mineral water mineral vasser

A little more, please. A bissel mer, zeit azoy gut.

That's enough. Shoyn genug.

The check, please. Dem cheshben, zeit azoy gut.

Is the tip included?   Iz dos trinkgelt areingerechent?

It was very good.   Es iz geven zaier gut.

WHEN YOU GO SHOPPING

I would like to buy this.   Ich volt gevolt dos koyfen.

And that   un dos

I am just looking around.   Ich kuk zich nor arum.

Something cheaper, please.   Epes biliger, zeit azoy gut.

It's too much.   Ez iz tsu fil.

What do you call this?   Vi haist dos?

Where is the department for   Vu is der optail far
    raincoats?   regen-mantlen?
    a hat?   a hitel?
    men's clothing?   menner klaider?
    women's clothing?   froyen klaider?
    underwear?   untervesh?
    shoes?   shich?
    a pair of gloves?   a por hentchkes?
    stockings?   zoken?
    socks?   shkar-peten?
    shirts?   hemder?

In America my size is . . .   In amerika mein moz iz . . .

Toys   shpitseig, shpilchelech, tsatskes

Perfume   parfum

Costume jewelry   kinstlech tsirung

Watches   zaigers

Sport articles   sport zachen

Show me.   Veist mir.

Another one   an anderer

A better quality   a bessereh kvalitet

Bigger   gresser

Smaller   klener

I don't like the color.   Der kolir gefelt mir nit.

I want that.   Ich vil dos.

in green. in grin.
yellow. gel.
blue. bioy.
red. royt.
gray. groy.
white. veis.
black. shvarts.
brown. broyn.
pink. rozeh.
lighter. heler, lichtiker.
darker. tunkeler.

I'll take it with me. Ich vel es nemen mit zich.

Please, have it delivered. Zeit azoy gut, brengt es tsu.

A receipt, please. A kaboleh, zeit azoy gut.

Where is there Vu iz do
  a book store? a bicher-krom?
  department store? universal gesheft?
  a flower shop? a blumen-krom?
  a food store? a shpaiz-krom?

Where can I buy Vu ken ich koyfen
  stamps? markes?
  toothpaste? tson-pasteh?

Sale! Oysfarkoyf!

WHEN YOU GO TRAVELLING

Bon voyage! Fort gezunterhait!

Taxi! Taksi!

Take me to the airport. Firt mich tsum fliplats.

Go slow! Pavolyeh! Pamelech!

Turn right. Farkerevet zich oyf rechts.
Turn left. Farkerevet zich oyf links.

Straight ahead. Fort gleich.

Not so fast! Nit azoy gich!

Stop here! Shtelt zich op doh!

How much is it to . . .? Vifil kost es tsu . . .?

And back? Un tsurik?

How-much by the hour? Vifil kost a sho?
 by the day? a tog?

What is that building? Vos iz der binyen?
Can it be visited? Meh ken es bazuchen?

I want to see the . . . Ich vil zaien di . . .

To the railroad station. Tsu der ban-stantsyeh.
 Tsum vagzal.

Wait for me. Vart oyf mir.

Porter! Treger!

A ticket to . . . a bilet tsu . . .

I have two bags. Ich hob tsvai valizes.

One way ain richtung

Round trip ahin un tzurik

First class ershteh klas

Second class tsvaiteh klas

When do we get to . . .? Ven kumen mir on kain . . .?

Where is the train to . . .? Vu iz der tsug kain . . .?
When does it leave? Ven fort er op?

Where is the dining-car? Vu iz der vagon-restoran?

Open the window. Effent dos fenster.
Close the window. Farmach dos fenster.

Where is the bus to . . .? Vu iz der otohbus tsu . . .?

I want to go to . . . Ich vil forn tsu . . .

Please tell me where to get off. Zeit azoy gut, zogt mir
 vu oystsushtaigen (. . . vu aroptsugaien).

Where is the gas station? Vu iz der gazolin stantsyeh?

I need gas. Ich darf hoben gazolin.

I need oil. Ich darf hoben ail.

Water vasser

Tires gumi reder

Something is wrong with the car. Epes iz kalyeh gevoren mit dem oyto.
Can you fix it? Kent ir es farrichten?

How long will it take? Vi lang vet es nemen?

Is this the road to . . .? Iz dos der veg kain . . .?

Have you a map? Hot ir a mapeh?

Where is the boat to . . .? Vu iz di shif kain . . .?

When does it leave? Ven gait zi op?

WHEN YOU WANT TO MAKE FRIENDS

Good day. Gut morgen.

My name is. Ich hais.

What is your name? Vi ruft men eich? Vos iz eier nomen? Vi haist ir?

I am delighted to meet you. Ich bin tsufriden eich tsu kenen.

It was a pleasure seeing you. Es iz geven a fargenigen tsu eich zen.

Do you speak English? Ret ir english?

I speak only a little. Ich red nor a bissel.

Do you understand? Tsi farshtait ir?

Please speak slowly. Zeit azoy gut, ret pavolyeh (pamelech).

I am from New York. Ich kum fun niew york.

Where are you from? Fu vanen kumt ir?

I like your country very much. Ich hob eier land zaier lib.

Your city eier shtot

Your house eier haim

Have you been in America? Tsi zeit ir geven in amerike?

This is my first visit here. Dos iz mein ershter bazuch do.

May I sit here? Meg ich doh avegzetsen?

May I take your picture? Meg ich nemen fun eich a bild?

This is a picture of my wife.   Dos iz a bild fun mein veib.

    husband.   man.
    son.   zun.
    daughter.   tochter.
    mother.   mameh.
    father.   tateh.
    sister.   shvester.
    brother.   bruder.
    brother-in-law.   shvoger.
    sister-in-law.   shvegerin.
    father-in-law.   shver.
    mother-in-law.   shviger.
    in-laws.   mechutonim.
    aunt.   mumeh.
    uncle.   feter.
    family.   mishpocheh.

Have you any children?   Hot ir kinder?

How beautiful!   Azoy shain!

Very interesting.   Zaier interesant.

Would you like a cigarette?   Tsi vilt ir a papiros?
    something to drink?   epes tsu trinken?
    something to eat?   epes tsu essen?

Sit down, please.   Zetst zich avek, zeit azoy gut.

Make yourself at home.   Macht zich bakvem.

Good luck!   Mazel tov!

To your health!   Tsu gezunt!

When can I see you again?   Ven ken ich eich zen noch a mol?

Where shall we meet?   Vu zollen mir zich treffen?

Here is my address.   Doh iz mein adres.

What is your address?   Vos iz eier adres.

What is your phone number?   Vos iz eier telefon-numer?

May I speak to . . .?   Ken ich reden mit . . .?

Would you like to have lunch?   Tsi volt is veln essen mitog?
    dinner?   vetshereh?
    a drink?   nemen a trunk?

Would you like to take a walk? Tsi vilt ir gaien shpatsiren?
>   **to go to the movies?** tsu gaien in kinoh?
>   **to the theatre?** in teater?
>   **to the beach?** tsu der plazhe?

With great pleasure! Mit grois fargenigen!

I am sorry. Es fardrist mich.

I cannot. Ich ken nit.

Another time an ander mol

I must go now. Ich muz itst gaien.

Thank you for a pleasant day. A dank far an angenemen tog.

Have you a match? Tsi hot is a shvebeleh?

Thank you for an excellent dinner. A dank eich far an oysgetsaichenten moltseit.

This is for you. Dos iz far eich.

A little souvenir a klainer ondenk

You are very kind. Ir zeit zaier gut-hartsik.

It's nothing really. Es iz be'emes gor nit.

With best regards mit di beste grussen

Regards home. A grus in der haim.

Congratulations! Mazel tov!

WHEN YOU ARE IN TROUBLE

Help! Gevald!

Police! Politsai!

Fire! Es brent!

Stop that man! Shtelt op dem man!

I have been robbed! Meh hot mich baroibt!

Look out! Hit zich!

Wait a minute! Vart a minut!

Stop! Hert oyf! Shtelt zich op!

Get out! Gait aroys!

Hurry up! Eilt zich! Shnell! Macht es gich!

Don't bother me! Tchepeh zich nit tzu mir!

What is going on? Vos tut zich doh?

I don't understand. Ich farshtai nit.

Please speak more slowly. Zeit azoy gut,
ret pamelecher.

Entrance areingang

Exit aroysgang

Danger! Sakoneh!

Keep out! Meh tor nit araingaien.

No smoking. Nit raicheren.

No parking. Nit parken.

Dead end blindh gessel

One way ain richtung

I am ill. Ich bin krank.

It hurts here. Es tut mir vai doh.

Please call a doctor. Zeit azoy gut, ruft a doktor.

Take me to the hospital. Nemt mich in shpitol.

Where is a drugstore? Vu is doh an apteik?

Where is a dentist? Vu iz a tson-doktor?

I have lost my bag. Ich hob farloyren mein valiz.
my wallet. mein beitel.
my passport. mein pass.
my camera. mein aparat.

I am an American. Ich bin an amerikaner.

Everything is all right. Alts iz gut.

TWO_____

Words
and Phrases
Alphabetized

A   a, an
Address   adres
Again   noch, noch a mol, vider, veiter
Airmail   luftpost
Airport   fliplats, luftport
All   alts, gants, aleh, alemen, ingantsen
All right   gut, gants gut
Already   shoyn
American   amerikaner
And   un
And this   un dos
Another   an andereh
Another time   an andereh tzeit, an andersh mol
Any   kain
Any mail for me?   Iz doh far mir a briv?
Any packages?   Zeinen doh peklech?
Anyone   emetser
Apothecary   apteik
Around   arum
Articles (goods)   artiklen, zachen

Aunt   mumeh

Automobile   oyto, otoh,

Bag (pocketbook, wallet)   beitel

(Go) back!   (Gai) tzurik!

Bad   kalyeh, shlecht

Bags   bagazh, valizes

Barber shop   razeer shtoob

Bath   bod, vanneh

Be well!   Zei gezunt!

Beach   plazheh

Beans   fasolyes, beblech, bubkes

Beautiful   shain

Beauty parlor   shainkeit-salon

Beef stew   rinderner-gulash

Beer   bir

A better quality   a bessereh aigenshaft, a bessereh
  kvalitet

Bigger   gresser

Bill   chesben

My bill, please.   Mein cheshben, zeit azoy gut.

Black   shvarts

Black coffee   shvartzeh kaveh

Blue   bloy

Boat   shif

Bon voyage!   Fort gezunterhait!

Book   buch

Book store   bicher-krom

Bother, v.   tchepen

Bread   broyt

Bread and butter   broyt mit putter

Breakfast   frishtik

Bring, v.   brengen

Bring me another fork. Brengt mir an anderen gopel.

Bring me some water. Brengt mir a bissel vasser.

Brother bruder

Brother-in-law shvoger

Brown broyn

Building binyen

Bus oytobus, otohbus

Butter putter

Buy koyfen

Cake lekech

To call rufen

Call a doctor. Ruft a doktor.

Call me at seven in the morning. Ruft mich ziben
a zaiger in der fri

Camera fotografir-aparat

Can you fix it? Kent ir es farrichten?

Car oyto, otoh

Carrots meren

Cauliflower kalafyoren

Ceiling sufit, pulip, stelyeh

Change (money), v. oysbeiten

Cheap bilig

Cheaper biliger

The check please. Dem cheshben, zeit azoy gut.

Cheese kez

Cheese cake kez-kuchen

Chicken hun

Children kinder

Cigarette papiros

City shtot

Class klas

Clean, adj. rain

Clean, v.   rainiken, oysrainiken

Clock   zaiger

Close the window.   Farmach dos fenster.

Clothing   klaider

Coat, topcoat   mantel

Cocktail   coktail

Coffee   kaveh

Coffee with cream   kaveh mit shmant

Color   kolir

Come   kumen

Come back   kumen tzurik

Come here.   Kumt aher.

Come in.   Kumt arein.

Comfortable   bakvem

Congratulations!   Mazel tov!

Cost   kost

Costume   kostyum

Costume jewelry   kostyum tsirung, kinstleche tsirung

Country   land, medinah

Cow   ku

Cream   krem, smeteneh, shmant

Cucumber   ugerkeh

Cutlets   kotleten

Darker   tunkeler

Daughter   tochter

Daughter-in-law   shnur

Day   tog (sing.), teg (pl.)

Dead end   blindeh gessel

Be delighted   zein tsufriden

Deliver   tsushtelen

Department (of a store)   optail

Dentist   tsondokter

Department store universal gesheft

Dining car vagon-restoran, vagon ess-tzimmer

Dinner vetshereh

Disappointment entoishung, genart

Do you have hot ir

Do you speak English? Tsi ret ir english?

Do you understand? Tsi farshtait ir?

Doctor dokter

Dollar dolar

Don't bother me! Tshepeh zich op fun mir!

Down the hatch! l'cheiyim

Drink, n. trunk troonk

Drink, v. trinken

Drug store apteik

Eat, v. essen

Eggs aier

Eight acht

Eighteen achtsen

Eighth achte(r)

Eighty achtsik

Eleven elef

Eleventh elfte(r)

Enough genug

Entrance areingang

Evening ovnt

Everything is all right. Alts iz gut.

Excellent oysgetsaichent

Excuse me. Zeit moichel, antshuldikt mir.

Exit aroysgang

Expect, await dervarten

Family mishpocheh

Fast gich

Father   tateh, foter
Father-in-law   shver
Fifteen   fuftsen
Fifth   finfte(r)
Fifty   fuftsik
Fire!   Es brent!
First   ershte(r)
First class   ershteh klas
Fish   fish
Five   finf
Fix   farrichten
Floor   dil, goren, podlogeh
Floor   goren (story level), dil, podlogeh, brik
Flower shop   blumen-krom
Food store   shpaiz-krom
For   far, oyf
For tomorrow   oyf morgen
Fork   gopel
Forty   fertsik
Four   fir
Fourteen   fertsen
Fourth   ferte(r)
Friday   freitik
Fried   gepregelteh
From   fun
From where   fun vanen
Fruit   frucht
Gasoline   gazolin
Gasoline station   gazolin-stantsyeh
Glad to meet you.   Tsufriden eich tsu kenen.
Gentlemen   menner
Get off   aropgaien

Get off aropgaien, aroptsugaien, oystsushtaigen

Glass gloz

Glass of beer a gloz bir

Gloves hentchkes

Go gaien

Go away! Gai avek!

Go slow! Pavolyeh! Pamelech!

Good gut

Good-by. A guten. Shalom.

Good day. Gut morgen.

Good evening. Guten ovent.

Good luck! Mazel tov!

Good morning. Gut morgen.

Good night. A guteh nacht.

Gray groy

Great. grois

Great pleasure grois fargeniven

Green grin

Hat hut, hitel

Have it delivered. Shikt es tsu. Brengt es tsu.

Have you a map? Hot ir a karte (mapeh)?

Have you been in America? Tsi zeit ir geven in amerike?

Have you children? Tsi hot ir kinder?

He er

Healthy gezunt

Hello! Haloh! Shalom!

Help! Gevald!

Here doh, aher, ot

Here are my bags. Ot iz mein bagazh.

Here is my address. Do is mein adres.

Here is my passport. Ot iz mein pass.

Home haim

Honey honik

Honey cake honik-lekech

Hospital shpitol

Hot water haiseh vasser

Hotel hotel

Hour sho

How viazoy

How are you? Vos macht ir?

How beautiful! Azoy shain!

How long will it take? Vi lang vet es nemen?

How much? Vifil?

How much by the day? Vifil kost a tog?
Vifil loitn tog?

How much by the hour? Vifil kost a sho?
Vifil loitn sho?

How much is it? Vifil kost es?

How much is it to . . .? Vifil kost es tsu . . .?

Hundred hundert

Hungry hungerik

Hurry, v. eilen zich

Hurry up! Eilt zich unter! Macht es shnell!
Macht es gich!

Hurt (pain) vai

Husband man

I ich

I am an American. Ich bin an amerikaner.

I am delighted to meet you. Es frait mich eich tsu
kenen.

I am disappointed. Ich bin entoisht. Ich fil zich genar'

I am expecting someone. Ich dervart emetsen.

I am from New York. Ich kum fun niew york.

I am hungry. Ich bin hungerik.

I am ill. Ich bin krank.

I am just looking around. Ich kuk zich nor arum.

I am sorry. Es fardrist mich. Es tut mir laid. Zeit moichl.

I cannot. Ich ken nit.

I come from ich kum fun

I do not understand. Pléase repeat. Ich farshtai nit. Zeit azoy gut, chazert es iber.

I don't know. Ich vais nit.

I don't like it. Es gefeit mir nit.

I don't like the color. Der kolir gefelt mir nit.

I don't understand. Ich farshtai nit.

I don't want any sauce. Ich vil nit kain gedempts.

I don't want it. Ich vil es nit.

I have been robbed! Meh hot mich baroibt!

I have lost my wallet (bag). Ich hob farloyren mein beitel (valiz).

I have two bags. Ich hob tsvai valizes.

I know. Ich vais.

Like, v. lib hoben; gefelen

I like it. Es gefelt mir.

I like your country very much. Eier land gefelt mir zaier shtark.

I must go now. Ich muz itst gaien.

I need gas. Ich darf hoben gazolin.

I need it for tonight. Ich darf es oyf heint ovent.

I need oil. Ich darf hoben ail.

I speak only a little. Ich red nor a bissel.

I want ich vil

I want a room. Ich vil a tsimmer.
    with bath. mit a vanneh.
    for one person. far ain mentsh.
    for two persons. far tsvai mentshen.
    for two days. oif tsvai teg.

for a week. oif a voch.
till Monday. biz montik.

I want five airmail stamps for the United States. Ich vil finf luftpost-markes far di farainikteh shtaten.

I want that. Ich vil dos.

I want to change some money. Ich vil oysbeiten a bissel gelt.

I want to eat. Ich vil essen.

I want to go to . . . Ich vil gain tsu . . .

I want to have this washed. Ich vil lozen dos oysvashen.
  pressed. oyspressen.
  cleaned. oysrainiken.

I want to see . . . Ich vil zaien . . .

I want to send a telegram. Ich vil shiken a telegrameh.

I would like ich volt veln

I would like to buy this. Ich volt gevolt dos koyfen.

Ice eiz

Ice cream eiz krem

If az, oyb, tomer, tsi

If anyone calls me, I'll be back at six. Oyb emetser telefonirt mir—ich vel kumen tsurik zeks a zaiger.

I'll take it with me. Ich vel es nemen mit zich.

I'm sorry. Es tut mir laid.

I'm thirsty. Ich bin dorshtik.

In in, arein, oyf

In America my size is in amerike iz mein moz

In the morning in der fri

In-laws (parental) mechutonim

Interesting interesant

Is iz

Is it ready? Es iz fartig?

Is the tip included? Iz dos trinkgelt areingerechent?

Is this the road to . . .? Iz dos der veg kain . . ?

Is this the train for . . .?   Iz dos der tsug kain . . .?

It   es

It hurts me.   Es tut mir vai.

It is very good.   Es iz zaier gut.

It was a pleasure seeing you.   Es is geven a fargenigen eich tsu zen.

It was very good.   Es iz geven zaier gut.

It's all right.   Es iz gants gut.

It's nothing really.   Es iz be'emes gornit.

It's too much.   Es iz tsu fil.

Jewelry   tsirung

Juice   zaft

Keep out!   Meh tor nit araingaien!

Key   shlisel

Key, please.   Mein shlisel, zeit azoy gut.

Knife   messer

Know (facts)   vissen

Know (people, languages, skills)   kenen

Ladies   froyen

Ladies room   washtsimmer far froyen

Lamb meat   shepsen-flaish

Later   shpetter

Leave, depart, v.   avek gaien

Left   links

Leg   fus

Leg of lamb   fus fun shepsen-flaish

Lemon   limeneh

Letter, mail   briv

Lettuce   salat

Lighter (color)   heler, lichtiker

Like, v.   lib hoben, gefelen

Little quantity   a bissel

Little size   klain

A little more, please.   A bissel mer, zeit azoy gut.

A little souvenir.   A klainer ondenk.

Long   lang

Look around   kuk arum

Look out, beware, watch out   hiten zich

Look out!   Hit zich!

Lose, v.   farliren

Love, v.   lib hoben

Luck   mazel, glik

Lunch   varrems, mitog

Mail, letter   post, briv

Make yourself at home.   Macht zich bakvem.

Make yourself comfortable.   Macht zich bakvem.

Man   man, mentsh

Map   karteh, mapeh

Match, light   shvebeleh

May I sit here?   Meg ich doh zich avekzetsen?
    speak to . . .?   reden tsu . . .?
    take your picture?   nemen fun eich a bild?

Me   mir

Meat   flaish

Meet   bagegenen

Men   menner, mentshen

Men's clothing   menner-klaider

Men's room   vashtsimmer far menner

Menu   shpaizkart, menyu

Milk   milch

Million   milyon

Mine   mein(er)

Mineral water   mineral vasser

Minute   minut, minoot

Monday montik

Money gelt

More mer

Morning morgen (also means tomorrow)

Morning (early) fri

Mother mameh

Mother-in-law shviger

Movies kinoh

My mein(er)

My name is ich hais

My size is mein moz iz

Name nomen

Need, v. darfen

Night nacht

Nine nein

Nineteen neintsen

Ninety neintsik

Ninth neinte(r)

No nain

No parking. Nit parken. Nit avekshtellen.

No smoking. Nit raicheren.

Not nit, nisht

Not any nit kain

Not so fast! Nit azoy gich!

Nothing gornit

Now itzt, shoyn

Number numer

O'clock a zaiger

Off, down arop

Oil ail

Omelet omlett, fein-kochen

One ains

One hundred hundert

One way ain richtung

  and back un tzurik

Oneself zich

Onions tsibeles

Only nor

Open, v. effenen

Open the window. Effen dos fenster.

Or oder

Orange marants, pomerants, oranzh

Orange juice marantsn-zaft

Out! Aroys!

Out (prefix) oys-

Package pekel

Pair por

Pair of gloves a por hentchkes

Park, v. parken, avekshtellen

Parlor salon

Passport pass

Pastry gebeks

Peas arbes

Pepper feffer

Perfume parfum

Person mentsh (sing.), mentshen (pl.)

Picture bild

Pie flodn

Pink rozeh

Plate teller

Pleasant time eingenemeneh tseit

Please.. Zeit azoi gut. Bitteh.

Please, v. gefelen

To be pleased zein tsufriden

Pleasure   fargenigen, fraid

Police!   Polits! Politsai!

Porter!   Treger!

Postage stamps   markes

Postcards   postkartlech

Potatoes   kartofles, bulbes

Press, v.   pressen, oyspressen

Put, place, v.   laigen

Put it there.   Laig es dorten.

Quality   kvalitet

Quickly   shnell, gich

Railroad   train, bahn

    To the railroad station.   Tsu der ban stantsyeh.

    Tsum vok-zal.

Rain   regen

Raincoats   regen-mantlen

Rare (meat)   nit debroten

Rate of (exchange)   koors, kurs

Ready   fartig

Receipt   kaboleh

Red   royt

Red wine   royter vein

Regards   grus, grussen

Regards home.   A grus in der haim.

Relatives   mishpocheh

Repeat   iberchazeren, nochzogen

Restaurant   restoran

Rice   reiz

Ride, v.   foren (verb)

Right (direction)   rechts

Right, correct   richtik, gerecht

Road   veg

Roasted chicken gebroteneh hun

Rob baroiben

Robbed baroibt

Rolls and Coffee bulkes un (mit) kaveh

Room tsimmer

Round trip ahin un tsurik

Salads salatn

Sale! Oysfarkoyf!

Salt and Pepper zalts un feffer

Sandwich sendvich

Saturday shabbes

Sauce gedempts

Second tsvaiteh (adj.), tsvaiter (n.)

Second class tsvaiteh klas

See you again. Meh vet zich zen.

Self zich

Send shiken

Send breakfast to room 702. Shikt frishtik tsum
    tsimmer ziben hundert un tsvai.

Seven ziben

Seventh zibete(r)

Seventy zibetsik

She zi

Shirts hemder

Shoes shich

show, v. veizen

Show me another room. Veist mir an anderer tsimmer.

Sickness krenk

Sister shvester

Sister-in-law shvegerin

Sit zitsen

Sit down. Zetst zich avek.

Six zeks

Sixteen zechtsen

Sixth zekste(r)

Sixty zechtsik

Size moz

Slow, slowly pavolyeh, pamelech

Small klain

Smaller klener

Smoke, v. raicheren

So long. Zeit gezunt. Shalom. Meh vet zich zen.

Soap zaif

Socks shkarpeten

Soda sodeh

Sold oysfarkoyft

Some etlecheh, a bissel

Some postcards elteceh postkartlech

Someone emetser

Something epes

Something cheaper, please. Epes biliger, zeit azoy gut.

Something is wrong with the car. Epes iz kalyeh in
dem oyto.

Something to drink? Epes tsu trinken?

Something to eat? Epes tsu essen?

Son zun

Son-in-law aidim

Have sorrow tun bank

Be sorry hoben fardross

Soup zup, yoych

Souvenir ondenk

Speak reden

Speak more slowly. Ret pamelecher.

Speak slowly. Ret pavoli (pamelech).

Spoon   leffel

Sport articles   shport artiklen

Stamps   markes

State   shtat

Steak   ku-flaish, oksen-flaish

Stew   gulash

Stockings   zoken

Stop!   Hert oyf! Shtelt zich op!

Stop here!   Oyfheren doh! Shtelt zich op doh!

Stop that man!   Farhalt dem man! Shtelt op dem man!

Store   krom

Straight   gleich

Straight ahead   fort gleich

Strawberry   trushkaveh

String, cord   shtrik

Sugar   tsuker

Sunday   zuntik

Swiss cheese   shvaitser kez

Table   tish

Table for two   a tish far tsvai

Take   nemen

Take me to the hospital.   Nemt mir in shpitol arein.
     to the hospital.   tsu a shpitol.

Taxi!   taksi!

Tea with lemon   tai mit limeneh

Telegram   telegrameh

Telephone   telefon

Tell   zogen

Tell him (her) to wait for me.   Zog im (ir)az er (zi) zol
     varten oyf mir.

Tell me, where there is a drug store?   Zogt mir vu iz do
     an apteik?

Tell me where to get off. Zogt mir vu aroptsugaien.

Ten tsen

Tenth tsente(r)

Thank you. A dank.

Thank you for a wonderful day. A dank far an angenemen tog.
>   **for an excellent dinner.** far an oysgetsaychenten moltseit.

That dos

That's enough. Shoyn genug.

Theatre teater

There dorten

Third dritte(r)

Thirsty durshtik

Thirteen dreitsen

Thirty dreisik

This dos

This is a picture of my wife. Dos iz a bild fun mein veib.

This is for you. Dos iz far eich.

This is my lrst visit here. Dos iz mein ershter bazuch doh.

Thousand toyzent

Three drei

Thursday donershtik

Ticket bilet

Time tzeit (hour), mol (interval)

Tip trinkgelt

Tires gumi reder

To tsu, tsum

To your health! Tsu gezunt! L'chaiyim!

Toilet klozet, vash-tsimmer

Tomatoes   tomaten, pomidoren

Tomorrow   morgen

Tonight   heint ovent, heint bei nacht

Too, also   oych, oychet

Too, excessive   tsu

Too much   tsu fil

Toothpaste   tsonpasteh

Towel   hantech

Tower   turem

Toys   shpiltszeig, shpilchelech, tsatskes

Train   tsug, ban

Tuesday   dinstik

Turn right.   Farkerevet zich oyf rechts.

Twelve   tsvelf

Twelfth   tsvelfte(r)

Twenty   tsvontsik

Twenty-one   ain un tsvontsik

Two   tsvai

Uncle   feter

Understand   farshtain

Underwear   untervesh

United States   farainikteh shtaten

Until   biz

Up   aroyf

Veal   kalb-flaish, kelberneh-flaish

Veal cutlets   kelberneh-kotleten

Vegetables   grins, grinvarg, grinsteig

Very   zaier

Very interesting   zaier interesant

Very well, thank you, and you?   Zaier gut, a dank, un
vos macht ir?

Village shtetel

Visit bazuch

Wait varten

Wait a minute! Vart a minut (minoot)!

Wait for me. Vart oyf mir.

Waiter! Kelner!

Waitress! Kelneren!

Walk, v. shpatziren

Wallet beitel

Wash, v. vashen, oysvashen

Watch, clock zaiger

Water vasser

Way, direction veg

Wednesday mitvoch

Week voch

Well, good, fine gut, fain

Well-done (meat) gut durchgebroten

What? Vos? Vossereh?

What do you call this? Vi haist dos?

What is going on? Vos tut zich?

What is good today? Vos iz gut heint?

What is that building? Vos iz der binyen?
  Can it be visited? Ken men in ihm areingain?

What is there for dessert? Vos hot ir far kompot?

What is the rate to the dollar? Vifil iz der koors fun dollar?

What is the telephone number? Vos iz der telefon-numer?

What is there for dessert? Vos hot ir far desert?

What is your address? Vos iz eier adres?

What is your name? Vos ruft men eich? Vos iz eier nomen? Vi haist ir?

What is your phone number? Vos is eier telefon-numer?

What time is it? Vifil halt der zaiger?

What vegetables? Vossereh grins?

When? Ven?

When can I see you again? Ven ken ich eich zen noch a mol?

When do we get to . . . Ven kumen mir on kain . . .

When does it leave? Ven for men op?

When will it be ready? Ven vet es zein fartig?

Where? Vu?

Where from? Fun vanen?

Where to? Vuhin?

Where are you from? Fun vanen kumt ir?

Where can I buy? Vu ken ich koyfen?

Where do I get off? Vu gai ich arop?

Where is a dentist? Vu iz doh a tson-dokter?

Where is a drugstore? Vu iz do an apteik?

Where is the gas station? Vu iz di gazolin-stantsyeh?

Where is a good hotel? Vu iz a guter hotel?

Where is a good restaurant? Vu iz do a guter restoran?

Where is the boat to . . . ? Vu iz di shif kain . . . ?

Where is the bus to . . . ? Vu iz der oytohbus kain . . . ?

Where is the department for . . . ? Vu iz der optail far . . . ?

Where is the dining car? Vu is der restoran vagon?

Where is the ladies' room? Vu iz dos vashtsimmer far froyen?

Where is the men's room? Vu iz dos vashtsimmer far menner?

Where is the telephone? Vu iz der telefon?

Where is the toilet? Vu iz der klozet?

Where is the train to . . . ? Vu iz der tsug kain . . . ?

Where is there...? Vu iz do...?

Where shall we meet? Vu zollen mir zich bagegenen?

Whiskey viski, shnaps, bronfen

Whiskey and soda viski mit sodeh

White veis

White wine veisser vein

Wife veib

Window fenster

Wine vein

With mit

With best regards. Mit di beste grussen.

With great pleasure mit a grois fargenigen

With or without sugar? Mit tsuker oder on tsuker?

With potatoes mit kartofles

Without on

Who ver

Wonderful vunderlich

Women's clothing froyen klaider

Would you like to have lunch? Tsi volt ir veln essen varrems?
    a cigarette? a papiros?
    dinner? vetshereh?
    a drink? a trunk (troonk)?

Would you like to go to the movies? Tsi volt ir veln gaien in kinoh?
    to the theatre? in teater?
    to the beach? tsu der plazhe?
    to take a walk? shpatsiren?

Wrong kalyeh

You understand? Farshtaist?

Yellow gel

Yes yoh

You du (sing.), ir, eich (pl.)

You are very kind.   Ir zeit zaier gut-hartsik (lib).

You are welcome.   Nit do far vos.

Your   eier

Your city   eier shtot

Your house   eier haim, eier hoiz, eier shtub

Your name?   Eier nomen? Vi haist ir?

Yourself   zich

THREE_____

Popular
Words, Idioms
and Colloquialisms

Absent-minded Aiver butel, oiver botel

Ache, n. vaitik

All at once inmitten drinnen, plootzim

All shoemakers go barefoot. Alleh shusters gaien borves.

Alphabet Alefbais (the first two letters of the Hebrew alphabet)

Amen ohmain

An unlucky person is a dead person. A mentsh on glik iz a toyter mentsh.

Ancestry Yichus

Angel of death der malech hamoves

Angry person kasnik

Animal, dull-witted human being behaimeh

Anniversary of the death of a person Yortseit

Annoy persistently nudgen

Annoying person nudnik, onshikenish

Another man's disease is not hard to endure. A makeh unter yenem's orem iz nit shver tsu trogen. (Lit., a boil in another's arm is not hard to endure.)

Antique altvarg, antik, tranteh

Anything worthless shmatteh (rag), bubkes (beans)

Are you crazy?   Tsi bistu meshugeh?

Are you in a hurry?   Shtaist abf ain fus? (Lit., are you on one leg?)

As futile as stomping on the earth!   Es iz nit vert a zets in drerd. (Lit., not worth a knock on the earth!)

As long as I can be with you.   Abi tsu zein mit dir.

Ask a sick man!   A kranken fregt men! (i.e., when a man is ill, you ask him what he wants to eat; a humorous reply to a host's offer of refreshments.)

Ask me something else!   Freg mich becherim! (Used when you don't know the answer or are indifferent.)

Assuredly   Takeh

Atonement   kaporeh

Attractive girl   tsatskeh (Lit., toy)

Authority   maivin

Average man   mittelmessiger

Aw, hell!   A broch!

Awkward person   klotz, kuneh-lemel

Back-handed slap   frask

Bad   shlecht

Bad person, someone capable of evil   vos-in-der-kort (Lit., represents every bad card in the deck)

Bad taste!   mein bobbeh's tam (Lit., my grandmother's taste)

Badger, v.   nudgen

Baked dumplings, filled with potato, meat, liver, or barley   knishes

Bang, n.   a chmalyeh, a klap, a zetz

Barely made it!   kom mit tsores! (Lit., barely avoided trouble!)

Bargain, n.   metsiyeh

Bargain, v.   handlen, dingen zich

Bastard   mamser, oisvurf

Be at pains to (please), make an effort   zei zich matriach (make an effort.)

Be happy! Zeit mir frailech!

Be so good zeit azoy gut

Be quiet! Zol zein shtil!

Be well! Zeit mir gezunt. Zeit gezunt!

Beautiful as the seven worlds. Shain vi di ziben velten.
(Legend has it that God made and destroyed the world
seven times before he finally made our world.)

Bedbug vantz

Beet soup borsht

Beggar shnorrer, bettler

Believe me! Gloib mir!

Belly-button pipek, pupik

Bewildered tsetoomelt

Big bargain groisseh metsiyeh

Big boss balebos

Big breadwinner (ironic, of a person who isn't) groisser
fardiner

Big deal! (ironic) Ain klainikeit! (Lit., one small matter)
Gantseh megilah! Groisseh gedillah! A glick hot dich
getrofen!

Big eater fresser

Big good-for-nothing groisser gornisht

Big healthy dame a gezunteh moid

Big mouth! Pisk!

Big noise tararam

Big shot knacker, gantser knacker, groisser shisser

Bit shtik, shtikel

Bitter person farbissener

Blabbermouth (female) yenteh

A black year! (A) shvartz yor!

Blessed with children. Gebentsht mit kinder.

A blessing on your head. A leben ahf dein kop.
(Idiomatically, well said! well done!) A brocheh ahf
dein kop.

Blinding the eyes! Es shvindilt in di oygen!

Bluff one's way out unterfonfen

Blundered farblonjet

Boarding house with cooking privileges koch-alain

Bologna vursht

Bon voyage! Fort gezunterhait!

Book of services for the first two nights of Passover
  hagadah, hagodeh (Lit., story)

Boor yold

Boorish young man grobber yung

Boorish or coarse person burvan

Bore nudnik

Born loser umglik

Brazenness chutzpeh

Break a leg! Brech a fus! Tsebrech a fus!

Bribe (slang) shmeer

Bride kalleh

Bride and groom chossen-kalleh

Bridegroom chossen

A Brunhilde a gezinteh moid

Buckwheat kashe

Buffoon shmegegi

Bum trombenik

Bungler klotz

Burglar goniff

Burst with frustration platsn

Business gesheft

Busy-body kochleffel

To butter up untershmeichlen

Buttocks hinten, inten (slang), toches (taboo)

Call me a "nut." Ruf mich knak-nissel [nut-cracker].
  (Fig., I don't care.)

Capable housewife and homemaker balebosteh, beryeh

Careless dresser shlump

Cash mezumen

Cash only! Don't ask for credit! Ribi-fish, gelt ahfen tish!

Certainly takeh

Circumcision bris

Charity tsedokeh

Chattering yatatata

Cheap billig

Cheap as soup, a real bargain billig vi borsht

Chopped liver gehakteh leber

Chopped meat hak-flaish

Chump yold

Clumsy person klotz, kuneh-lemel

Clutched at the heartstrings klemt beim hartz

Coarse person grobber yung

Coat, as with butter shmeeren

Coffee cake, pastry gebeks

Come now! Gait, gait!

Come to the point! Macht es keilechdik un shpitsik. (Lit., make it round and pointy.)

Come-upper oyfgekumener, alrightnik (American)

Commandment mitsveh

Common sense, good sense saichel

Compassion rachmones

Complain kvetshen

Complain (when there is nothing to complain about) A chissoren di kaleh iz tsu shain. (Lit., the bride is too pretty.)

Complainer kvetsher, kloger

Complete details gantseh megillah (slang)

Compulsive eater fresser

Conceited   ongeblozzen

Confusing work   ongepatshket (Lit., muddled)

Confusion   kashe (slang) (Lit., mush cereal, buckwheat, or porridge), mishmash, tumel

Congratulations!   Mazel tov!

Connoisseur   maivin

Continuous eater of snacks   nasher

Corny   shmaltzik

Costly   teier

Could be   ken zein

Countryman, fellow townsman   landsman

Crazy   meshugeh, tsidrait

Crazy antics or actions, a craze or madness   meshugass

Crazy as a loon   meshugeh ahf toyt

Crazy man   meshugener

Crazy woman   meshugeneh

Crazy world   a meshugeneh velt

Cream   smetteneh, shmant (for coffee)

Creep, n.   zhlob

Criminal, thief, racketeer   gazlen

Cripple   kalyekeh

Crook   goniff, ganev

Crooked actions   Ganaivisheh shtiklech

A curse on my enemies   A klog tsu meineh sonim.

A curse on you.   A broch ahf dir. A choleryeh ahf dir. A finster yor ahf dir.

Customary gifts exchanged on Purim, usually candy, cake   shalach mohnes

Cut it short!   On langeh hakdomes! (Lit., without long introductions)

Cute (girl)   lyalkeh, tsatskeh (Lit., plaything, doll)

Daddy   tateh

Dairy food   milchiks (n.), milechdik (adj)

Damn it! A broch!

Darling neshomeleh, teiers

Dear teier

Delicacy meichel

Delicious tasting geshmak

The devil with him! Ich hob im in bod!

Dietary laws kashress

Diminutive, affectionate term for children kinderlach

Diplomacy saichel, diplomatyeh

Dipped eingetunken

Dirt shmuts

Disappointment entoishung, fardross

Do it fast! Mach es shnell!

Do it for my sake. Tu mir tsulib.

Do me a favor. Tu mir tsulib. Tu mir a toiveh.

Do me a favor and drop dead! Folg mich a gang un gai in drerd!

Do you want? Vilstu?

Doll lyalkeh, tsatskeh, krassavitseh (beautiful girl)

Dolt shnook

Don't be a damn fool! Zei nit kein vyzosoh!

Don't be a fool! Zeit nit kain nar! Zeit nit kain goilem!

Don't bleed me! Tsap mir nit dos blut! (Fig., don't aggravate me.)

Don't bother me! Drai mir nit kain kop! Hak mir nit kain tsheinik! Tshepeh zich nit tsu mir! Tshepeh zich op fun mir!

Don't complain. Zindik nit. Baklog zich nit.

Don't do me any favors. Tu mir nit kain toyves.

Don't double-talk. Nisht gefonfet.

Don't envy. Zindik nit. Zai nit mekaneh.

Don't fool around. Nisht gefonfet.

Don't give me an evil eye. Gib mir nit kain einoreh (eiyin horeh).

Don't make a big deal out of it! Mach nit kain tsimmes [sweet carrot compote] fun dem!

Don't mix up the prayers. Farmisht nit di yotsres.

Don't threaten me! Strasheh mich nit!

Don't twist my head! Drai mir nit kain kop!

Don't worry! Deigeh nisht! Hob nit kain deiges! Nisht gedeiget! Zorg zich nit!

Door post container of parchment on which is written Deuteronomy VI, 4-9 and XI, 13-21 Mezuzeh

Dope shmendrik, yold

Dopey, clumsy person shlemiel

Double-talk, v. fonfen

Dowdy, gossipy woman barederkeh, recheelisnitseh

Dowry nadan

Drop dead! Geharget zolstu verren! Ver derharget! Ver geharget! Ich hob dich! Zolst ligen in drerd!

Drunkard shicker

Dullard temper kop

Dull person, clumsy and sluggish Goilem

Dull-witted behaimeh (Lit., domesticated animal)

Dumb like a piece of wood! Shtik holtz!

Dumbbell, dunce, dumb head dumkop, shtik holtz

Eat voraciously, like an animal fressen

Eat in good health! Ess gezunterhait!

Embittered person farbissener

Enough is enough! Genug is genug!

The end of the world. Ek velt.

Endearing term bubeleh, bubee

Engaged couple chossen-kalleh

Esteem koved

Erudite person lamden

Exciting person   kasnik

Excuse me.   Zeit (mir) moychel.

Exhausted   oysgehorevet, oysgematert

Expensive   teier

Expert   maivin

Extreme pleasure   fargenigen

Fairy tale   bobbeh meisseh (Lit., grandmother's story)

Fait accompli   a nechtiger tog (Lit., a yesterday's day), farfallen

Fall guy   shlump

False or forced laugh.   Me lacht mit yashtsherkes.

Family   mishpocheh

The faster the better.   Vos gicher alts besser.

Fat   shmaltz

Father-in-law   shver

Feces, dung   drek (taboo)

Female infant (affectionate term)   pisherkeh (Lit., little urinator)

Female tricks   veiberishe shtik

Festive   yontefdik

Fidget   Sitzen ahf shpilkes. (Lit., to sit on pins and needles)

Filthy rich   shtain reich (Lit., gem rich)

Finicky   aidel gepatshket (adj.), pritsteh (fem. n.)

Fiftieth wedding anniversary   goldeneh chasseneh

Fine   balebatish

Flattery   shmaltz (slang), komplimenten

Flavor   ta'am

Food forbidden under Jewish dietary laws   traif

Food that meets rules of Jewish dietary laws   kosher

Fool, n.   nar, shlemiel, shmendrik, shmegegi, behaimeh

A fool feels nothing.   A nar filt nit.

Foolish (fruitless) question   klotz kasheh

Foolishness narishkeit

For better, for worse tsum glik, tsum shlimazel

For nothing umzist

Forget him! Ich hob im in bod! (Lit., I have him in the bath)

Fractured English tsebrochener english

Friendly face haimisher ponim

From your mouth to God's ear! Fun eier moyl in Gots oyeren.

Fuss over nothing, n. tsimmes

Gadabout kochleffel

Gall chutspeh

Garden of Eden, paradise ganaiden

Get a move on! Gib zich a shockel! Gib zich a traisel! Eilt zich!

Get away from me! Tshepeh zich op fun mir!

Get killed! Ver derharget! Ver geharget!

Get lost! Go away! Ver farblondjet! Trog zich op!

Getting senile aiver butel, oiver botel

Gimmick machareikeh

Girl of marriageable age kalleh-moid

Gizzard pipek, pupik

Glass of tea glezel tai

Gnawing, grinding person grizhidiker

Go away! Gai avek!

Go bang your head against the wall! Gai klop zich kop in vant!

Go break a leg! Tsebrech a fus!

Go drive yourself crazy! Fardrai zich dein aigenem kop!

Go flap your ears! Ich hob dich! (Lit., I have you [somewheres!])

Go jump in a lake! Nem zich a vanneh! (Lit., take a bath.)

Go mix yourself up, not me! Gai fardrai zich dein aigenem kop!

Go peddle your fish elsewhere! Gai feifen ahfen yam! (Lit., go whistle on the ocean)

Go take a bath! Nem zich a vanneh!

Go to hell! Gai in drerd arein! Ich hob dich in drerd! Gai kabenyeh matyereh!

Go to the devil! A ruach in dein taten's tateh!

Goad utz

Go-between mekler

God forbid! Cholileh! Got zol uphiten! Nisht gedacht! Chas vesholem!

God in Heaven, Master of the Universe! Roboynoy shel oylom!

God knows Got vaist

God should hear you and favor you! Fun eier moyl in Got's oyeren!

God watches out for fools. Got hit op di naronim.

God will punish. Got vet shtrofen.

God willing! Im yirtseh hashem! Mirtsishem!

Going into labor to give birth gaien tzu kind

The golden count y. Goldeneh medina.

Good deed mitsveh

Good for nothing! Toigen ahf kapores!

Good health to you! A gezurt ahf dein kop!

Good holiday! Gut yontev!

Good Jew shainer yid, a getrayer yid

Good luck! Zol zein mit glik.

Good luck to you! A glik ahf dir!

The good old days mellech sobyetskis yoren (Lit., the years of King Sobieski)

Good Sabbath Gut shabbes.

Good taste taam

Gossip reden rechiless

Gourmet's delight   meichel

Grandfather   zaideh

Gratification, as from children   naches

Grease   shmaltz

Great pleasure, great satisfaction   mecheiyeh

Groans   krechts

A guilty person is always sensitive.   Ahfen goniff brent dos hittel. (Lit., on a thief burns his hat.)

A guy who doesn't smell too good   a shtinker

Hanger-on   nuchshlepper, tsutsheppenish

Happy Sabbath.   Gut shabbes.

Happy-go-lucky, lively world.   A lebedikeh velt.

Having a ball!   Lebt a tog! (Lit., lives a day)

Hard-luck guy who is a sucker for anything, an incompetent, a misfortunate   shlimazel

Hard-working, efficient, housewife   beryeh, balebosteh

Have respect!   Hob derech erets!

He bluffs his way out.   Er fonfet unter.

He eats like a horse.   Er esst vi a ferd.

He eats like a man who has recovered from a sickness.   Er esst vi noch a krenk.

He has a cold!   Er hot a farshtopteh nonjeh. (Lit., he has a stuffed nose.) Er iz farkeelt.

He has strange ways.   Er hot modneh drochim.

He has nothing at all.   Er hot a makeh [boil]. Er hot kadoches.

He hasn't got a worry.   Er hot nit kain zorg.

He is barely able to creep.   Kam vos er kricht.

He makes a lot of trouble for me.   Er macht mir a shvartzeh chasseneh. (Lit., he makes me a black wedding.)

He repeats himself, he re-hashes things over and over again.   Er molt gemolen mel.

He ruins it.   Er macht a tel derfun.

He should drop dead! Paigeren zol er!

He should go to hell! Er zol gaien in drerd! Er zol einemen a misseh meshuneh! (Lit., he should meet a strange death!)

He should have lots of trouble! Er zol zain ahf tsores! Er zol ainemen a miesseh meshuneh!

Having no end of trouble hoben tsu zingen un tsu zogen (Lit., having [enough] to sing and to recite)

He talks himself into a sickness. Er ret zich ein a krenk.

He talks nonsense. Er ret in der velt arein.

He turns the world upside down. Er kert iber di velt.

Hebrew school talmud torah

The hell with it! Ich hob es in drerd!

He's a low-down good-for-nothing. Er iz a nider trechtiker yung. Er iz an oysvurf.

He's thick. Er hot a farshtopten kop. (Lit., he has a stuffed head.)

He's worthless. Er toyg ahf kapores.

Headache Kop-vaitik

Healthy as a horse gezunt vi a ferd

Heartache hartsvaitik

Hearty laugh hartsik gelechter

Help! Oy gevald! (cry of anguish, distress, suffering, or frustration)

Hole in the head loch in kop

Holiday yontiff, yom tov, yontev (n.), yontefdik (adj.)

Honor, n. koved

Honorable balebatish, choshev

Horrible ending finsterer sof (Lit., dark end)

Horrible year finster yor

Hot bath haiseh vanneh

Hot-head kasnik

Competent housewife beryeh, balebosteh

How are things? How goes it?   Vi gaits? Vos hert zich?

How should I know?   Freg mich becherim!

How's business?   Vi gait dos gesheft?

Hurry up!   Eilt zich! Mach es shnell!

I am disappointed.   Ich bin entoisht. Ich feel zich opgenart.

I am fainting.   Es vert mir finster in di oygen. (Lit., it's getting dark before my eyes.)

I despise you.   Ich hob dich in bod. (Lit., I have you in the bath.)

I don't envy you.   Ich bin dir nit mekaneh.

I don't give a care. I don't give a hang.   A deigeh hob ich.

I don't know.   Ich vais nit.

I do not begrudge you.   Ich bin dich nit mekaneh.

I hate him.   Ich hob im feint.

I have a choice?   A braireh hob ich?

I have a heartburn.   Es brent mir ahfen harts.

I have no use for it.   Ich darf es ahf kapores.

I haven't the faintest idea!   Zol ich azoy vissen fun tsores! (Lit., May I know about troubles [as I know about what you're asking].)

I like it.   Es gefelt mir.

I need it like a hole in my head!   Ich darf es vi a loch in kop.

I need it like a wart on my nose.   Ich darf es vi a lung un leber ahfen noz. (Lit., I need it like a lung and liver on my nose.)

I predicted it. My heart told me.   Dos harts hot mir gezogt.

I should know from trouble as much as I know about that.   Zol ich azoy vissen fun tsores.

I should have such good luck.   Az a glik ahf mir.

I should worry.   A deigeh hob ich.

Idler   laidik-gaier

Idiot shmegegi (slang)

I'm dying for it. Mein cheiyes gait oys.

I'm making a fool of myself. Ich mach zich narish.

I'm not in a hurry. Ich yog zich nit.

I'm sorry. Es tut mir bank. Es tut mir laid.

Impossible! A nechtiker tog! Ummeglich!

Inexpensive billik, billig

Infant pisherkeh (f.), pisher (m.) (colloq.)

Inferior merchandise or work shlak

In-law (parent) mechuten (sing.), mechutonim (pl.)

In the middle of in mitten drinnen

Insincere talk shmaltz (slang)

In spite of everything you do, it still comes out wrong.
Ahf tsu luches. Ahf tsu lehaches.

In trouble ahf tsores

Is it my worry? A deigeh hob ich?

Is that how you talk to a father? Azoy ret men tsu a
taten?

Is that so? Azoy zogstu? (Lit., that's what you say?)

Is that so? Really? Takeh?

Israel eretz yisroel

It appears to me es veist zich mir oys

It could be. Es ken zein.

It doesn't matter to me. Es macht mir nit oys.

It doesn't work! Es gait nisht! Gait es nit!

It gives me a great pleasure! (also ironic) Es tut mir a
groisseh hanoeh!

It hurts me. Es tut mir vai.

It is not fitting. Es past nit.

It is said. Meh zogt.

It is very expensive. Es is zaier teier.
    inexpensive. billig.

It isn't proper. Es past nit.

It isn't running smoothly! Es gait nit.

It seems veist oys

It makes no difference. It doesn't matter. Es macht nit oys.

It never happened. Es iz nit geshtoigen un nit gefloigen. (Lit., it didn't stand and it didn't fly.)

It pleases me. Es gefelt mir.

It should be that way. Alevei.

It should happen to me! Ahf mir gezogt gevorn! Alevei ahf mir! Mirchishem bei mir!

It shouldn't come to pass! Nit gedacht gevorn!

It shouldn't happen! Nit gedacht!

It shouldn't happen to us! Nit oyf undz gedacht!

It shouldn't happen to you! Nit oyf eich gedacht!

It sorrows me. Es tut mir bang. (bank)

It stinks. Es gait a raiech. Se hert zich a raiech.

It will all work out. Es vet zich alts oispressen.

It will heal before the wedding. Es vet zich oyshailen far der chasseneh.

It will help like blood-cupping on a dead body. Es vet helfen vi a toiten bankes!

It won't hurt in making a catch. Nit shaten tsum shiddech.

It's a shame for the children. Es iz a shandeh far di kinder.

It's a steal. A metsiyeh fun a goniff. (Lit., a bargain from a thief)

It's bad manners. Es past zich vi a patsh tsu gut shabbes.

It's delicious! Meh ken lecken di finger!

It's good for nothing! Es toig ahf kapores! need it for a [profitless] sacrifice.)

It's great! S'iz mir gut! Es iz mir gut!

It's hardly worth the trouble. Folg mich a gang. (Scoffing statement, lit., follow me on a [useless] errand.)

It's not to the point. Es past zich vi a patch tzu gut shabbes.

It's O.K. with me. Bei mir poilst du.

It's on his (her) mind. Es ligt im (ir) in zinnen.

It's perfect. Kosher veyosher.

It's tough to make a living. Shver tzu machen a leben.

It's useless! Gai klop zich kop in vant! (Lit., go bang your head against the wall.)

It will take a long, long time. Till doomsday. A yor mit a mitvoch. (Lit., a year and a Wednesday)

It's worth nothing. Es toig ahf kapores.

Jewish head yiddisher kop

Jewish native of Galicia galitsianer

Jewish parochial school yeshiva

Jewish prayer shawl tallis

Joy, as from children naches

Joyous occasion: birth, bar mitzvah, engagement, marriage simcheh

Just made it. Kam derlebt.

Keep moving! Drai zich!

Keep quiet! Shveig!

Knock on wood, no evil eye. Kain enoreh. Kain eiyin horeh.

Know-it-all (ironic) maivin

Kosher condition kashress

Leave me alone! Loz mich tsu ru!

Lecherous old man alter kacker (taboo)

Let it be! Zol zein!

Let me be in peace! Loz mich tsu ru!

Let's end it! A sof, a sof!

Let's have some quiet! Zol zein shtil!

Liar ligner

Listen here! Hert zich ein!

Littered   ongevorfen

Little bird   faigeleh

Little bride   kallehnyu

Little cakes dipped in honey   taiglech

Little girl (affectionate diminutive)   maideleh

A little joy   a shtik naches

Little ones   pitsilech

Little prig   klainer gornisht

Livelihood   parnosseh

Lively world   lebedikeh velt

Living doll   yungeh tsatskeh

Living high off the hog!   Leben a chazerishen tog!

Long coat worn by religious Jews   kapotah, kaftan

Look at him!   Kuk im on!

Loquacious   Yatatata

Lost   farblondjet

A lot to tell, little to hear.   A sach tsu reden, vainik tsu heren.

Loudmouth   pisk

Lousy   nit gut

Lout   grobber yung

Low-life   parech (Lit., scab headed, having sores on the scalp)

Lump of sugar   shtik tsukeı

Madness   meshugass

Make a living   machen a leben
       livelihood   parnosseh

Make it snappy!   Mach es shnell!

Making an outcry   machen a gevald

Man built like an ox   boorvan

Man who constantly builds castles in the air, man who starves by his wits   luftmentsh

Manure   drek (taboo)

The marriage is off! Oys shiddech!

Marriage broker shadchen

May God help me! Zol Got mir helfen!

May he break a leg! Zol er tsebrechen a fuss!

May he rest in peace. Olov hasholem. (Lit., in Hebrew, upon him be peace.)

May it not come upon you. Lo alaichem.

May no evil befall us! Kain einoreh!

May she rest in peace. Oleho hasholem.

May you live long. Lang leben zolt ir.

May we meet on happy occasions. Mir zollen zich bagegenen ahf simches.

Mean person paskudnyak

Meat or meat products flaishik (n.), flaishidick (adj.)

Meddlesome spectator kibbitzer

Mercy rachmones

Mess (slang) kashe, mishmash, hekdish

A middleman, one who is neither smart nor dumb mittelmessiger

Miserable finster un glitshik (Lit., dark and slippery)

Misery tsores

Misfortune umglik

Mix-up kashe (slang)

Mixed up tsidrait, farmisht, tsetoomelt

Mixture mishmash

Moans, v. krechts, kvetsht zich

Money gelt, mezumen

Money goes to money. Gelt gait tsu gelt.

Money thrown out, wasted aroysgevorfeneh gelt

Money tied in a corner of a handkerchief knippel

Moron zhlobb

Mortally insane! Meshugah ahf toyt!

Mother-in-law shvigger

Mother's favorite   tsatskeleh der mamehs

Mourning period (seven days)   shiva

Mouth   pisk (slang)

Mr. Slowpoke   Kam vos er kricht.

Mr. Upside Down (a person who does everything wrong)
  moisheh kapoyer

Much ado about nothing!   Ahfen himmel a yarid! (Lit.,
  in heaven there's a fair!)

Muddled   ongepatshket

My enemies should live so!   Meineh sonim zollen azoy
  leben!

My heart told me!   Dos harts hot mir gezogt!

My money went down the drain!   In drerd mein gelt!
  (Lit., into the earth [went] my money!)

Naive person   kuneh-lemel

Narrowly achieved   kam derlebt

Nasty fellow   paskudnyak

Ne'er-do-well.   zhlook, trombenik

Neighbor from the old country   landsman (sing.)
  landsleit (pl.)

Neutral food, neither meat nor dairy   parveh

Nibble between meals   nash

Nibbler, especially between meals   nasher

Nincompoop   zhlook, shmendrik

No evil eye.   Kain einoreh.

No-gooder   trombenik

Nobody, a pitiable person   nebbach (nebbish), vantz
  (Lit., bedbug)

Noise   tumel

Noise-maker   tumler

Non-kosher   traif

Non-Jew   goy (m), goyeh (f.)

**Non-Jew who does work forbidden to observant Jews
  on the Sabbath**   Shabbes goy

Non-Jewish boy shaigetz

Non-Jewish girl shikseh

Nonsense! A nechtiker tog! (Lit., a yesterday's day)

Noodle or bread suet pudding kugel

Noodles lokshen

Not good nish gut, nit gut

Not really at all! Chas v'cholileh!

Not so bad nishkosheh

Not today, not tomorrow. Nit heint, nit morgen.

Nothing came of it! Es hot zich oysgelozen a boydem! (Lit., there's nothing there but a small attic.)

Nothing, of small value kreplach (Slang, lit., ravioli), bobkes

Nothing to be sorry for. A shaineh, raineh, kaporeh (Lit., a beautiful, clean sacrifice).

Nothing will help you! Es vet dir gornit helfen!

Nouveau riche oyfgekumener (Lit., come-upper)

Nuisance nudnik, a tsutsheppenish

The nuisance is here already! Er iz shoyn do, der nudnik!

"Nutty" tsidrait

O.K. zaier-gut; zol zein azoy

Obey me. Folg mich.

Oh, God! Gottenyu!

Old acquaintance an alter bakanter

Old witch an alteh machashaifeh

Old wreck an alter trombenik

On the level, true emes

One who is helpless on a job a kalyekeh

One who drops whatever he touches a gelaimter

One who stirs up trouble kochleffel

One who tends to confuse you draikop

Only God knows. Nor Got vaist!

Onions should grow from your navel! Zol vaksen tsibelis fun pupik!

Other world yeneh velt

Out of this world Ek velt

Overdressed woman iberzaltseneh tsatskeh

Over-praise shmaltz (slang)

Overflow with pride and happiness kvellen

Owner balebos

Pale as a sheet. Blaich vi di vant. (Lit., pale as the wall.)

Palsy-walsy aderabe-ve'aderabe

Panhandler shnorrer

A patsy shnook, shlump

Parvenu oyfgekumener g'vir

Pauper kaptsen

Pedigree yichus

Peeved, pouting ongeblozen

Perfect kosher (slang)

Person from Lithuania litvak

Person who butts into everything kochleffel

Person with a sweet tooth nasher

Pest tsutsheppenish

Pesty nagger nudnik

Philanthropic spirit tsedokeh

Phylacteries (worn on head and left arm each weekday morning while praying) tefillen

Pig, piggish person chazzer

A pig remains a pig. A chazzer bleibt a chazzer.

Pig's feed, bad food chazzerei

Piece shtik

Piece of luck glick, mazel

A piece of luck happened to you! A glick hot dich getrofen!

Pious person tsaddik

Pity rachmones

A plague! A finsternish! (Lit., a darkness!)

Plaything tsatskeh

Pleasantly plump and pretty woman zaftig (adj.)

Please. Ich bet eich. Zeit zich matriach. Zeit azoy gut.

Please forgive me. Zeit (mir) moichel.

Please, I beg you. Ich bet eich, bitteh.

Policeman shames (Slang, lit., a synagogue sexton.)

Poor box in the home for odd coins, usually deposited on Friday afternoon, before the Sabbath begins pushkeh

Porridge kashe

Poverty orem-keit

Prayer book sidder

Prayer in honor of the dead kaddish
(begins: Yiskadal veyiskadash)

Pretends to be ignorant. Macht zich nit vissendik.

Prettier ones they bury! The girl is ugly. Sheners laigt men in drerd.

Procrastinating Kum ich nit heint, kum ich morgen!
(Lit., if I don't come today, I'll come tomorrow!)

Proper kosher (slang)

Prostitute nafkeh, kurveh

Proud shtoltz

Puffed up, peeved ongeblozzen

Pull, or carry an unnecessary object shleppen

Punch chmalyeh, klap, zets

Punk, (n.) paskudnyak

Push shtup

Put up or shut up! Toches ahfen tish! (taboo)

Quickly, quickly shnell

Quiet! Shveig! Sha!

Quite a job! Folg mich a gang!

Rabbi's wife rebbetsin

Rabid fan, ardent participant farbrenter

Racketeer gazlen (Slang, lit., thief), untervelt mensh

Rag shmatteh

Raise cain hulyen

The real article, the real McCoy richtiker chaifets, di emeseh skhoireh

Real bargain billik vi borsht (Lit., cheap as beet soup)

Really! Is that so! Tahkeh!

Reciting prayers over lit candles bentshen lecht

Reciting the afternoon prayers Davenen mincheh

Relatives mishpocheh, kroivim

Relatives through marriage, in-law mechuten (sing.) mechutonim (pl.)

Religious functionary who performs the circumcision moihel

Remember? Gedainkst?

Respect koved, derech erets

Responsible balebotish

Reverence koved

Right kosher (slang)

Righteous person tsaddik

Ritual bath (part of the bride's wedding preparation) mikveh

Ritual slaughterer of animals and fowl shochet

Rogue yungatsh

Rude young man grobber yung

Become ruined verren a tel

Sacrifice kaporeh

Satisfactory nishkosheh

To ruin you, to make a nothing out of you machen a tel fun dir

Scatterbrain draikop

Scholar lamden

School shul

Scram! Gai shoyn, gai!

Scream kvitsh

Screwy tsidrait

Scroll, or Book, of Esther; slang for meaningless rigamarole megillah

Second-rater shlump

Selfmade fool shmok (taboo)

Senile aiver butel, oiver botel

Sentimental shmaltzik, zeeslech

Serves him right! Gut oyf im!

Shame and disgrace a shandeh un a charpeh

Sharp practices genaivisheh shtiklech

She has all the virtues. Alleh meiles hot zi,

Shoddy shlok

To shout for help machen a gevald

Shove, v. shtuppen

Show-off, n. knacker

Shrew shlecht veib

Shriek kvitsh

Shut up! Sha! Shveig!

Shy person nebbach (nebbish)

Sick krank

Sickness krenk

Sickness that hangs on a farshlepteh krenk (Lit., a drawn-out sickness)

Silence! Zol zein shtill!

Simpleton nebbach (nebbish), shlemiel

Sit in mourning zitsen shiveh ([Lit., to sit seven,] the number of days in the mourning period)

Sitting on pins and needles zitsen ahf shpilkes

Skin someone alive reissen flaish

Skull cap worn during prayers, and at all times by Orthodox Jews to indicate that God is present above yarmelkeh

Slam! Chmalyeh!

Slap, smack patsh

Slightly drunk farshnoshkit

Slime, dirt shmuts

Slob zhlob

Slow as molasses. Kam vos er kricht.

Small pieces of baked dough taiglech

Small pockets of dough filled with chopped meat or cheese kreplach

Smell shmek

Smell badly farshtunken

A smell and a taste (ironic, in expressing inordinately small amounts) a lek un a shmek

Smelled bad, as food shtark gehert (Lit., strongly hear)

Smoked salmon lox, laks

Snack nash

So? Well? Nu?

So I guessed wrong! Nit getrofen!

So I made a mistake, so what! Hostu bei mir an avleh!

So it goes. Azoy gait es.

Something delicious mecheiyehdik, geshmak

Soul neshomeh

Sour cream zoiyereh smetteneh, shmant

Speak nasally, unclearly fonfen

Special bit of acting shtik

Spectator who offers unsolicited advice kibbitzer

Spirit neshomeh

Spitefully ahf tsu lehaches

Split your guts! Plats!

Sponger shnorrer, shlepper

"Stacked" (slang) zaftig

Starved toit hungerik

Steam bath a shvitz bod

Stinks, rotten ipish (Aramaic for rotten)

Stomach ache boych-vaitik

Stop annoying me. Drai mir nit kain kop! (Lit., don't turn my head); Hak mir nit kain tsheinik! (Lit., don't knock me any tea-kettle!)

Stop bending my ear! Hak mir nit in kop (Lit., don't knock me in the head!)

Stop talking! Shveig!

A strange death. A miesseh meshuneh. (Fig., it shouldn't happen to a dog.)

Strong kreftig, shtark

Strong character shtarker charakter

Strong as a horse shtark vi a ferd

Stuffed farshtopt, ongeshtopt

Stuffed derma kishkeh

Stuffed fish, usually made of chopped fish, onions and seasoning and cooked in salt water gefilteh fish

Stuffed shirt (slang) ongeblozzener

Sweet cream smetteneh

Swill chazzerei

Sucker shlump, shnook, shlemiel

Suffix denoting diminutive or affection el, elleh

Summer boarding house with cooking privileges koch-alain

Sweet carrot compote tsimmes

Sweetheart neshomeleh (my soul), geleebteh

Sweet soul ziseh neshomeh

To swindle shmeikel

Swindler ganef, shvindler

Swollen, puffed up geshvollen

Synagogue shul

Tact saichel, takt

Take it easy! Chap nit!

Talk, n. shmooz, shmuess

Talk onself into sickness! Zich einreden a krenk!

Talk to the wall (for all the good it will do you)! Red tsu der vant!

Talk your heart out! Red zich oys dos harts!

Tall story bobbeh meisseh

Tasty geshmak

Teamster balagoleh

Teats tsitskes (taboo)

Teen-age girl yung maidel

A terrible thing! Gevaldikeh zach! Shrekliche zach!

Thank God! Danken Got! Got tsu danken! Boruch Hashem!

Thanks for nothing! A shainem dank in pupik! A gezunt in dein pupik! (Lit., thanks in your belly-botton)

That's all. Dos is alts.

That's how it goes. Azoy gait es.

That's nothing. Ez iz bloteh. (Lit., it is mud)

That's worthless. Ez iz bloteh.

There's a buzzing in my head! Es zshumet mir in kop!

They don't let you live! Meh lost nit laiben!

They say! Meh zogt.

Thief goniff, ganef, gazlen

This pleases me. Dos gefelt mir.

This too is a living? This you call a living? Oych mir a leben?

This was a pleasure! Dos is geven a mecheiyeh!

Tickle a kitsel

Tipsy farshnoshkit

Tired out oysgematert

Too bad! Az och un vai!

Too bad the bride is too pretty; a novel complaint A chissoren di kaleh iz tsu shain.

Too late! Noch ne'eleh! Tsu shpait!

Tough guy a shtarker

Tough•luck! Az och un vai!

Tragedy umglik

Treasury of Jewish law interpreting the Torah (five books of Moses) into livable law talmud

Tricky doings genaivisheh shtiklech

Treat meichel, nash

Triflings bobkes

Troubles tsores

Uncouth grob

Uncouth young man grobber yung

Ugly mies

Unfortunate person an umgliklecher mentsh

Ungraceful person klotz

Unkempt, sweaty shlumperik

Unlucky one umglik

An unlucky person is a dead person. A mentsh on glik iz a toyter mentsh.

Unmarried girl maidel (young), moid (older)

Untidy person an opgelozener mentsh

Unwanted follower nuchshlepper

Uproar tumel

Urine pishechtz (taboo)

Utter misery gehakteh tsores

Vicious animal (usually, an inhumane person) baizeh cheiyeh

Vulgar, unmannered man grobyan

Wail of sorrow Gevald! Och un vai!

Wallop klap

Wandered around arumgevalgert

Watch out, to mind varfen an oyg (Lit., to cast an eye on)

We shall say grace. Mir vellen bentshen.

Weakling nebbach (nebbish)

Wear it in good health! Trog es gezunterhait!

Well done! Well said! A leben ahf dein kop! (Lit., life to your head!)

Well said. Zaier shain gezogt.

What a sober man has on his mind (lit., lung), a drunkard has on his tongue. Vos bei a nichteren oyfen lung, is bei a shikkeren oyfen tsung.

What are you talking my head off for? Vos hakst du mir a kop? (Lit., what are you knocking [at] my head?)

What are you saying? Vos zogt ir?

What are they lacking? Vos failt zai?

What did I need it for? Vos hob ich dos gedarft?

What difference does it make? Vos macht dos oys?

What difference does it make as long as he makes a living? Nifter-pifter a leben macht er? ("Nifter" means a dead man)

What does it matter? Vos zol es arren?

What does it lead to? Vos iz der tachlis?

What does it matter to you? Vos art es eich?

What does it mean? Vos maint es?

What else? Vos noch?

What is going on? What's cooking? Vos tut zich?

What is the name of? Vi ruft men? Vos haist es?

What will be, will be. Vos vet zein, vet zein.

What's new. Vos hert zich epes neiyes?

What's on his mind is on his tongue. Vos iz in kop iz ahfen tsung!

What's wrong with you? Vos iz mit dir?

What's the outcome? What's the point? Vos iz di untershteh shureh?

What's the purpose? Vos iz der tachlis?

What's the trick? Vos iz di chochmeh?

Where are you going? Vuhin gaistu?

Where does it hurt? Vu tut dir vai?

Where the devil says good morning vu der ruach zogt gut morgen

Whom are you kidding? Vemen barestu?

Whine, n. klog

Whiskey bronfen, shnapps

Who knows! Freg mich becherim! Ver vaist?

Who would have believed it? Ver volt dos geglaibt?

Whole works shmeer, megillah (slang)

Why should I do it? Folg mich a gang. (Scoffing; lit., follow me on a [useless] errand.)

Wild man! Vilder mentsh!

Wisdom chochmeh

Wise guy knacker

Wise man chochem

Witticism vitz, chochmeh (also used ironically)

Woe is me! Oy, vai iz mir. A klog iz mir!

Worked to death oysgemutshet, oysgematert tsum toit

Worn out oysgematert

Would that it comes true! Alevei!

Very wealthy, stuffed with money ongeshtopt (slang)

Yearly remembrance of the dead yortzeit

You can go crazy! Meh ken meshugeh veren!

You can vomit from this! Meh ken brechen!

You don't frighten me! Gai strashe di gens! (Lit., go frighten the geese)

You don't have to be pretty if you are charming. Meh darf nit zein shain, nor chainevdik.

You don't show a fool something half finished. A nar veist men nit kain halbeh arbet.

You fool, you! Nar ainer!

You please me a great deal. Ir gefelt mir zaier.

You should choke on it! Dershtikt zolstu veren!

You should get a stomach cramp! Zol dich chapen beim boych!

You should swell up like a mountain! Zolst geshvollen veren vi a barg!

You shouldn't know bad things! Zolst nit vissen fun kain shlechts.

You should live (and be well)! A laiben ahf dir!

You should live so! Zolstu azoy laiben!

You understand? Farshtaist?

You're all set! Ir zeit ahfen ferd! (Lit., you're on top of the horse!)

You're not making sense. Nisht geshtoigen un nisht gefloigen. (Lit., you're not standing and you're not flying.)

You're nuts! Bist meshugeh! Bist tsedrait!

1001 Yiddish Proverbs

Introduction

MY STUDY of Yiddish proverbs has proved to be a fascinating and intriguing adventure. The fabric of Jewish proverbial wisdom woven over the centuries now has become a magnificent tapestry of maxims, aphorisms, and pithy sayings reflecting the devious course of Jewish history. In it can be described the longings and strivings, the trials and tribulations, the joys and griefs of the Jewish people.

Yiddish proverbs deal with many subjects, ranging from the homely happenings of everyday life to man's highest aspirations; they mirror the philosophy, wisdom, and culture that safeguarded the Jews' sanity and preserved their identity through millennia of suffering, affliction, expropriation, expulsion, persecution and holocaust.

The Jews ridiculed themselves and others in their proverbs, they rejoiced over glad tidings, and they hid their grief in the face of adversity. The proverbs were a mask, a crutch, a guidepost, a hope. They reveal the warmth of a people and, above all, their indominatable humor, well expressed in the proverb, "Suffering makes you laugh too."

Yiddish proverbs are usually restrained and gentle in their satire. They represent a seeking for social standards, a search for spiritual insights and ethical solutions to human conduct. In their proverbial wisdom the Jews also reveal great understanding of psychology. As Dr. A. A. Roback has said, the Jews had to become psychologists, of course, for it improved their chances of survival!

In the words of the Holy Bible, "Acquaint thyself with proverbs, for of them thou shalt learn instruction."

FRED KOGOS

PRONUNCIATION GUIDE

VOWELS

> *a* as in f*a*ther
> *i* as in l*i*t
> *e* as in b*e*d
> *o* as in h*o*t
> *u* as in p*u*t

DIPHTHONGS

> *ai* as in s*ay* or m*ai*n
> *ei* as in b*y* or h*ei*ght
> *oi* or *oy* as in b*oy* or v*oi*ce
> (When two other vowels appear together, pronounce them separately.)

CONSONANTS

> *dz* as in soun*ds*
> *g* as in *g*o
> *ch* as in lo*ch* or Ba*ch*
> *r* soft (no trill)
> *ts* as in pa*ts*
> *tsh* or *tch* as in *ch*urch
> *zh* as in sei*z*ure

AS TO ACCENT

In words of two syllables, the accent usually falls on the first syllable. In words of three syllables or more, the accent usually falls on the second syllable. Words elongated by prefixes or suffixes retain the original accent. (I hope that is not too *ongepatchket* [muddled] for you!)

1001 Yiddish Proverbs

1

A badchen macht alemen frailech un alain ligt er in drerd.
The wedding jester makes everyone laugh; he alone is miserable.

2

A baizeh tsung iz erger fun a shlechter hant.
A wicked tongue is worse than an evil hand.

3

A barg mit a barg kennen zich nit tsuzamen kumen, ober a
mentsh mit a mentsh kennen.
Mountains cannot meet, but men can.

4

A behaimeh hot a langen tsung un ken kain brocheh nit zogen.
An animal has a long tongue, yet he can't recite a blessing.

5

A behaimeh hot a langen tsung un ken nisht reden; der mentsh
hot a kurtseh un tor nisht reden.
*Animals have long tongues but can't speak; men have short
tongues and shouldn't speak.*

6

A bisseleh chain iz shoin nit gemain.
A little charm and you are not ordinary.

7

A bitter hartz redt a sach.
An embittered heart talks a lot.

8

A bocher a shadchen, a moid a bobbeh—konnen nisht zein.
*A bachelor a matchmaker, a spinster a grandmother—these
cannot be.*

9

A chissoren, di kalleh iz tsu shain.
A fault-finder complains even that the bride is too pretty.

10

A chossen a yaden gait nit on naden.
You can't have a learned bridegroom without a dowry.

11
A dank ken men in kesheneh nit legen.
You can't put "thank you" in your pocket.

12
A dokter un a kvores-man zeinen shutfim.
Doctors and gravediggers are partners.

13
A falsheh matba'ieh farliert men nit.
A bad penny always turns up.

14
A farshporer iz besser vi a fardiner.
A saver is better than an earner.

15
A foilen iz gut tsu shiken nochen malech-hamoves.
It's a good idea to send a lazy man for the Angel of Death.

16
A freint bekamt men umzist; a soineh muz men zich koifen.
A friend you get for nothing; an enemy has to be bought.

17
A freint bleibt a freint biz di kesheneh.
A friend remains a friend up to his pocket.

18

A freint darf men zich koifen; sonem krigt men umzist.
A friend you have to buy; enemies you get for nothing.

19

A fremdeh tsoreh iz kain tsibeleh nit vert.
The troubles of a stranger aren't worth an onion.

20

A fremdeh bissen shmekt zis.
Another man's tidbit smells sweet.

21

A fremdeh pelz varemt nit.
Another's cloak does not keep you warm.

22

A fremder nar iz a gelechter; an aigener—a shand.
A strange fool is a laughing stock; your own—a shame.

23

A froi, zogt men bei undz, hot langeh hor un kurtsen saichel.
A woman, they say, has long hair and short sense.

24

A gast iz vi regen az er doi'ert tsu lang, vert er a last.
A guest is like rain: when he lingers on, he becomes a nuisance.

25

A ganef fun a ganef iz potter.
It's no crime to steal from a thief.

26

A gelechter hert men veiter vi a gevain.
Laughter is heard farther than weeping.

27

A gemachteh machashaifeh iz erger fun a geborener.
A woman turned witch is worse than one who is born so.

28

A geshvir iz a guteh zach bei yenem untern orem.
A boil is fine as long as it's under someone else's arm.

29

A guteh tochter iz a guteh shnur.
A good daughter makes a good daughter-in-law.

30

A guten helft a vort; a shlechten helft afileh kain shteken oich nit.
A word helps a good person; but even a stick can't help the bad.

31

A guten vet der shaink nit kalyeh machen, un a shlechten vet der bes-hamedresh nit farichten.
A good man can't be corrupted by the tavern nor a bad one reformed by the synagogue.

32

A guter freint iz oft besser fun a bruder.
A good friend is often better than a brother.

33

A guter vort iz karanter fun a nedoveh.
A kind word is better than alms.

34

A guter Yid darf nit kain briv, a shlechten Yidden helft nit kain briv.
A good person doesn't need a letter of recommendation; for a bad one, it would do no good.

35

A halber emes iz a gantser ligen.
A half truth is a whole lie.

36

A halber entfer zogt oichet epes.
Half an answer also says something.

37

A halber nar iz a gantser chochem.
A half-fool is a very wise man.

38

A hartz iz a shlos: me darf dem richtiken shlisel.
A heart is a lock: you need the right key to it.

39

A hartz iz a shlos, ober a shlos efent men oich mit a noch-gemachten shlisel.
A heart is a lock, but a lock can be opened with a duplicated key.

40

A hunt iz a mol getrei'er fun a kind.
A dog is sometimes more faithful than a child.

41

A hunt on tsain iz ois hunt.
A dog without teeth is just not a dog.

42

A hunt on tsain varft zich oich oif a bain.
A dog without teeth also attacks a bone!

43

A katz meg oich kuken oifen kaisser.
A cat may also look at a king.

44

A katz vos m'yavket ken kain meiz nit chapen.
A meowing cat can't catch mice.

45

A kechin fardarbet zich nit.
A cook does not upset her own stomach.

46

A kind in shtub, ful in alleh vinkelech.
With a child in the house, all corners are full.

47

A kind vert geboren mit kulyaken un a man shtarbt mit ofeneh
hent.
*A baby is born with clenched fists and a man dies with his
hands open.*

48

A kind ken zein erger vi a gazlen, un men tantst noch oif zein
chasseneh.

A child may be worse than a robber, yet people (the parents) dance at his wedding.

49
A kindersher saichel iz oichet a saichel.
A child's wisdom is also wisdom.

50
A klaineh veibeleh ken oich hoben a groisseh moil.
A small woman can also have a big mouth.

51
A klap fargait, a vort bashtait.
A blow passes on, a spoken word lingers on.

52
A kloleh iz nit kain telegrameh: zi kumt nit on azoi gich.
A curse is not a telegram: it doesn't arrive so fast.

53
A kluger farshtait fun ain vort tsvai.
A wise man hears one word and understands two.

54
A kluger gait tsu fus un a nar fort in a kareteh.
A wise man walks on foot and a fool rides in a coach.

55
A kluger kop halt zich nit lang.
A smart head does not last long.

56
A kluger vaist vos er zogt, a nar zogt vos er vaist.
A wise man knows what he says, a fool says what he knows.

57
A lecherdiken zack ken men nit onfillen.
One can't fill a torn sack.

58
A ligen tor men nit zogen; dem emess iz men nit m'chuyev zogen.
A lie you must not tell; the truth you don't have to tell.

59
A ligner darf hoben a guten zechron.
A liar must have a good memory.

60
A ligner glaibt men nit, afileh az er zogt dem emess.
No one believes a liar even when he tells the truth.

61
A ligner hert zich zeineh ligen azoi lang ein biz er glaibt zich alain.
A liar tells his story so often that he gets to believe it himself.

62
A lustiger dales gait iber alles.
Happy poverty overcomes everything.

63

A maidel darf zich putsen far fremdeh bachurim un a veibel far'n aigenem man.

A maiden should pretty herself for strange bachelors and a young wife for her own husband.

64

A maidel iz vi samet—aderabeh, gib a glet!

A maiden is like velvet—come on, fondle her!

65

A makeh in yenem's orem iz nit shver tsu trogen.

Another man's disease is not hard to endure.

66

A mameh iz a dektuch (zi fardekt di chesroines fun di kinder).

A mother is like a veil (she hides the faults of her children).

67

A mentsh iz a mol shtarker fun eizen un a mol shvacher fun a flieg.

Man is sometimes stronger than iron and at other times weaker than a fly.

68

A melocheh iz a melucheh!

A craft is a kingdom!

69

A man, az er iz shener fun dem teivel, iz er shoin shain.
A man is handsome if he is only better looking than the devil.

70

A melocheh iz a melucheh, ober men hot nit kain minut
menucheh.
  A trade makes you a king but robs you of leisure.

71

A mentsh tracht un Got lacht.
Man thinks and God laughs.

72

A mentsh zol leben shoin nor fun neigerikeit vegen.
A man should stay alive if only out of curiosity.

73

A miesseh moid hot feint dem shpiegel.
A homely girl hates the mirror.

74

A mol iz der meshores mer yachsen vi der poretz.
Sometimes the servant is nobler than the master.

75

A mol iz der refueh erger fun der makeh.
Sometimes the remedy is worse than the disease.

76

A moshel iz nit kain rai'eh.
An example is no proof.

77

A nacht on shlof iz di gresteh shtrof.
A sleepless night is the worst punishment.

78

A nar bleibt a nar.
A fool remains a fool.

79

A nar darf hoben a sach shich.
A fool needs a lot of shoes.

80
A nar darf kain mosser nıt hoben.
A fool needs no informer.

81
A nar farlirt un a kluger gefint.
A fool loses and a clever man finds.

82
A nar gait in bod arein un fargest zich dos ponim optsuvashen.
A fool goes to the baths and forgets to wash his face.

83
A nar gait tsvai mol dort, vu a kluger gait nit kain aintsik mol.
A fool makes two trips where a wise man makes none.

84
A nar git un a kluger nemt.
A fool gives and the clever one takes.

85
A nar ken a mol zogen a gleich vort.
Sometimes a fool can say something clever.

86
A nar ken fregen mer frages in a sho vi a kluger ken entferen in a yor.
A fool can ask more questions in an hour than a wise man can answer in a year.

87

A nar vakst on regen.
A fool grows without rain.

88

A nar vert nit elter un kalteh vasser vert nit kalyeh.
A fool doesn't age and cold water doesn't spoil.

89

A nei'er bezim kert gut.
A new broom sweeps clean.

90

A nemmer iz nit kain gibber.
A taker is not a giver.

91

A nevaireh kost oich gelt.
It costs money to sin.

92

A nogid a nar iz oich a har.
A foolish rich man is still a lord.

93

A nogid kumt op un an oreman kumt oif, iz noch nit gleich.
A rich man's fortune down and a poor man's fortune up—
they are still not even.

94

A noventer groshen iz besser vi a veiter kerbel.
A penny at hand is worth a dollar at a distance.

95

A patsh farhailt zich un a vort gedenkt zich.
A slap heals but a harsh word is remembered.

96

A pusten fas hilcht hecher.
An empty barrel reverberates loudly.

97

A sach mentshen zehen, nor vainik fun zai farshtai'en.
Many people see things but few understand them.

98

A shaineh froi iz a halbeh parnosseh.
A pretty wife is half a livelihood.

99

A shaineh maidel iz a karanteh shtikel s'choireh.
A pretty girl is the kind of goods that's always in demand.

100

A shain ponim kost gelt.
A pretty face costs money.

101

A shlecht veib iz noch tomid gerecht.
A shrewish wife can also be right.

102

A shlechteh mameh iz nitto.
There is no such thing as a bad mother.

103

A shlechteh sholem iz besser vi a guter krig.
A bad peace is better than a good war.

104

A shlimazel falt oifen ruken un tseklapt zich dem noz.
A fool falls on his back and bruises his nose.

105

A shlimazel kumt oich a mol tsu nutz.
Sometimes a piece of ill luck comes in handy.

106

A shloss iz gut nor far an orentlechen mentshen.
A lock is good only for an honest man.

107

A shpigel ken oich zein der grester farfirer.
A mirror can be the biggest deceiver.

108

A shtikel mazel iz vert merer vi a ton gold.
A little bit of luck is better than a ton of gold.

109

A shver hartz redt a sach.
A heavy heart talks a lot.

110

A shverer beitel macht a leicht gemit.
A heavy purse makes a light-hearted spirit.

111

A smagler regen iz gut far di felder un shlecht far di vegen.
A heavy rain is good for the fields and bad for the roads.

112

A toiber hot gehert, vi a shtumer hot dertsailt, az a blinder hot gezen, vi a krumer iz gelofen.
A deaf man heard how a mute told that a blind man saw a cripple run.

113

A toiten bevaint men ziben teg, a nar dem gantsen leben.
One mourns for the dead seven days, but for a fool a whole lifetime.

114

A tsaddik vos vais az er iz a tsaddik iz kain tsaddik nit.
A righteous man who knows he is righteous is not righteous.

115
A tserissen gemit iz shver tsum hailen.
A broken spirit is hard to heal.

116
A tsoreh kumt nit alain.
Trouble doesn't come alone.

117
A tsvaiteh veib iz vi a hiltserner fus.
A second wife is like a wooden leg.

118
A vaicher vort brecht a bain.
A gentle word can break a bone.

119
A veibeleh iz a teibeleh un a teiveleh.
A wife is a little dove and a little devil.

120
A vort iz azoi vi a feil—baideh hoben groisseh eil.
A word is like an arrow—both are in a hurry to strike.

121
A vort iz vert a sileh; shveigen iz vert tsvai.
Talk is worth a shilling; silence is worth two.

122

A veib a marsha'as iz a nega-tsora'as.
A shrewish wife is a scourge.

123

A yosem est a sach un a bitter hartz redt a sach.
An orphan eats too much, a bitter heart talks too much.

124

A yoven vert klug noch varmes.
A soldier becomes smart after eating some warm food.

125

A yung baimeleh baigt zich; an alter brecht zich.
A young tree bends; an old tree breaks.

126

A zaiger vos shtait iz besser vi a zaiger vos iz kalyeh; veil afileh a zaiger vos shtait derveizt di richtikeh tseit tsvai mol a tog.

A watch that has stopped is better than a watch that works badly; for even a watch that has stopped shows the correct time twice a day.

127

Abi gezunt—dos leben ken men zich alain nemen.

Be sure to stay healthy—you can kill yourself later.

128

Aider azoi foren iz besser tsu fus gaien.

Better walk than ride like that.

129

Aider es kumt di nechomeh, ken oisgaien di neshomeh.

Things may get worse before they get better.

130

Aider gemain, besser alain.

Rather alone than with a lowly mate.

131

Aider me zogt arois s'vort, iz men a har; dernoch iz men a nar.

Before you utter a word you are the master; afterwards you're a fool.

132

Ain foiler epel farfoilt di ander.
One rotten apple spoils the other.

133

Ain Got un azoi fil sonim.
One God and so many enemies.

134

Ain hartz fielt di andereh.
One heart feels another's affections.

135

Ain kind iz azoi vi ain oig.
Having an only child is like having one eye.

136

Ain man hot lib smetteneh un der anderer maftir.
One man likes sour cream and the other prayer.

137

Ain mol a saichel, dos tsvaiteh mol chain, dem dritten mol git
men in di tsain.
*The first time it's smart, the second time it's cute, the third
time you get a sock in the teeth.*

138

Ain nar iz a maivin oifen anderen.
One fool is an expert on the other.

139
Ain nar ken mer fregen aider tsen klugeh kenen entferen.
One fool can ask more than ten wise men can answer.

140
Ain nar macht a sach naronim.
One fool makes a lot of fools.

141
Ain tatteh tsen kinder derner; tsen kinder ain tatteh iz shver.
One father can support ten children; but it is difficult for ten children to support one father.

142
Aineh villen leben un kennen nit, un andereh kenen leben un villen nit.
Some want to live well and cannot, while others can live well and will not.

143
Ainem dacht zich az bei yenem lacht zich.
One always thinks that others are happy.

144
Ainem's mazel iz an anderen's shlimazel.
One's good luck is another's misfortune.

145
Ainer bovet un der anderer voint.
One builds the house and the other lives in it.

146

Ainer hakt holts un der anderer shreit: ei!
One chops the wood and the other shouts: oh!

147

Ainer iz a ligen, tsvai iz ligens, drei iz politik.
One lie is a lie, two are lies, but three is politics!

148

Ainer iz a maivin oif a p'shetel, der tsvaiter oif chazzer-hor,
ober alleh zeinen m'vinim oif a chazzen.
*One is an expert on scholarly discourse, another on bristles, but
all are experts on cantors.*

149

Ainer krigt far a k'nip a glet un a tsvaiter far a glet a patsh.
*One gets a caress for a pinch and the other for a caress gets
a slap!*

150

Ainer nait; der tsvaiter gait.
One sews the garment, the other wears it.

151

Ainer vaist nit dem anderens krenk.
One doesn't know another's sorrow.

152

Alain iz di neshomeh rain.
Don't depend upon others—do it yourself.

153

Alleh finger tuen gleich vai (alleh kinder zeinen gleich tei'er).
All fingers hurt alike (all children are equally dear to parents).

154

Allehs fleken ken men aroisnemen mit a bisseleh gold.
All spots can be removed with a little gold.

155

Alleh kalles zeinen shain; alleh maissim zeinen frum.
All brides are beautiful; all the dead are pious.

156

Alleh maissim hoben ain ponem.
All corpses have the same look.

157

Alleh meiles in ainem, iz nito bei kainem.
No one person possesses all the virtues.

158

Alleh shtumeh villen a sach reden.
All deaf-mutes have a great deal to say.

159

Alleh yiden kenen zein chazonim, ober maistens zeinen zai haizerik.
Every Jew is a cantor, but he is hoarse most of the time.

160

Alleh shusters gaien borves.
All shoemakers go barefoot.

161

Alts drait zich arum broit un toit.
Everything revolves around bread and death.

162

Alts iz gut nor in der tseit.
Everything is good but only in its time.

163

Amol flegen di eltern lernen di kinder reden; heint lernen di kinder di eltern shveigen.
Once parents used to teach their children to talk; today children teach their parents to keep quiet.

164
An aizel derkent men bei di langeh oi'eren, a nar bei der langer tsung.
You can recognize a donkey by his long ears, a fool by his long tongue.

165
An alter freint iz besser vi a nei'eh tsvai.
One old friend is better than two new ones.

166
An iberik vort hot nit kain ort.
A superfluous word has no place.

167
An ofter gast falt tsu last.
A frequent guest becomes a burden.

168
An opgeshailteh ai falt oich nit alain in moil arein.
A peeled egg doesn't leap into the mouth by itself.

169
An oreman iz vi a lecherdiker zak.
A poor man is like a torn sack.

170
An oreman vil oich leben.
Even a poor man wants to live.

171

Arein iz di tir brait, un arois iz zi shmol.
The door to evil-doing is wide, but the return gate is narrow.

172

Aroif kletert men pavolyeh; arop kolert men zich shnell.
Uphill one climbs slowly; downhill one rolls fast.

173

Az a kluger redt tsu a nar, reden tsvai naronim.
When a wise man talks to a fool, two fools are talking.

174

Az a nar gait in mark, fraien zich di kremer.
When a fool goes shopping, the storekeepers rejoice.

175

Az a nar shveigt, vaist men nit tsi er iz a nar tsi a chochem.
When a fool keeps quiet, you can't tell whether he is foolish or smart.

176

Az a narishkeit gerot afileh amol, iz es fort a narishkeit.
When foolishness sometimes succeeds, it is still follishness.

177

Az alleh zuchen shaineh kalles, vu kumen ahin di miesseh maidlech?
If everybody looks for pretty brides, what's to become of the ugly girls?

178
Az a nar halt di ku bei di herner, ken zi a kluger melken.
If a fool holds the cow by the horns, a clever man can milk her.

179
Az an oreman macht chasseneh, krigt der hunt kadoches.
When a poor man makes a wedding, the dog gets the shivers!

180
Az der chossen iz der bagerter, darf di kalleh nit kain verter.
When the groom is desired, the bride doesn't need words.

181
Az der kluger failt, failt er veit!
When a clever man makes a mistake, does he make a mistake!

182

Az der kop iz a nar, ligt der gantser guf in der erd.
When the head is a fool, the whole body can go to hell.

183

Az der malamed kright zich mit der veib iz az och un vai tsu di talmidim.
When the teacher and his wife quarrel, the scholars get the worst of it.

184

Az der man iz tsu gut far der velt, iz er tsu shlecht far'n veib.
If a man is generally charitable, he will be unkind toward his wife.

185

Az der mogen iz laidik iz der moi'ech oich laidik.
When the stomach is empty, so is the brain.

186

Az der oirach hust, felt im a leffel.
When the guest coughs, he's lacking a spoon.

187

Az der oks falt, sharfen alleh di messer.
When the ox falls, everyone sharpens their knife.

188

Az der milner shlogt zich mitten koimen-kerer, vert der milner shvarts un der koimen-kerer veis.

When the miller fights with the chimneysweep, the miller becomes black and the chimneysweep white.

189

Az der soineh falt, tor men zich nit fraien, ober men haibt im nit oif.

When your enemy falls, don't rejoice; but don't pick him up either.

190

Az der talmid iz a voiler, iz der rebbi oich a voiler.

If the student is successful, the teacher gets the praise.

191

Az der tatteh shainkt dem zun, lachen baideh; az der zun
shainkt dem tatten, vainen baideh.
*When the father gives to his son, both laugh; but when the son
gives to his father, both cry.*

192

Az der yeger ken nit shissen, bleibt oich der hunt on a bissen.
If the hunter can't shoot, even his hound is left without a bite.

193

Az di balabosteh iz a shtinkerin, iz di katz a fresserin.
When the housewife is a slattern, the cat is a glutton.

194

Az di balabosteh iz brait, bakt zi braiteh broit.
If the housewife is stout, the loaves she bakes are large.

195

Az di hatslocheh shpilt, gilt ersht di chochmeh.
If luck plays along, cleverness succeeds.

196

Az di kalleh ken nit tantsen, zogt zi az di klezmorim kennen
nit shpilen.
If the bride can't dance, she finds fault with the musicians.

197

Az di muter shreit oifen kind: "mamzer," meg men ir gloiben.
When a mother shouts at her child: "Bastard," you can believe her.

198

Az di velt zogt, zol men gloiben.
If everybody says so, there's some truth to it.

199

Az di vort iz in moil, iz men a har; az me lozt zi arois, iz men a nar.
While the word is still in your mouth, you are a lord; once you utter it, you are a fool.

200

Az dos hartz iz ful, gai'en di oigen iber.
When the heart is full, the eyes overflow.

201

Az dos mazel gait, kelbt zich der oks.
With luck, even your ox will calve.

202

Az drei zogen meshugeh, darf der ferter zogen, "Bim bom."
The majority rules.

203

Az du gaist oifen laiter, tsail di treplech.
When you climb a ladder, count the rungs.

204

Az du krigst zich, krig zich azoi du zolst zich kennen iberbeten.
In a quarrel, leave the door open for a reconciliation.

205

Az du kukst oif hoicheh zachen, halt tsu di hittel.
If you look up to high things, hold on to your hat.

206

Az du vest foren pamelech, vest du shneller onkumen.
If you drive slowly, you'll arrive more quickly.

207

Az es bashert ainem dertrunken tsu verren, vert er dertrunken
in a leffel vasser.
If one is fated to drown, he will drown in a spoonful of water.

208

Az es klingt, iz misstomeh chogeh.
When people talk about something, it is probably true.

209

Az es kumt der basherter, vert es in tsvai verter.
The right mate comes with the first date.

210

Az es kumt tsonvaitik fargest men kopvaitik.
When a toothache comes, you forget your headache.

211

Az es reg'nt mit gold, shtait der oreman untern dach.

When there's a shower of gold, the poor man stays under the roof.

212

A regen treibt arein in shtub un a baizeh veib treibt arois fun shtub.

Rain chases you into the house and a quarrelsome wife chases you out.

213

Az es vert geboren a maidel, iz a hatslocheh in der mishpocheh.

When a girl is born, it's a good omen for the family.

214

Az es vert nit besser, vert memaileh erger.

If it doesn't get better, depend on it, it will get worse.

215

Az es volt geven vainiker chazairim, volt geven vainiker mamzairim.

If there were fewer swine, there would be fewer bastards.

216

Az es zeinen nito kain andereh meiles, iz a zumer-shprinkeleh oich a meileh.

If a girl has no other virtues, even a freckle can be considered one.

217

Az Got git broit, giben mentshen puter.
When God gives bread, men give butter.

218

Az Got vil ainem dos hartz opshtoissen, git er im a groissen saichel.
When God wants to break a man's heart, he gives him a lot of sense.

219

Az Got vil, shist a bezim.
If God wills it, even a broom can shoot.

220

Az Got vil nit geben, ken men zich alain nit nemen.
If God does not give, one cannot take.

221

Az Got volt gelebt oif der erd, volt men im alleh fenster oisgeshlogen.
If God lived on earth, all his windows would be broken.

222

Az ich vel zein vi yener, ver vet zein vi ich?
If I would be like someone else, who will be like me?

223

Az in dem kufert ligt samet un zeid, ken men in trantes aroisgain far leit.

If velvet and silk are stored in the chest, one may appear among people in rags.

224

Az in droissen iz a vint, flit dos mist hoich.
When there is wind outside, the garbage flies high.

225

Az me chapt a patsh, bakumt men noch a soineh dertsu.
If one gets a slap in the face, one acquires an enemy as a bonus.

226

Az me est chazzer, zol rinnen fun bord.
If you're going to do something wrong, enjoy it!

227

Az me est nit kain k'nobel, shtinkt men nit.
If you don't eat garlic, you won't smell bad.

228

Az me handelt mit a nodel, gevint men a nodel.
If you invest a needle, you'll realize a needle.

229

Az me est op dem baigel, bleibt in kesheneh di loch.
If you eat your bagel, you'll have nothing in your pocket but the hole.

230

Az me est Shabbes kugel, iz men di gantseh voch zat.
If you eat pudding on the Sabbath, you'll be full all week.

231

Az me fregt a sheileh, vert traif.
If you ask the Rabbi a question, he will surely find something wrong.

232

Az me fregt, blonzhet men nisht.
If one asks, one does not err.

233

Az me gait tsevishen leiten, vaist men vos se tut zich in der haim.
When you go to your neighbors, you find out what is happening at home.

234

Az me ganvet avek dem ferd, farshliest men ersht di shtal.
After the horse has been stolen, the stable door is locked.

235

Az me gait gleich, falt men nit.
If you walk straight, you will not stumble.

236

Az me git, nem; az me nemt, shrei: "Gevalt!"
If you are given something, take it; if some one tries to take from you, cry "Help!"

237

Az me git ois a tochter, iz arop a horb fun der plaitseh.
When you marry off a daughter, a hump is off your back.

238

Az me grubt a grub far yenem, falt men alain arein.
If you dig a pit for someone else, you fall in it yourself.

239

Az me hot nit in kop, hot men in di fis.
If one hasn't got it in his head, he has it in his legs.

240

Az me hot nit tsu entfern, muz men farshveigen.
If one has nothing to answer, it is best to shut up.

241

Az me iz foil, hot men nit in moil.
The lazy person acquires no food.

242

Az me ken nit ariber, gait men arunter.
If you can't go over, go under.

243

Az me hot a sach tsu tun, laigt men zich shlofen.
If you have a lot to do, go to sleep.

244

Az me hot gelt, iz men klug un shain un men ken gut zingen.
*If you have money, you are wise and good-looking and can
sing well too.*

245

Az me ken nit vi me vil, tut men vi me ken.
If you can't do as you wish, do as you can.

246

Az me klingt, iz oder a chsogeh oder a paiger.
When bells toll, it's either a holiday or a funeral for Gentiles.

247

Az me kumt iber di planken, bakumt men andereh gedanken.
If you cross over the fence, you acquire other ideas.

248

Az me kumt noch yerusheh, muz men oft batsolen k'vureh gelt.
*If you come for the legacy, you often have to pay for the
funeral.*

249

Az me kumt traisten a yungeh almoneh, kvapet men zich nit
tsu fardinen a mitsveh.
*When one comes to comfort a young widow, he does not mean
to perform a good deed.*

250

Az me laight arein kadoches, nemt men arois a krenk.
If you invest in a fever, you will realize a disease.

251

Az me laigt arein, nemt men arois.
If you put something in, you can take something out.

252

Az me laigt zich nit gegessen, tsailt men di stolovanyes.
*If you go to sleep with an empty stomach, you will count the
beams on the ceiling.*

253

Az me lebt mit a teivel, vert men a teivel.
He who lives with a devil, becomes a devil.

254

Az me ligt oif der erd, ken men nit fallen.
If you lie on the ground, you cannot fall.

255

Az me muz, ken men.
When one must, one can.

256

Az me redt a sach, redt men fun zich.
If you talk a lot, you talk of yourself.

257

Az me redt, derredt men zich.
*If you keep on talking, you will end up saying what you didn't
intend to say.*

258

Az me lozt a chazzer aruf af'n bank, vil er af'n tish.
Give a pig a chair, he'll want to get on the table.

259

Az me redt a sach, ken men zich oisreden a narishkeit.
When one talks too much, one talks foolishness.

260

Az me redt zich arop fun hartsen, vert gringer.
When one pours out his heart, he feels lighter.

261

Az me shikt a nar oifen mark, frai'en zich di kremers.
When you send a fool to the market, the merchants rejoice.

262

Az me shloft mit hint shtait men oif mit flai.

If you lie down with the dogs, you get up with the fleas.

263

Az me shlogt di veib mit a kulteveh, vert derfun di gret nit veis.

Beating your wife with a paddle does not make the linen white.

264

Az me shmirt, fort men.

When you grease the palm, everything goes easy.

265

Az me shport nit dem groshen, hot men nit dem rubel.

If you don't save the penny, you'll not have the dollar.

266

Az me shveigt iz men a halber nar; az me redt iz men a gantser nar.

He who keeps quiet is half a fool; he who talks is a complete fool.

267

Az me tantst oif alleh chassenes, vaint men noch alleh maissim.

If you dance at every wedding, you'll weep at every funeral.

268

Az me trinkt alleh mol esik, vais men nit az es iz do a zisereh zach.

When one always drinks vinegar, he doesn't know that anything sweeter exists.

269

Az me tut zich loden, kumt men sei vi nit tsum shoden.
From litigation you can never recover your loss.

270

Az me vaint zich ois, vert gringer af'n hartz.
After a good cry, your heart is lighter.

271

Az me varft dem sod arein in yam, varft im der yam arois.
If you cast your secret into the sea, the sea will cast it out.

272

Az me vil a hunt a zets geben, gefint men a shteken.
When you want to beat a dog, be sure to find a stick.

273

Az me vil nit alt verren, zol men zich yungerhait oifhengen.
If you want to avoid old age, hang yourself in youth.

274

Az me zait gelt, vaksen naronim.
When you sow money, you reap fools.

275

Az me zetst arein a gandz in hober, shtarbt zi fun hunger.
Let a goose loose in oats and she will starve to death.

276

Az me zingt aider me shtait uf, vet men vainen aider me gait shlofen.

Sing before seven, cry before eleven.

277

Az me zogt meshugeh, zol men gloiben.

When people say someone is crazy, believe it.

278

Az me zucht, gefint men.

If you seek, you will find.

279

Az men antloift fun fei'er, bagegent men dos vasser.

When you flee from fire, you run into water.

280

Az men baizert zich op, gait op der ka'as.

When you give vent to your feelings, your anger leaves you.

281

Az men chazert tsu fil iber vi gerecht men iz, vert men umgerecht.

If you repeat often enough that you're right, you will discover you're wrong.

282

Az men dermont zich on dem toit, iz men nit zicher miten leben.
If you start thinking of death, you are no longer sure of life.

283

Az men falt bei zich, falt men oich bei andereh.
If you lose your self-respect, you also lose the respect of others.

284

Az men ganvet a sach ai'er, ken men oich verren a nogid.
If one steals a lot of eggs, one can also become rich.

285

Az men hot a gilderneh hentel, hot men dem leberel fun entel.
With golden hands, one can always afford the choicest delicacies.

286

Az men hot a shaineh veib iz men a shlechter chaver.
When you have a pretty wife, you are a bad friend.

287

Az men hot an ainikel, hot men tsvai kinder.
When you have a grandchild, you have two children.

288

Az men hot di matbai'eh, hot men di dai'eh.
If you have the money, you have the "say"!

289

Az men hot nit kain klinger, bleibt men ainer alain vi a finger.

If you have no dough, you are alone as a finger.

290

Az men iz a meister, iz ful der teister.

If you are a craftsman, your wallet is full.

291

Az men iz biz tsvantsik yor a kind, iz men tsu ain-un-tsvantsik a behaimeh.

If you're a child at twenty, you're an ass at twenty-one.

292

Az men ken nit beissen, zol men nit veizen di tsain.

Those who can't bite should not show their teeth.

293

Az men ken nit iberhar'n dos shlechteh, ken men dos guteh nit derleben.

If you can't endure the bad, you'll not live to witness the good.

294

Az men krigt zich miten rov, muz men sholem zein miten shainker.

If you're at odds with your rabbi, make peace with your bartender.

295

Az men lebt, derlebt men zich alts.
If you live long enough, you will live to see everything.

296

Az men maint, genart men zich.
To assume is to be deceived.

297

Az men shert di shaf, tsitteren di lemmer.
When the sheep are shorn, the lambs tremble.

298

Az men zitst in der haim, tsereist men nit kain shtivel.
If you stay at home, you won't wear out your shoes.

299

Az meshiach vet kumen, vellen alleh krankeh oisgehailt verren;
nor a nar vet bleiben a nar.
*When the Messiah comes, all the sick will be healed; only a
fool will stay a fool.*

300

Az m'iz hungerik est men broit.
If you're hungry enough, you can eat dry bread.

301

Az nito kain klaineh, iz nito kain groisseh.
When there are no small ones, there are no big ones.

302

Az oif dem hartsen iz bitter, helft nit in moil kain tsuker.
If there's bitterness in the heart, sugar in the mouth won't make life sweeter.

303

Az s'a regenboigen, veizt Got dem simen, az er iz undz moichel.
When there's a rainbow, it's a sign that God has forgiven our sins.

304

Az se brent, iz a fei'er.
Where there's smoke, there's fire.

305

Az se dunert in vinter iz der simen fun a zol.
Thunder in the winter is a sign of coming plenty.

306

Az s'iz in droissen a bloteh, frai'en zich di shusters.
When the streets are muddy, the cobblers rejoice.

307

Az s'iz nito in top, iz nito in teller.
If there's nothing in the pot, there's nothing on the plate.

308

Az tsvai zogen as du bist shikker, darf men zich laigen shlofen.
When two say you're drunk, it's best to go to sleep.

309

Azoi gait af der velt; ainer hot di beitel, der tsvaiter hot di gelt!
So it goes in this world: one has the purse, the other has the money.

310

Bainer on flaish iz do; flaish on bainer iz nito.
Bones without meat is possible; meat without bones is not possible.

311

Barat zich mit vemen du vilst; un tu miten aigenem saichel.
Ask advice from everyone, but act with your own mind.

312

Bei a shveren vogen iz gring tsu gain tsu fus.
Alongside a heavy wagon, it's easy to walk.

313

Bei nacht hert zich veit.
Prayer is heard best at night.

314

Beim glezel gefint men a sach guteh freint.
Over a glass of wine, you find many good friends.

315

Bei sholem—bayis iz men tsufriden mit a k'zayis.
When there is peace in the house, a bite suffices.

316

Beim oiskern di shtub gefint men alts.

When you sweep the house, you find everything.

317

Beitog tsum get, beinacht tsum bet.

By day they're ready to divorce, by night they're ready for bed.

318

Besser a gantser nar aider a halber chochem.

Better a complete fool than half wise.

319

Besser a guter soineh aider a shlechter freint.

Better a good enemy than a bad friend.

320

Besser a hon in hant aider an odler in himmel.

Better a hen in the hand than an eagle in the sky.

321

Besser a hunt in friden vi a zelner in krig.

Better a dog in peacetime than a soldier in war.

322

Besser a krummer fus aider a krumer kop.

Better a crooked foot than a crooked mind.

323

Besser a loit mazel aider a funt gold.
An ounce of luck is worth more than a pound of gold.

324

Besser a miesseh lateh aider a shaineh loch.
Better to have an ugly patch than a beautiful hole.

325

Besser a reicher shochen aider an oremer balabos.
Better a rich tenant than a poor landlord.

326

Besser a vaitik in hartz aider a charpeh in ponem.
Better a pain in your heart than shame before men.

327

Besser a yid mitun a bord, vi a bord mitun a yid.
Better a Jew without a beard than a beard without a Jew.

328

Besser ain alter freint vi a nei'eh tsvai.
One old friend is better than two new ones.

329

Besser ain freint mit gekechts aider hundert mit a krechtz.
*Better one friend with a dish of food than a hundred with a
sigh.*

330
Besser ain ku in shtal aider tsen in feld.
Better one cow in the stable than ten in the field.

331
Besser alter vein aider alter koiches.
Better old wine than old strength.

332
Besser der soineh zol bei mir guts zen aider ich bei im shlechts.
Better that my enemy should see good in me than I should see evil in him.

333
Besser di t'no'im tsereissen aider di ketubeh.
Better to break off an engagement than a marriage.

334
Besser dos shlechteh fun guten aider dos guteh fun shlechten.
Better a bad deed of a good person than a good deed of a bad one.

335
Besser gornisht tsu machen aider tsu machen gornisht.
Better to do nothing than to make something into nothing.

336
Besser dos kind zol vainen aider der foter.
Better the child should cry than the father.

337

Besser fri'er bevorent aider shpeter bevaint.
Better caution at first than tears afterwards.

338

Besser fun a gratsh a patsh aider fun a nar a kush.
Better a blow from a wise man than a kiss from a fool.

339

Besser gut un a bissel aider shlechts un a fuleh shissel.
Better good and a little rather than bad and a lot of it.

340

Besser heint an ai aider morgen an ox.
Better an egg today than an ox tomorrow.

341

Besser herren kloles aider herren nebech.
Better to hear curses than to be pitied.

342

Besser mit a klugen in gehenem aider mit a nar in ganaiden.
It's better to be with a wise man in hell than with a fool in paradise.

343

Besser oif der velt nit tsu leben aider onkumen tsu a kind.
It is better not to live than to be dependent on children.

344
Besser tsu shtarben shtai'endik aider tsu leben oif di k'ni.
Better to die upright than to live on your knees.

345
Besser zich tsu vintshen aider yenem tsu shelten.
Better to pray for yourself than to curse another.

346
Bistu erlech mit dein veib, hostu a gezunteh leib.
If you're faithful to your wife, you'll have a healthy body.

347
Bitochen tsit tsum himmel, koved tsit tsu der erd.
Trust draws to heaven, honor to earth.

348
Biz zibetsik yor lernt men saichel un men shtarbt a nar.
Up to seventy years of age we learn wisdom and then we die fools.

349
Blut iz dicker fun vasser.
Blood is thicker than water.

350
Borgen macht zorgen.
Borrow causes sorrow.

351
Brecht zich a ring, tsefalt di gantseh kait.
One link snaps and the whole chain falls apart.

352
Bris, bar mitsveh, chasseneh, k'vureh-gelt—bald nossenen!
Circumcision, confirmation, wedding, burial fee—all too soon
to be paid!

353
Chain gait iber shain.
Charm is better than beauty.

354
Chasseneh gehat oif gich un geblibben in shtich.
Married in a hurry and stuck for good!

355
Chavershaft iz shtarker vi brudershaft.
Friendship is stronger than kinship.

356
Chutspeh gilt!
Nerve succeeds!

357
Darf men honig ven tsuker iz zis?
Who needs honey when sugar is sweet?

358

Dem bitersten mazel ken men farshtellen mit a shmaichel.
The bitterest misfortune can be covered up with a smile.

359

Dem ligner gloibt men afileh an emess oich nit.
The liar is not believed even when he tells the truth.

360

Dem oreman's yaitzer-horeh iz a skorinkeh broit.
The poor man's temptation is a loaf of bread.

361

Dem rosheh gait oif der velt, dem tsaddik oif yener velt.
The wicked fare well in this world; the saints in the life to come.

362

Dem rov's tochter tor nit vos dem beder's tochter meg.
The Rabbi's daughter is forbidden what the bath-house keeper's daughter is allowed.

363

Der barimer bleibt shteken in bloteh.
The boaster gets stuck in the mud.

364

Der bester ferd darf hoben a beitsh, der klugster man an aitseh un di frumsteh nekaiveh a man.
The best horse needs a whip, the wisest man advice and the chastest woman a man.

365

Der bester ferd iz nor a padleh ven er paigert.
The best horse is just a carcass when it dies.

366

Der cholem iz a nar un der shlof iz der har.
The dream is a fool and sleep's the master.

367

Der dales farshtelt di chochmeh.
Poverty hides wisdom.

368

Der dales hot a grobeh kop.
Poverty has a thick head.

369

Der dales laigt zich tsum ershten oifen ponem.
Poverty reveals itself first on the face.

370

Der derech hayosher iz alleh mol kosher.
The just path is always the right one.

371

Der doktor hot a refueh tsu altz, oder nit tsu dales.
The doctor has a remedy for everything but poverty.

372

Der emess hot alleh meiles, ober er iz a shemevdiker.
The truth has charm but it's shy.

373

Der emess iz a kricher.
Truth is a slowpoke.

374

Der emess iz der bester ligen.
Truth is the safest lie.

375

Der emess iz in di oigen, der ligen iz hinter di oigen.
The truth is in sight; the lie is behind the eyes.

376

Der emess ken arumgain a naketer, dem sheker darf men baklaiden.
The truth may walk around naked; the lie has to be clothed.

377

Der emess kumt arois azoi vi boimel oif der vasser.
The truth surfaces like oil on water.

378

Der emess lebt nit, der emess shtarbt nit, der emess matert zich!
The truth is not alive, the truth is not dead, it struggles!

379

Der emess shtarbt nit ober er lebt vi an oreman.
The truth doesn't die but it lives like a poor man.

380

Der ershter broigez iz der bester broigez.
The first quarrel is the best quarrel.

381

Der ganev hot a gringer melocheh un shlechteh chaloimes.
The thief has an easy job and bad dreams.

382

Der gehenem iz nit azoi shlecht vi dos kumen tsi im.
Hell is not so bad as the way to it.

383

Der grester rachmones iz oif an oremeh moid vos ligt in kimpet.
The most to be pitied is a poor maiden in childbirth.

384

Der grester shvimmer kon zich trenken.
Even the best swimmer can drown.

385

Der gleichster veg iz ful mit shtainer.
The smoothest way is full of stones.

386

Der guf iz a shvom, di neshomeh a t'hom.
The body is a sponge, the soul an abyss.

387

Der gvir hot dem saichel in teister.
The rich man has his brains in his billfold.

388

Der 'Innu-hadin iz erger vi der din alain.
Suspense is worse than the ordeal itself.

389

Der iz klug vos zein mazel gait im noch.
Who is smart? He whose fortune follows him.

390

Der ka'as un der tsoren farkirtzen di yoren.
Bad temper and anger shorten the years.

391

Der kluger bahalt dem saichel; der nar veist zein narishkeit.
A wise man conceals his intelligence; the fool displays his foolishness.

392

Der klugster mentsh benart zich.
The wisest man is guilty of folly.

393

Der koved iz fun dem vos git im, un nit fun dem vos krigt im.

Honor is measured by him who gives it, not by him who receives it.

394

Der leben iz di gresteh metsi'eh—me wrigt es umzist.

Life is the biggest bargain—we get it for nothing.

395

Der mazel macht klug, veil der mazel macht reich.

Fortune makes you smart, because fortune makes you rich.

396

Der mentsh fort un Got halt di laitses.

Man rides, but God holds the reins.

397

Der mentsh hot tsvai oigen, tsvai oiren, ober nor ain moil.

Man has two eyes, two ears, but only one mouth.

398

Der mentsh iz tsum shtarben geboren.

Man is born to die.

399

Der mentsh iz vos er iz, ober nit vos er iz geven.

Man is what he is, but not what he used to be.

400

Der mentsh tracht, un Got lacht.
Man thinks and God laughs.

401

Der mentsh tut hofen biz er vert antshlofen.
Man keeps hoping till he goes to his eternal slumber.

402

Der miesteh leben iz besser fun shensten toit.
The ugliest life is better than the nicest death.

403

Der mogen halt besser a sod vi di hartz.
The stomach keeps a secret better than the heart.

404

Der oilem iz a goilem.
The masses are asses.

405

Der oisher hot nit kain yoisher.
The rich have no sense of justice.

406

Der oks vais nit fun zein gevureh.
The ox is not aware of its strength.

407

Der oreman hot vainik feint, der reicher hot vainiker freint.
The poor man's enemies are few, the rich man's friends are
even fewer.

408

Der oreman tracht, der nogid lacht.
The poor think, the rich laugh.

409

Der ponem zogt ois dem sod.
The face tells the secret.

410

Der poretz iz gut un in hant iz di rut.
The master is kind but his hand holds the cane.

411

Der reicher est dos flaish un der oreman di bainer
The rich eat the meat; the poor the bones.

412

Der remez shlogt shtarker vi der emess.
A hint hits harder than the truth.

413

Der saichel fort oif oksen.
Wisdom travels by oxen.

414

Der saichel kumt noch di yoren.
Wisdom comes with the years.

415

Der shainker hot lib dem shikker, ober di tochter vet er im nit geben.
The saloonkeeper loves the drunkard, but he wouldn't give him his daughter in marriage.

416

Der shlof iz a ganev.
Sleep is a thief.

417

Der shlof iz der bester dokter.
Sleep is the best doctor.

418

Der shuster beim kapul un der top iz ful.
If the cobbler sticks to his last, his pot is full.

419

Der shuster redt fun der kapoteh; der backer fun der lopeteh.
The shoemaker speaks of his last and the sailor of his mast.

420

Der shversteh ol iz a laidikeh kesheneh.
The heaviest burden is an empty pocket.

421

Der shpigel nart kainem nisht op, nor dem miessen.
The mirror fools none but the ugly.

422

Der tsoren iz in hartsen a doren.
Anger is like a thorn in the heart.

423

Der veister veg iz der tsu der kesheneh.
The longest way is the one to the pocket.

424

Der vint flit avek un di kerpes bleiben.
The storm blows over but the driftwood remains.

425

Der volf hot nit moireh faren hunt, ober es gefelt im nit zein bilen.

The wolf is not afraid of the dog, but he hates his bark.

426

Der vos farshtait zein narishkeit iz a kluger.

He who is aware of his folly is wise.

427

Der vos gleicht tsu nemen, gleicht nit tsu geben.

He who likes to take does not like to give.

428

Der vos hot nit farzucht bittereh, vaist nit voz zies iz.

He who has not tasted the bitter does not understand the sweet.

429

Der vos shveigt maint oich epes.

He who is silent means something just the same.

430

Der vos zucht leichteh arbet gait zai'er mid tsu bet.

He who looks for light work goes very tired to bed.

431

Der yaitser-horeh shloft bei a maidel un iz oif bei a veibel.

Temptation in a maiden is asleep; in a wife it's awake.

432
Di alteh kei'en un di yungeh shpei'en.
What the old chew the young spit out.

433
Di boich farshlingt di kop miten saichel.
The stomach swallows up the head with the mind.

434
Di chasidem'lech zollen frailech zein, trinkt der rebenyu ois dem vein.
The rabbi drinks up the wine and orders his followers to be gay.

435
Der emess hot a sach ponimer.
The truth has many faces.

436
Di epeleh falt nit veit fun baimeleh.
The apple doesn't fall far from the tree.

437
Di ergsteh rechiles iz der emess.
The worst libel is the truth.

438
Di ershteh veib iz fun Got; di tsvaiteh iz fun mentshen.
Marriage with the first wife is made in Heaven; with the second, it's arranged by people.

439

Di ga'aveh ken fardarben, ober fun a ta'aveh vet men nit shtarben.

Haughtiness can do harm but you can't die from loving pleasure.

440

Di gantseh velt iz ful mit shaidim; treib zai chotsh fun zich arois.

The whole world is full of demons; you just exorcise them out of yourself.

441

Di gantseh velt iz nit meshugeh.

The whole world isn't crazy.

442

Di gantseh velt iz aim ganev.

The whole world is one thief.

443

Di gresteh narishkeit fun a nar iz vos er maint az er iz klug.

The biggest folly of the fool is that he thinks he is smart.

444

Di gresteh tsoreh—a veib a klafteh.

The biggest trouble—a shrewish wife.

445

Di grub iz shoin ofen un der mentsh tut noch hofen.

The grave is already dug and man still continues to hope.

446

Di hun hert dem hon's drosheh un zucht zich a kernd'l proseh.

The hen listens to the rooster's sermon and goes to look for a grain of corn.

447

Di kan fun blecher iz ful mit lecher.

The tinsmith's can is full of holes.

448

Di kats hot lib fish, nor zi vil di fis nit einnetsen.

The cat likes fish but she doesn't want to wet her paws.

449

Di klainer hartz nemt arum di groisseh velt.

The heart is small and embraces the whole wide world.

450

Di klensteh nekomeh farsamt di neshomeh.

The smallest vengeance poisons the soul.

451

Di klugeh gai'en tsu fus, un di naren foren.

Wise men go on foot and fools ride.

452

Di kro flit hoich un zetst zich oif a chazzer.

The crow flies high but settles on a hog.

453

Di libeh iz zis, nor zi iz gut mit broit.
Love is sweet, but it's nice to have bread with it.

454

Di lichtikeh velt iz fun shlimazel farshtelt.
The world is good, only bad luck casts a pall over it.

455

Di oi'eren heren nit vos dos moil redt.
The ears don't hear what the mouth utters.

456

Di oigen zollen nit zen, volten di hent nit genumen.
If the eyes wouldn't see, the hands wouldn't take.

457

Di pod-panes zeinen erger fun di panes alain.
Underlings are worse than masters.

458

Di roitsteh epel hot a vorm.
The reddest apple has a worm in it.

459

Di shich fun oreman's kind vaksen miten fisel.
The shoes of the poor man's kids grow with their feet.

460

Di shtileh vasserlech reissen ein di breges.
Quiet streams tear away the shores.

461

Di shversteh arbet iz arumtsugain laidik.
The hardest work is to go idle.

462

Di tefileh gait aroif un di brocheh gait arop.
The prayer ascends and the blessing descends.

463

Di varemsteh bet is di mames.
The warmest bed is mother's.

464

Di toireh hot kain grund nit.
The Scriptures have no bottom.

465

Di toireh leicht, di toireh brent, ober varemen varemt der kerbel.
The Torah gives light, the Torah burns, but only the dollar gives warmth.

466

Di toireh voint a mol in a churveh un biz'n haldz iz di purveh.
The Torah often dwells in a hovel, up to the neck in dirt.

467

Di toi'ern fun treren zeinen kain mol nit farshlossen.
The gates of tears are never shut.

468

Di tseit brengt vunden un hailt vunden.
Time brings wounds and heals them.

469

Di tseit iz der bester doktor.
Time is the best physician.

470

Di tseit ken alts ibermachen.
Time can alter everything.

471

Di tsung iz di feder fun hartsen.
The tongue is the pen of the heart.

472

Di vegen fun teshuveh zeinen nit vainiker farborgen vi di vegen fun zind.
The ways of repentance are as much hidden as the ways of sin.

473

Di veib oiket un der hunt kanoiket, dos kind chlipet, un der dales ripet.
The wife wails and the dog whimpers and the child whines and poverty howls!

474

Di velt hot feint dem massernik un dem mussernik.
The world hates the informer and the moralist.

475

Di velt iz a hekeleh: ainer darf tsum anderen.
The world consists of cogs: one depends on the other.

476

Di velt iz ful mit tsores, nor yederer fielt nor zeineh.
The world is full of troubles, but each man feels his own.

477

Di velt iz grois, ireh tsores noch gresser.
The world is big, its troubles still bigger.

478

Di velt zogt a vertel: besser mit a klugen farliren aider mit a
nar gevinen.
*The world has a saying: better to lose with a wise man than to
win with a fool.*

479

Di zun sheint lichtiker noch a regen.
The sun shines brighter after a shower.

480

Di zorgen laig op oif morgen.
Put off your worries for the morrow.

481

Dort vu men hot dich lib, gai vainik; vu men hot dich feint, gai gor nit.

Where people love you, go rarely; where you are hated, go not at all.

482

Dorten iz gut vu mir seinen nito.

That place seems good where we are not.

483

Dos besteh epel chapt ois der chazzer.

The pig snatches the best apple.

484

Dos gantseh leben iz a milchomeh.

All of life is a struggle.

485

Dos harts iz a halber novi.

The heart is something of a prophet.

486

Dos hindel vert miten shochet gevoint.

Fowls are inured to the killing.

487

Dos leben iz di gresteh metsi'eh—men krigt es umzist.

Life is the greatest bargain—you get it for nothing.

488

Dos leben iz nit mer vi a cholem, ober vek mich nit oif.
Life is no more than a dream, but don't wake me up!

489

Dos leben iz vi kinderhemdel—kurtz un bash.
Life is like a child's undershirt—short and soiled.

490

Dos mazel hot hazel.
Fortune provides shelter.

491

Dos oibershteh klaid fardekt di untershteh leid.
The outergarment conceals the inner torment.

492

Dos veremel nart op, un nit der fisher oder di vendkeh.
It's the bait that lures and not the fisherman or the tackle.

493

Drei zachen kon men nit bahalten: libeh, husten un dales.
Three things cannot be hidden: love, coughing and poverty.

494

Drei zachen vaksen ibernacht: revochim, diregelt un maiden.
Three things grow overnight: profits, rents and girls.

495

Durch shveigen ken men nit shteigen.
You can't get ahead with keeping quiet.

496

Durchlernen gantz shas iz a groisseh zach: durch lernen ain mideh iz a gressereh zach.
To learn the whole Talmud is a great accomplishment; to learn one good virtue is even greater.

497

Ehreh iz fil tei'erer far gelt.
Honor is much dearer than money.

498

Elteren kenen alts geben, nor kain mazel kenen zai nit geben.
Parents can provide everything except good luck.

499

Emess iz in sidder.
Truth one finds only in the prayerbook.

500

Emess iz nor bei Got un bei mir a bissel.
Truth is found only with God, and with me only a little.

501

Er glaibt nit in Got un bet zein genod.
He doesn't believe in God, yet asks His mercy.

502

Er hot avekgeganvet dem chumesh mit dem "loi sig-noiv."
He stole the Bible containing "Thou shalt not steal."

503

Er hot di vert fun a paim un far'reist di kop vi a baim.
He is worth a penny, yet he holds his head high like a tree.

504

Er hot dos leben fun Got un dos essen fun mentshen.
He owes his life to God and his living to men.

505

Er iz a seredniak—nit no'ent tsu a chochem un nit veit fun a
nar.
He is mediocre—not near to a wise man, not far from a fool.

506

Er lebt mit der veib vi a brukiner mit a shtain.
He lives with his wife like a stonemason with a stone.

507

Er reit oif der kotshereh un zi reit oif dem fartach.
He rides the coach and she rides the apron.

508

Es iz a mitsveh a chazzer a hor arois tsu reissen.
It is a virtuous deed to pull a hair out of a pig.

509

Es iz besser a shandeh in ponem aider a vaitik in hartsen.
It is better to be embarrassed than heartbroken.

510

Es iz besser tsu leben in naches aider tsu shtarben in tsar.
It is better to live in joy than to die in sorrow.

511

Es iz bitter vi gal, un on gal ken men nit leben.
It's bitter like bile and without bile one cannot live.

512

Es iz bitter un shlecht ven der rabim iz umgerecht.
It's bitter and bad when the public is wrong.

513

Es iz groi di pai'eh un narish di dai'eh.
The temples are grey yet the mind is childish.

514

Es iz gut tsu fasten mit a polkeh fun a gandz un mit a pus-butelkeh.
Fasting is easy with a chicken leg and a half-bottle of wine.

515

Es iz gut tsu zein a gvir: der rov alain macht dem hesped.
It's good to be rich: the Rabbi himself makes the eulogy at your funeral.

516

Es iz leichter bei andereh chesroines tsu gefinen vi bei zich
meiles.

It is easier to find faults in others than virtues in oneself.

517

Es iz nit azoi gut mit gelt vi es iz shlecht on dem.

It is not so good with money as it is bad without it.

518

Es iz nit azoi tei'er der geshank vi der gedank.

The gift is not as precious as the thought.

519

Es iz nit varem fun dobreh raideleh, nor fun dobreh maineleh.

Sweet talk doesn't make you warm but sweet meaning does.

520

Es iz shver tsu trogen, un avekvarfen tut bang.

It's too heavy to carry and too precious to throw away.

521

Es ken nit verren tsen ven ains iz nito.

You can't make ten when there isn't one to start with.

522

Es ken zein an erlecher shenker un a shefer a ganev.

There may be an honest saloon-keeper and a dishonest shepherd.

523
Es ken zein harb, oich di reichsteh arb.
The richest inheritance might become a burden.

524
Es kumen mekabel ponem zein dem oreman—a kalter vint un a baizeh hunt.
Who comes to greet a pauper? A cold wind and wild dogs.

525
Es lacht zich alain un es vaint zich alain.
One laughs alone and weeps alone.

526
Es libt zich alain, shemt zich alain.
He who praises himself will be humiliated.

527
Es shlogen zich aleh far di shtikeleh challeh.
All fight for a piece of bread.

528
Es shtait doch geshribben: chochmoh—shtikoh.
It is written: silence is wisdom.

529
Es shtumeh di tsinger ven du host in kesheneh klinger.
Evil tongues are silenced by the tinkle of coins in your pocket

530
Es stayet di bobben chasseneh tsu machen.
Great wealth will marry off even an old woman.

531
Es tut zich nit azoi gut vi es redt zich.
It isn't done as easily as it's said.

532
Es vais di katz vemes flaish zi hot oifgegessen!
The cat knows whose meat she ate!

533
Es bainer, vest du hoben a veissen chossen.
Chew on bones and you'll have a handsome husband.

534
Ess nit di lokshen far shabbes.
Don't eat the noodles before Sabbath.

535
Falen falt men alain, ober oiftsuhaiben zich darf men a hant fun a freind.
To fall down you manage alone but it takes friendly hands to get up.

536
Far a bissel libeh batsolt men miten gantsen leben.
For a little love you pay all your life.

537

Far a tsap hot men moireh fun forent, far a ferd fun hinten, far a nar fun alleh zeiten.

Every one fears a goat from in front, a horse from the rear and a fool on every side.

538

Far an akshen iz kain refueh nito.

For the disease of stubborness there is no cure.

539

Far der klenster toiveh vert men a ba'al-choiv.

For the smallest favor you become a debtor.

540

Far der teliyeh hoben mentshen mer moireh vi far Got alain.

Men fear the gallows more than God himself.

541

Far der velt muz men yoitseh zein vi far Got alain.

It's more important to please people than to please God.

542

Far gelt bakumt men alts, nor kain saichel nit.

Money buys everything except brains.

543

Far Got hot men moireh; far mentshen muz men zich hiten.

Fear God, but be wary of men.

544

Far kinder tsereist men a velt.
For your children's sake you would tear the world apart.

545

Far mein tir vet oich a mol zein a bloteh.
There may be mud before my door, too, some day.

546

Far morgen vet Got zorgen—un heint ver vet mir borgen?
Let God worry about the morrow—and for today, who will give me a loan?

547

Far umkoved antloif, ober yog zich nit noch koved.
Run away from an insult but don't chase after honor.

548

Far ziseh raidelech tsegai'en di maidelech.
Sweet talk makes the girls melt.

549

Faran dareh gvirim un feteh oremeleit.
Rich men are often lean and poor men fat.

550

Faren doktor un faren beder zeinen nito kain soides.
From a doctor and from a bathhouse-attendant, there are no secrets.

551

Farloreneh yoren iz erger vi farloreneh gelt.
Lost years are worse than lost dollars.

552

Farvos feift der dales? Veil er hot nor a dudeh!
Why does poverty whistle? Because it has nothing but a pipe!

553

Farvos klapt der dales? Veil er gait in klumpes!
Why does poverty knock? Because it walks in wooden shoes!

554

Fun a nar hot men tsar.
From a fool you have trouble.

555

Fun a vort vert a kwort.
One cross word brings on a quarrel.

556

Fun ain oks tsit men kain tsvai fellen nit arop.
From one ox you can't skin two hides.

557

Fun ain tifeh grub hot men mer vasser vi fun tsen flacheh.
From one deep ditch comes more water than from ten shallow ones.

558

Fun akshones vegen gait men amol fun ganaiden in gehenem arein.

Out of stubborness many a man goes from heaven to hell.

559

Fun an alteh moid vert a getrei'eh veib.
An old maid becomes a faithful wife.

560

Fun an ek fun a chazzer ken men nit machen a shtreimel.
You can't make a hat out of a pig's tail.

561

Fun blut vert kain vasser nisht.
Blood doesn't turn into water.

562

Fun dein moil in Got's oi'eren arein.
From your mouth into God's ears!

563

Fun dem ber in vald zol men dos fel nit farkoifen.
Don't sell the skin off the bear that's still in the forest.

564

Fun eilenish kumt kain guts nisht arois.
No good comes out of hurrying.

565

Fun glik tsum umglik iz a shpan; fun umglik tsum glik iz a shtik veg.

From fortune to misfortune is a short step; from misfortune to fortune is a long way.

566

Fun handlen in gas mit klaineh zachen ken men kain groisseh gliken nit machen.

From peddling small goods on the streets you don't make big fortunes.

567

Fun hunger shtarbt men nor in a hunger-yor.

You can die of hunger only in a year of famine.

568

Fun iberessen cholyet men mer vi fun nit deressen.

From overeating one suffers more than from not eating enough.

569

Fun itlechen hoiz trogt men epes arois.

If you mix around, you learn quite a bit.

570

Fun kin'ah vert sin'ah.

Envy breeds hate.

571

Fun krimeh shiduchim kumen arois gleicheh kinder.

From bad matches good children are also born.

572

Fun loiter hofenung ver ich noch meshugeh.
Stuff yourself with hope and you can go crazy.

573

Fun naches lebt men nit; fun tsores shtarbt men nit.
One is not kept alive by joy, nor does sorrow alone cause death.

574

Fun rachmones un fun pachdones ken men zich nit ois'hailen.
For compassion and for cowardice there is no remedy.

575

Fun rechiles un soides antloif vi fun shaidim.
From tale-bearing and secrets run as from ghosts.

576

Fun shikker and fun shenker shtinkt mit bronfen.
The drunkard and the bartender both smell of whisky.

577

Fun sholem vegen meg men afileh a ligen zogen (ober sholem
tor kain ligen nit zogen).
*For the sake of peace one may even lie (but the peace itself
should not be a lie).*

578

Fun tsar vert der bain dar.
Sorrow makes the bones grow thinner.

579

Fun veiten nart men leiten; fun der noent, zich alain.
From afar you fool others; nearby, only yourself.

580

Fun yener zeit planken hot men andereh gedanken.
On the other side of the fence, you have a change of heart.

581

Ga'aveh un a laidiker teister zeinen nit kain por.
Conceit and an empty purse are no companions.

582

Gadles ligt oifen mist.
Pride lies on the dungheap.

583

Gai farshtai a maidel: zi vart oif di chasseneh un vaint tsu di chupeh.
Go understand a girl: she looks forward to her wedding and weeps as she walks to the marriage ceremony.

584

Ganaiden un gehenem ken men baideh hoben oif der velt.
Heaven and hell can both be had in this world.

585

Ganveh nit un fast nit.
Rob not, repent not.

586

Ganvet mein bruder, hengt men dem ganev.
If my brother steals, it is the thief who is hanged.

587

Geborgter saichel toig nit.
Borrowed brains have no value.

588

Gebroteneh teibelech fli'en nit in moil arein.
If you want something, you have to work for it!

589

Geganvet un opgegeben tsedokeh—haist geganvet.
Stealing and giving away for charity is still stealing.

590

Gehakteh leber iz besser vi gehakteh tsores.
Chopped liver is better than miserable troubles.

591

Gelebt vi a har un geshtorben vi a nar.
Lived like a lord and died like a fool.

592

Gelt brengt tsu ga'aveh un ga'aveh tsu zind.
Money causes conceit and conceit leads to sin.

593

Gelt farloren, gor nit farloren; mut farloren, alts farloren.
Money lost, nothing lost; courage lost, everything lost.

594

Gelt fiert di gantseh velt!
Money rules the world!

595

Gelt gait tsu gelt.
Money goes to money.

596

Gelt iz di besteh zaif vos nemt arois dem gresten flek.
Money is the best soap—it removes the biggest stain.

597

Gelt tsu fardinen iz gringer vi tsu halten.
It's easier to earn money than to keep it.

598

Gelteleh baleicht vi zun mein velteleh.
Money lights up my little world like the sun.

599

Geredt iz nit gebulen.
Talking isn't barking.

600
Gelt iz keilechdik—amol iz es do, amol iz es dort.
Money is round, it rolls away from you.

601
Geshmak iz der fish oif yenems tish.
Tasty is the fish from someone else's table.

602
Geshvindkeit iz nor gut floi tsu chapen.
Speed is only good for catching flies.

603
Gezunt kumt far parnosseh.
Health comes before making a livelihood.

604

Gleicher mit a haimishen ganev aider mit a fremden rov.
Rather with a hometown thief than a strange rabbi.

605

Glik on saichel iz a lecherdiker zak.
Luck without sense is a perforated sack.

606

Gold probirt men mit fei'er; a froi mit gold.
Gold is tested with fire; a woman with gold.

607

Gold sheint fun bloteh.
Gold glitters even in the mud.

608

Gornisht iz nisht shver—men badarf nor kenen.
Nothing is too difficult—you only have to know it.

609

Got alain iz nit reich—er nemt nor bei ainem un git dem
anderen.
*God is not rich; all He does is take from one and give to the
other.*

610

Got handelt nit un Got vandelt nit.
God does not bargain and God does not change.

611

Got helft dem oreman: er farhit im fun tei'ereh avaires.
God helps the poor man: He protects him from expensive sins.

612

Got hit op di naronim.
God watches over fools.

613

Got hot gegeben dem nar hent un fis un hot im gelozt loifen.
God gave the fool hands and feet and let him run.

614

Got hot lib dem oreman un helft dem nogid.
God loves the poor and helps the rich.

615

Got hot zich bashafen a velt mit klaineh veltelech.
God created a world full of many little worlds.

616

Got iz a foter; dos mazel iz a shtif-foter.
God is a father; luck is a stepfather.

617

Got nemt mit ain hant un git mit der andereh.
God takes with one hand, and gives with the other.

618

Got shikt di kelt noch di klaider.
God send the weather according to your needs.

619

Got shikt di refueh far der makeh.
God sends the remedy for the disease.

620

Got shtroft, der mentsh iz zich noikem.
God punishes but man takes revenge.

621

Got shtroft mit ain hant, un bentsht mit der anderen.
God punishes with one hand and blesses with the other.

622

Got zitst oiben un poret unter.
God sits on high and makes matches below.

623

Got zol hiten fun ain hemd, ain oig un ain kind.
God save us from having one shirt, one eye, and one child.

624

Got zol mich bentshen, ich zol nit broichen mentshen.
God should bless me so that I don't need people.

625

Gring iz tsu krigen a soineh; shver iz tsu krigen a freind.
It's easy to acquire an enemy; hard to acquire a friend.

626

Gring tsu zogen, shver tsu trogen.
Easy to promise, hard to fulfill.

627

Gringer iz herren a sod aider hiten a sod.
It is easier to hear a secret than to keep it.

628

Guteh p'sures hert men fun der veitens.
Good tidings are heard from far away.

629

Guteh freint fun veiten.
You are better friends at a distance.

630

Guteh tsolen, shlechteh monen.
The good ones pay, the bad ones demand.

631

Guts gedenkt men, shlechts filt men.
Kindness is remembered, meanness is felt.

632

Gutskeit iz besser fun frumkeit.
Kindness is better than piety.

633

Halten shabbes iz gringer vi machen shabbes.
To observe the Sabbath is easier than to make it.

634

Handelshaft iz kain brudershaft.
Don't mix business with pleasure.

635

Himmel un erd hoben geshvoren az kain zach zol nit zein farloren.
Heaven and earth have sworn that the truth shall be disclosed.

636

Hint beissen zich iber a bain un availim iber a yerusheh.
Dogs fight over a bone and mourners over an inheritance.

637

Hiten zol men zich far di freind, nit far di feint.
Beware of your friends, not your enemies.

638

Hob lib dem tsvaiten un loz zich nit naren fun dem ershten.
Love the other fellow and don't let yourself be fooled by the first.

639

Hob mich vainik lib nor hob mich lang lib.
Better love me little, but love me long.

640

Hob nit kain moireh ven du host nit kain ander braireh.
Don't be scared when you have no other choice.

641

Hof oif nissim un farloz zich nit oif a nes.
Hope for miracles but don't rely on one.

642

Hofen un haren machen klugeh far naren.
Hoping and waiting makes fools out of clever people.

643

Honik oifen tsung, gall oifen lung.
Honey on the tongue, gall in the heart.

644

Host broit mit puter, iz der mazel a guter.
If you have bread and butter, you have good luck.

645

Host du, halt; vaist du, shveig; kenst du, tu!
If you have, hold on to it; if you know, be silent; if you can, do!

646

Iber a tsvikel macht men kalyeh kain hemd.
One doesn't spoil a shirt because of one corner.

647

Ibergekumeneh tsores iz gut tsu dertsailen.
It's good to talk about troubles that are over.

648

In a guter sho tsu reden; in a baizer sho tsu shveigen.
In a lucky time it's good to talk; in an unlucky time, it's better to be silent.

649

In a shainem epel gefint men amol a vorem.
In a good apple you sometimes find a worm.

650

In bod zeinen alleh gleich.
At the baths all are equal.

651

In der yugent a behaimeh; oif der elter a ferd.
In youth a cow; in old age a horse.

652

In shissel ken nit zein mer vi in top.
You can't have more in the plate than you have in the pot.

653

In shlof zindikt nit der mentsh, nor zeineh chaloimes.
In sleep, man doesn't sin, but his dreams do.

654

In shpigel zet itlecher zein besten freind.
In the mirror everybody sees his best friend.

655

In toch iz yeder tsad gerecht.
In a quarrel, each side is right.

656

In yenems moil tsailt men nit di tsain.
You don't count the teeth in someone else's mouth.

657

Itlecheh bas-yechideh hot zich ir chaindel.
Every only daughter has her charms.

658

Itlecheh shtot hot ir meshugenem.
Every town has its fool.

659

Itlecher mentsh hot zich zein shigoyen.
Every man has a madness of his own.

660

Iz di shteig enger, hodeven zich di gendz besser.
When the coop is secure, the geese will grow fatter.

661

Iz do a braireh, darf nit zein kain moireh.
When there is a way out, there is no need for fear.

662

Kadeges klepen zich tsu klaider un krenk tsum guf.
Thistle sticks to clothes and disease to the body.

663

Kain braireh iz oich a braireh.
No choice is also a choice.

664

Kain naronim badarf men nisht tsu zai'en; zai vaksen alain.
Fools don't have to be sown; they grow up by themselves.

665

Kain umzister soineh iz nito; me batsolt far im.
There are no enemies for free; you have to pay for them.

666

Kainer bahalt nit; nit der rosheh zein rishes, nit der nar zein narishkeit.
No one hides—neither the wicked his wickedness nor the fool his folly.

667

Kainer hot nit kain legoteh tsu hoben charoteh.
Nobody has a monopoly on regret.

668

Kainer iz nit azoi toib vi der vos vil nit herren.
There's no one as deaf as he who will not listen.

669

Kainer vaist nit vemes morgen es vet zein.
No one knows what the morrow will bring.

670

Kainer vaist nit vemen der shuch drikt.
You never know the other fellow's troubles.

671

Kainer zogt nit "Oi" az se tut nit vai.
One doesn't cry "Ouch" if he's not in pain.

672

Kargeh leit dinen der avoideh-zoreh.
Misers are idol worshippers.

673

Kargen iz erger vi ganvenen.
To be miserly is worse than to steal.

674

Kenen toireh iz nit kain shter tsu avaireh.

Knowledge of the Torah is no deterrent to sin.

675

A kind's treren reissen himlen.

A child's tears reach the heavens.

676

Kinder brengen glik, kinder brengen umglik.

Children bring good fortune, children bring misfortune.

677

Kinder un gelt iz a shaineh velt.

Children and money make a nice world.

678

Kirtzer geshlofen, lenger gelebt.

The less you sleep, the more you get out of life.

679

Klaider bahalten dem mum.

Clothes conceal the blemish.

680

Klaider machen dem mentshen.

Clothes make the man.

681
Klaineh genaivim hengt men; groisseh shenkt men.
Petty thieves are hanged; big thieves are pardoned.

682
Klaineh kinder, klaineh fraiden; groisseh kinder, groisseh laiden.
Little children, little joys; bigger children, bigger sorrows.

683
Klaineh kinder lozen nit shlofen; groisseh kinder lozen nit ruen.
Small children don't let you sleep; big children don't let you rest.

684
Klaineh lozen nit kei'en; groisseh lozen nit banei'en.
Little ones don't let you chew; big ones don't let you buy anything new.

685
Klugheit iz besser fun frumkeit.
Wisdom is better than sanctimony.

686
Kolzman es rirt zich an aiver, klert men nit fun kaiver.
As long as one limb stirs, one does not think of the grave.

687
Kratsen un borgen iz nor gut oif a veil.
Scratching and borrowing is only good for a while.

688

Kreplach essen vert oich nimis.
One gets tired of eating only kreplach.

689

Krich nit tsu hoich, vestu nit darfen falen.
Don't climb too high and you won't have to fall.

690

Laig nit op oif morgen vos du kenst heint bazorgen.
Don't put off till tomorrow what you can do today.

691

Laig zich nit mit a gezunter kop in a kranken bet.
Don't lie down with a healthy head in a sick bed.

692

Leichteh libes, shvereh shodens.
Easy loves, heavy damages.

693

Lei'en darf men mit aides, geben zol men on aides.
Lending should be done with witnesses; giving, without witnesses.

694

Libeh iz vi puter, s'iz gut mit broit.
Love is like butter, it's good with bread.

695

Libeh un hunger voinen nit in ainem.
Love and hunger don't dwell together..

696

Loif nit noch dem koved, vet er alain tsu dir kumen.
Honors will come to you by themselves if you don't run after them.

697

Loshen horeh iz di ergsteh mideh un gresteh tsoreh.
Gossiping is the worst habit and the biggest calumny.

698

Loz zein an ergerer, abi an anderer.
Let it be worse, as long as it's a change.

699

Men farshpetikt nit chasseneh hoben un shtarben.
Marrying and dying are two things for which one is never late.

700

Man un veib zeinen ain leib.
Husband and wife are like one flesh.

701

Mazel un chain koift men nit in kremel.
Luck and charm cannot be purchased in a store.

702

Me darf nit zein shain, nor chainevdik.
You don't have to be pretty if you are charming.

703

Me ken dem barg mit a shpendel nit avektrogen.
A mountain cannot be moved with a splinter.

704

Me darf leben un lozen leben.
Live and let live.

705

Me ken dem yam mit a kendel nit ois'shepen.
The ocean cannot be emptied with a can.

706

Me ken nit foren oif alleh yariden oif ain mol.
You can't ride in all directions at one time.

707

Me ken nit iberloifen di levoneh.
You can't outrun the moon.

708

Me ken nit tantsen oif tsvai chassenes oif ain mol.
You can't dance at two weddings at the same time!

709

Me lernt zich biz zibetsik un shtarben shtarbt men a nar.
Man learns till seventy but still dies an ignoramus.

710

Me tor nit veizen a nar halbeh arbet.
You don't show a fool a job half-done.

711

Me zogt: a nar hot lib ziseh zachen—dos hoben klugeh oisgetracht.
The saying that fools like sweets is an invention of smart people.

712

Me zol nit darfen onkumen tsu kinder.
Pray that you may not be a burden to your children.

713

Me zol nit gepruft verren tsu vos me ken gevoint verren.
Pray that you may never have to endure all that you can learn to bear.

714

Melocheh bez deigeh.
To have a trade is to be free of worry.

715

Men bagrist noch di klaider, men baglait nochen saichel.
When you enter you are greeted according to your dress; when you leave, you are bade farewell according to your wisdom.

716

Men iz dir moichel di t'shuveh, nor tu nit di avaireh.
Never mind the remorse, don't commit the sin.

717

Men ken handlen mit trantes un zich klaiden in samet.
You may deal in rags and dress in velvet.

718

Men ken machen dem cholem gresser vi di nacht.
You can make a dream bigger than the night.

719

Mer a chessorin, mer nadan.
More blemish, more dowry.

720

Miesseh maiden lozen zich raiden.
Homely girls let themselves be seduced.

721

Mit a barsht un a nodel bahalt men dem dales.
With a brush and a needle poverty can be covered up.

722

Mit a foilen shteken ken men nit aroistreiben dem dales.
With a lazy stick you cannot chase away want.

723

Mit a groissen roifeh gait a groisser malech.
A great doctor is accompanied by a great angel.

724

Mit a guten gast frait men zich ven er kumt arein; mit a shlechten gast, ven er gait avek.
With a good guest, you are happy when he arrives; with a bad one, when he leaves.

725

Mit a krechtz batsolt men nit a choiv.
You cannot pay a debt with a sigh.

726

Mit a meisseh un mit a ligen ken men nor kinder farvigen.
With a fairy tale and with a lie you can lull only children to sleep.

727

Mit a nar tor men nit handlen.
With a fool you have no right to do business.

728

Mit a yid iz gut kugel essen, ober nit af ain teller.
It's good to eat pudding with a Jew, but not from one plate.

729

Mit ain hant shtroft Got un mit der anderer bentsht er.
With one hand God punishes and with the other he blesses.

730

A ligner glaibt kainmol nit.
A liar never believes anyone else.

731

A shveigendiker nar is a halber chochem.
A quiet fool is half a sage.

732

Bei nacht zeinen alleh ki shvartz.
At night all cows are black.

733

Nitzochen farshikert on vein.
Success intoxicates without wine.

734

Zingen ken ich nit, ober a maivin bin ich.
I can't sing, but I'm an expert on it.

735

Onkuken kost kain gelt.
It costs nothing to look.

736

Tachrichim mach men on keshenes.
Shrouds are made without pockets.

737

Ven di bobbeh volt gehat a bord, volt zi geven a zaideh.
If your grandmother had a beard, she'd be your grandfather.

738

Vos toig dir der chaner cholem, ven der frimorgen iz kalt?
What's the use of a beautiful dream, if the dawn is chilly?

739

Mit alleh meiles iz nito.
Nothing is perfect.

740

Mit di yoren verren shvacher di tsain un der zikoren.
As the years go by, the teeth and the memory grow weaker.

741

Mit emess kumt men far Got.
With truth man reaches God.

742

Mit fremdeh hent iz gut fei'er tsu sharren.
It's good to poke the fire with somebody else's hands.

743

Mit fremden saichel ken men nit leben.
With another's common sense one cannot live.

744

Mit geduld shept men ois a k'val.
With patience you can drain a brook.

745

Mit geduld boi'ert men durch afileh a kizelshtain.
With patience you can even bore through granite.

746

Mit gelt ken men alles.
Money can do everything.

747

Mit gelt tor men nit stolzieren, veil me ken es gleich farlieren.
Don't boast of your money because you can easily lose it.

748

Mit Got tor men zich nit shpilen. Ershtens, tor men nit, un tsvaitens, lozt er nit.
You don't play around with God! First, it's not allowed and second, He won't let you.

749

Mit honik ken men chapen mer fligen vi mit essik.
With honey you can catch more flies than with vinegar.

750

Mit ligen kumt men veit, ober nit tsurik.
With lies you will go far, but not back again.

751

Mit mazel ken men alles.
With luck, everything is possible.

752

Mit rugzeh fort men nit veit.
With anger you don't get too far.

753

Mit shnai ken men nit machen gomolkes.
You can't make cheesecakes out of snow.

754

Mit toireh vert men in ergets nit farfalen.
With knowledge you are nowhere lost.

755

Mit vos far an oig men kukt oif ainem, aza ponem hot er.
The way you look at a man so he appears to you.

756

Mit zabonges chapt men faigelech un mit matones—maidelech.
With nets you catch birds and with presents—girls.

757

Mit z'chus-oves batsolt men nit kain choives.
You cannot pay a debt with a noble pedigree.

758

Miten malach hamovess treibt men nit kain katovess.
You can't jest with the Angel of Death.

759

Naches fun kinder iz tei'erer fun gelt.
Pride in children is more precious than money.

760

Nadan kenen elteren geben, ober nit kain mazel.
Parents can give a dowry but not luck.

761

Naronim un kropeveh vaksen on regen.
Fools and weeds grow without rain.

762

Nein rabonim kenen kain minyen nit machen ober tsen shusters yoh.
Nine rabbis cannot make a quorum but ten shoemakers can.

763

Nisht azoi gich macht zich vi es tracht zich.
Things are not as quickly achieved as conceived.

764

Nisht alleh tsores kumen fun himmel.
Not all troubles come from heaven.

765

Nit als vos glanst iz gold.
All that glitters is not gold.

766

Nit der reicher tsolt; der erlecher tsolt.
Not the rich who pay; the honest pay.

767

Nit der shteken helft, nor der guter vort.
It's not the stick that helps but the kind word.

768

Nit dos iz shain vos iz shain, nor dos vos gefelt.
Not that which is beautiful but that which pleases is beautiful.

769

Nit far klugeh iz gelt, nit far shaineh iz klaider.
Not the wise have money, not the beautiful have (nice) clothes.

770

Nit fun a shaineh tsurkeh vert a guteh veib.
A pretty face doesn't make for a good wife.

771

Nit in z'chus-oves, nit in yerusheh—in zich zuch kedusheh.
*Not in the merit of ancestors, nor in inheritance—in yourself
you search for holiness.*

772

Nit itlecher vos zitst oiben-on iz a pan.
Not all who sit at the head-table are aristocrats.

773

Nit kain entfer iz oich an entfer.
No answer is also an answer.

774

Nit kain groisser chochem, nit kain klainer nar.
He's no great sage and no small fool.

775

Nit mit shelten un nit mit lachen ken men di velt ibermachen.
Neither with curses nor with laughter can you change the world.

776

Nit af alleh mol shlecht, un nit af alleh mol gut.
Things can't be bad all the time, nor good all the time.

777

Nit yeden mesles treft zich a nes.
Miracles don't happen every day.

778

Nit yeder hartz vos lacht iz frailech.
Not every heart that laughs is really cheerful.

779

Nit yeder iz tsufriden mit zein ponem, ober mit zein saichel iz yeder tsufriden.
Not everybody is content with his looks, but everyone is content with his brains.

780

Nit yederer oif vemen hunt bilen iz a ganev.
Not everyone the dogs bark at is a thief.

781

Noch dem oreman shlept zich der shlimazel.
Bad fortune follows the poor man.

782

Noch di chupeh iz shpet di charoteh.
After the wedding it's too late to have regrets.

783

Nochen toit vert men choshev.
After death one becomes important.

784

Nor bei zein aigenem tish ken men zat verren.
Only at your own table can you be sated.

785

Nor in cholem zeinen meren vi beren.
Only in dreams are the carrots as big as bears.

786

Nor naronim farlozen zich oif nisim.
Only fools rely on miracles.

787

Noit brecht eizen.
Necessity breaks iron.

788

Oder es helft nit oder men darf es nit.
Either it doesn't help or it isn't needed.

789

Oder gor oder gornit.
All or nothing.

790

Oib der shuch past, kenst im trogen.
If the shoe fits, wear it.

791

Oib di velt vet verren oisgelaizt, iz es nor in z'chus fun kinder.
If the world will ever be redeemed, it will be only through the merit of children.

792

Oib zein vort volt gedint als brik, volt men moireh hoben aribergain.
Were his word a bridge, it would be risky to pass over it.

793

Oif a meisseh fregt men kain kasheh nit.
Don't ask questions about fairy tales.

794

Oif a mentshen iz nit kain rachmones; a rachmones iz oif nit a mentshen.
A man is not to be pitied; pitiable is one who is not a man.

795

Oif a fremder bord iz gut zich tsu lernen sheren.

It's good to learn to barber on someone else's beard.

796

Oif a nar iz kain kasheh nit tsu fregen un kain pshat nit tsu zogen.

You should not ask a fool a question nor give him an explanation.

797

Oif a nar tor men nit faribel hoben.

You must not take offense at anything a fool does.

798

Oif shainem iz gut tsu kuken; mit a klugen iz gut tsu leben.

It's good to behold beauty and to live with wisdom.

799

Oif a tserisseneh freintshaft ken men kain lateh nit laigen.
You can't patch up a torn friendship.

800

Oif a vund tor men kain zalts nit shiten.
You mustn't pour salt on a wound.

801

Oif aigeneh kinder iz yederer a blinder.
When it comes to one's own children, then everybody is blind.

802

Oif der shpitz tsung ligt di gantseh velt.
On the tip of the tongue, lies the fate of the entire world.

803

Oif der tir fun derfolg iz ongeshriben "shtup" un "tsi."
The door of success is marked "push" and "pull."

804

Oif fremder erd boit men nit.
One doesn't build on foreign ground.

805

Oif gelt shtait di velt.
The world stands on money.

806

Oif Got tor men kain kasheh nit fregen.
Trust in God.

807

Oif itlechen terets ken men gefinen a nei'eh kasheh.
To every answer you can find a new question.

808

Oif mist iz geroten korn.
Corn can grow on manure.

809

Oif morgen zol Got zorgen.
Let God worry about tomorrow.

810

Oif nisim tor men zich nit farlozen.
Don't depend on miracles.

811

Oif drei zachen shtait di velt: oif gelt, oif gelt, un oif gelt.
The world stands on three things: money, money, and money.

812

Oifen balken ken kain korn nit geroten.
You can't grow corn on the ceiling.

813

Oif tsedokeh iz oich do chazokeh.
Charity is also a habit.

814

Oif vemens vogen me zitst, zingt men dem lied.
People always sing the tune that pleases their host (or bene-factor).

815

Oif "volt ich" un "zolt ich," borgt men nit kain gelt.
No one lends money on "I could have" and "I should have."

816

Oif yenems simchah hot men a guten appetit.
At other people's parties one eats heartily.

817

Oif zeineh raid ken men nit boien kain binyen.
On his words no building could be built.

818

Oifen goniff brent dos hittel.
A guilty man is always self-conscious.

819

Oifen goniff in a tsilinder brent nit dos hittel.
A thief with connections is not self-conscious.

820
Oif nichteren mogen ken men kain zach nit fartrogen.
An empty stomach cannot tolerate anything.

821
Oisbrukirt mit tsores iz der veg tsum bais-hakvores.
The road to the cemetery is paved with suffering.

822
On gelt iz kain velt.
Without money, it is no world (to live in).

823
On a teretz iz gor kain derech-eretz.
Without an excuse there's no respect.

824
On a tsung iz vi on a glok.
Without a tongue is like without a bell.

825
On mazel toig gor nit.
Without luck, nothing will succeed.

826
On mo'es iz tomid a to'es.
Being without money is always a mistake.

827

Orem iz nit kain shandeh, abi nit shmarkateh.
Poverty is no disgrace, just so it isn't filthy.

828

Orem iz nit kain shand, ober oich kain groisser koved nit.
Poverty is no disgrace, but also no great honor.

829

Parnosseh iz a refueh tsu alleh krenk.
A good livelihood is a cure for all ills.

830

Patsh zich nit in beicheleh, ven fisheleh iz noch in teicheleh.
Don't rub your belly when the little fish is still in the pond.

831

Protsent fun kinder iz tei'erer vi protsent fun gelt.
Dividends from children is more precious than from money.

832

Purim iz kain yontev nit un kadoches iz nit kain krenk.
Purim is no holy day and fever is no disease.

833

Rachmones hot raineh kavones.
Pity has pure intentions.

834

Red besser vegen zich guts vider vegen dem andern shlechts.
It's better to praise yourself than to disparage others.

835

Reden iz gut, shveigen noch besser.
Speech is good, silence even better.

836

Reden iz shver un shveigen ken men nit.
Speech is difficult, but silence is impossible.

837

Reden iz zilber, shveigen iz gold.
Speech is silver, silence is golden.

838

Reboineh-shel-oilem, haib mich nit uf, varf mich nit arop.
Father in heaven, don't raise me up, don't cast me down.

839

Reboineh-shel-oilem: kuk arop fun dem himmel un kuk dir on dein velt.
Father in heaven, look down from heaven and see your world.

840

Rov oder beder, alleh hoben soinem.
Whether a rabbi or a bath-house keeper, all have enemies.

841

Saichel iz an aideleh zach.
Wisdom is a precious thing.

842

Saichel krigt men nisht oif di berzeh.
Wisdom can't be purchased in the market.

843

Shabbes hot der rosheh in gehenem oich ru.
On the Sabbath even the wicked in hell have rest.

844

Shaineh shveigen iz shener vi shain reden.
Dignified silence is better than dignified speech.

845

Shlimazel, vohin gaist du? Tsum oreman!
Bad fortune, where goest thou? To the poor man!

846

Shpeiz kocht men in top un koved krigt der teller.
The food is cooked in a pot and the plate gets the honor.

847

Shpilt tsu di shoh, iz kain zind nito.
If done at the right time, it is not a sin.

848

Shpor, shpor; kumt der shvartz yor un nemt tsu gor!
Save, save; comes the evil year and takes it all away!

849

Shrei'en helft nit, ober a shteken helft.
Scolding won't help, but the stick would.

850

Shtarben un chasseneh hoben farshpetigt men nit.
It's never too late to die or get married.

851

Shtil vasser grobt tif.
Still waters run deep.

852

Shveigen haist geret.
Silence gives consent.

853

S'iz shlecht tsu essen fremden broit.
It's hard to eat a stranger's bread.

854

Tinken haist nit trinken.
Dipping isn't drinking.

855
Tint trikent shnell ois; treren nisht.
Ink dries quickly; tears don't.

856
Toireh iz di besteh s'choireh.
Knowledge of the Scriptures is the best wares.

857
Toireh kumt nit b'yerusheh.
Learning cannot be inherited.

858
Tsedokeh zol kain gelt nit kosten un g'milas-chassodim zolen
kain agmas-nefesh nit farshafen, volten geven di velt fil
tsadikim.
*If one could do charity without money and favors without
aggravation, the world would be full of saints.*

859
Tsevishen yidden vert men nit farfalen.
One does not perish among Jews.

860
Tsores mit yoich iz gringer tsu fartrogen vi tsores on yoich.
Worries are easier to bear with soup than without it.

861
Tsores tsezegen di hartz.
Trouble cuts up the heart.

862

Tsores vi holtz, un mit vos eintsuhaitsen dem oiven iz nito.
Troubles (as plenty) as firewood, but you can't heat the oven with them.

863

Tsores vil men nit tsunemen; mitsves ken met nit tsunemen.
Nobody is willing to take away your troubles; nobody can take away your good deeds.

864

Tsores zeinen shtarkeh tropens, es toig nit a sach mit a mol.
Trouble is like strong medicine—too much at a time is harmful.

865

Tsu fil anives iz a halber shtoltz.
Too much modesty is half conceit.

866

Tsu fil essen un trinken in dales zinken.
Too much eating and drinking leads to poverty.

867

Tsu gut iz umgezunt.
Anything in excess is unhealthy.

868

Tsu hoben gelt iz a guteh zach; tsu hoben dai'eh iber di gelt, iz noch besser.
To have money is a good thing; to have a say over the money is even better.

869

Tsu fil koved iz a halbeh shand.
Too much glory is half disgrace.

870

Tsu itlechen nei'em lid ken men tsupassen an alten nigen.
To every new song one can find an old tune.

871

Tsu shain iz amol a chissoren.
Too much of anything is undesirable.

872

Tsulib ton kost tomid tei'er.
Trying to please is always costly.

873

Tsum glik badarf men kain chochmeh nit.
You don't have to be wise to be lucky.

874

Tsum guten vert men bald gevoint.
It doesn't take long to get used to good things.

875

Tsum shlimazel muz men oich mazel hoben.
Even for bad luck one needs luck.

876

Tsum shtain zol men klogen nor nit bei zich zol men trogen.
Better pour out your troubles to a stone, but don't carry them within yourself.

877

Tsum shtarben darf men kain luach nit hoben.
No calendar is needed for dying.

878

Tsuzogen un lib hoben kost nit kain gelt.
It doesn't cost anything to promise and to love.

879

Tsvai falen tsu last: der nar tsevishen klugeh un der kluger tsevishen naronim.
Two are embarrassed: the fool in the company of wise men and the wise man in the company of fools.

880

Tsvai kabtzonim kenen kain ain shabbes nit machen.
Two beggars together cannot afford to prepare for one Sabbath.

881

Tsvai mol a yor iz shlecht dem oreman: zumer un vinter.
Twice a year the poor are badly off: summer and winter.

882

Umglik bindt tsunoif.
Misfortune binds together.

883

Umzist krigt men nor mist.

Only refuse is to be gotten free.

884

Untergenumen haist zich farkoift.

Pledge yourself and you've sold yourself.

885

Vainiker a vort, abi dem emess.

A word less, as long as it's the truth.

886

Varf nit arois di shmutsikeh aider du host di raineh.

Don't throw away the soiled until you have the clean.

887

Veiber hoben nein mos raid.

Women have nine measures of talk.

888

Vellen zein kliger fun alleh iz di gresteh narishkeit.

Trying to outsmart everybody is the greatest folly.

889

Vemen Got vil erkvicken, kenen mentshen nit dershticken.

Whom God wishes to succor, men cannot destroy.

890

Ven a ferd volt gevust vi klain der mentsh iz akegen im, volt er im doires geven.

If a horse knew how small a man is compared to it, it would trample him.

891

Ven a shikker hot nit kain bronfen redt er chotsh fun bronfen.

When a drunkard has no whiskey, he will at least talk of whiskey.

892

Ven a shlimazel koilet a hon, gait er; drait er a zaiger, shtait er!

When a luckless fool kills a rooster, it still hops; when he winds a clock, it stops!

893

Ven a yosem leidt, zet kainer nit; ven er frait zich, zet di gantseh velt.

When an orphan suffers, nobody notices; when he rejoices, the whole world sees it.

894

Ven ain zelner volt gevust vos der anderer tracht, volt kain krig nisht geven.

If one soldier knew what the other thinks, there would be no war.

895

Ven alleh mentshen zollen tsien oif ain zeit, volt zich di velt ibergekert.
If all men pulled in one direction, the world would topple over.

896

Ven der man iz a balagoleh, hot er nit moireh far di veib's kloleh.
When the husband is a coachman, he is not afraid of his wife's curses.

897

Ven der nar volt nit geven mein, volt ich oich gelacht.
If the fool did not belong to me, I would also laugh.

898

Ven di avaireh iz zis, iz nit bitter di t'shuveh.
When the sin is sweet, the repentance is not bitter.

899

Ven di kalleh iz oif der tseit, kuken di mechutonim on a zeit.
When the bride is expecting, the wedding guests look away.

900

Ven di licht iz krum, iz der shoten krum.
When the light is crooked, the shadow is crooked.

901

Ven di maidel iz aidel, iz di veibel a teibel.
When the girl is refined, the wife is a little dove.

902
Ven di katz shloft, tantsen di meiz.
When the cat is asleep, the mice dance around.

903
Ven di oigen ze'en nit, tut nit vai di hartz.
When the eyes don't see, the heart doesn't ache.

904
Ven di veib trogt di hoizen, vasht der man di spodnitzen.
When the wife wears the pants, the husband washes the floor.

905
Ven di veib vil, az der man zol zein in shtub, redt zi vainiker
un gist vasser mer.
*When the wife wants the husband to stay at home, she talks
less and cleans more.*

906
Ven dos hartz iz bitter, helft nit kain tsuker.
When the heart is bitter, sugar won't help.

907
Ven dos mazel kumt, shtel im a shtul.
If fortune calls, offer him a seat.

908
Ven es felt puter tsu broit, iz es noch nit kain noit.
When you lack butter for the bread, it is not yet poverty.

909
Ven es flit arein der hunger durch der tir, flit arois di libeh durchen fenster.
When hunger slips in through the door, love flies out through the window.

910
Ven es gait gleich, vert men reich.
When things go right, you become rich.

911
Ven es vakst der teister, vaksen di baderftikaiten.
As the wallet grows, so do the needs.

912
Ven es zol helfen Got betten, volt men shoin tsugedungen mentshen.
If it would help to pray to God, then people would be hiring others to pray for them.

913

Ven frait zich a hoiker? Ven er zet a gresseren hoiker far zich.
When does a hunchback rejoice? When he sees one with a larger hump.

914

Ven frait zich an oreman? Ven er farlirt un gefint.
When does a poor man rejoice? When he has lost something and found it again.

915

Ven frait zich Got? Az an oreman gefint a metsieh un git es op.
When does God rejoice? When a poor man finds a treasure and returns it.

916

Ven hungert a nogid? Ven der doktor haist im!
When does a wealthy man go hungry? When the doctor orders him.

917

Ven me lacht ze'en alleh; ven me vaint zet kainer nisht.
When you laugh, all see; when you cry, no one sees.

918

Ven me zol Got danken far guts, volt nit zein kain tseit tsu baklogen zich oif shlechts.
If we thanked God for the good things, there wouldn't be time to weep over the bad.

919

Ven men darf hoben moi'ach, helft nit kain koi'ach.
When brains are needed, brawn won't help.

920

Ven men fort arois vaist men, ven men kumt tsurik vaist men nit.
We know when we start out; when we'll return, we know not.

921

Ven men hot an ainikel, hot men tsvai kinder.
When you have a grandchild, you have two children.

922

Ven men lebt fun der pushkeh iz laidik di kishkeh.
When one lives out of the alms box, his stomach remains empty.

923

Ven nit di moireh, volt geven zis di avaireh.
If not for the fear of punishment, it would be sweet to sin.

924

Ven nit di shaineh maidlech, volt men gehat dem yaitzer-horeh in der'erd.
If not for pretty girls, temptation would be unheeded.

925

Ven nit di shein, volt kain shoten nit geven.
If not for the light, there would be no shadow.

926

Ven s'farleshen zich di licht, haiben on tantsen di meiz.
When the lights go out, the mice begin to dance.

927

Ven tsores laigt zich nit oifen ponem, laigt zich es oifen hartsen.
When distress doesn't show on the face, it lies on the heart.

928

Ven tsu a krenk iz do a refueh, iz dos a halbeh krenk.
When there's a remedy for an ailment, it's only half an ailment.

929

Ven tsvai shpilen, muz ainer gevinen un ainer farliren.
When two play a game, there must be a winner and a loser.

930

Ver es darf hengen vert nisht dertrunken.
He who is destined to hang won't drown.

931

Ver es hot di hak, git dem k'nak.
He who has the ax gives the whacks.

932

Ver es hot di matbai'eh, der hot di dai'eh.
He who has the money has the authority.

933

Ver es hot gegeben tsain, der vet geben broit.
He who has given teeth, will give bread.

934

Ver es hot gelt hot di gantseh velt!
He who has money has the whole world!

935

Ver es hot lib di melocheh iz im leicht di melocheh.
He who likes his work, to him work comes easy.

936

Ver es kon kain pulver nit shmeken, der zol in der malchumeh
nit gai'en!
*He who cannot stand the smell of gunpowder should not engage
in war!*

937

Ver es lacht fun an oreman, der vet veren oif gelechter.
He who laughs at the poor will become the butt of others' jokes.

938

Ver es poret zich mit staleh, shmirt zich ein di hent.
If you deal with tar, expect your hands to get dirty.

939

Ver es toig nit far zich, der toig nit far yenem.
He who is no good to himself is no good to another.

940

Ver es varft oif yenem shtainer krigt tsurik in di aigeneh bainer.

He who throws stones on another gets them back on his own bones.

941

Ver es vert umzist baroiges, vert umzist vider gut.

He who becomes angry for no reason becomes friendly again for no reason.

942

Ver shemt zich fun zeineh mishpocheh, oif dem iz kain brocheh.

Whoever is ashamed of his family will have no luck.

943

Verem essen toiterhait un deiges lebedikerhait.

Worms eat you up when dead and worries eat you up alive.

944

Verter muz men vegen un nit tsailen.

Words must be weighed and not counted.

945

Vest vellen zich oisfeinen far leit, vestu shtarben far der tseit.

If you want to please everybody, you'll die before your time.

946

Vi ainer iz tsu ziben, azoi iz er tsu zibetsik.

As one is at seven, so is he at seventy.

947

Vi dem klugen iz bitter iz der nar alts frailech.
What a wise man bewails, makes the fool happy.

948

Vi me bet zich ois, azoi darf men shlofen.
As you make your bed, so will you sleep in it.

949

Vi men iz gevoint oif der yugend, azoi tut men oif der elter.
That which is practiced in youth will be pursued in old age.

950

Vi zaif faren guf iz a trer far di neshomeh.
Like soap for the body, so are tears for the soul.

951

Vibald du farshtaist dein narishkeit, bistu a kluger!
As long as you understand your foolishness, you are smart!

952

Vildeh grozen vaksen iber nacht.
Crabgrass grows overnight.

953

Voil iz dem vos hot nit kain gelt tsu borgen zeineh freint; er shaft zich nit kain soinim.
He is well off who has no money to lend to friends; he doesn't create enemies.

954

Voil tsu dem mentshen vos baglikt oif der elter.
Fortunate is the man who has a happy old age.

955

Volt der mentsh nor azoi fil vert geven, vi Got ken helfen.
If only man would deserve as much as God can help.

956

Vos a kind zol nit der'raiden, vet di muter im farshtain.
Whatever a child babbles, its mother will understand.

957

Vos a nar kon kalyeh machen, konen tsen chachomim nit
farrichten.
What a fool can spoil, ten wise men cannot repair.

958

Vos a toiber derhert nit, dos tracht er zich ois.
What a deaf man doesn't hear, he imagines.

959

Vos bei a nichteren oif dem lung, iz beim shikker oif der
tsung.
What a sober man thinks, a drunkard speaks.

960

Vos der mentsh ken alts ibertrachten, ken der ergster soineh im nit vintshen.
What a man thinks up for himself, his worst enemy couldn't wish for him.

961

Vos di oig zet nit, di hartz fielt nit.
What the eye doesn't see, the heart doesn't feel.

962

Vos Got tut basheren, ken kain mentsh nit farveren.
What God decrees, man cannot prevent.

963

Vos Got tut, iz mistomeh gut.
What God does is probably for the best.

964

Vos iz billik iz tei'er.
Cheapest is dearest.

965

Vos me hot, vil men nit; un vos me vil, hot men nit.
What one has, one doesn't want; and what one wants, one cannot have.

966

Vos mer gevart, mer genart.
He who hesitates is lost.

967

Vos oif der lung, dos oif der tsung.
What's on his mind, is on his tongue.

968

Vos toig shainkeit on mazel?
What use is beauty without good luck?

969

Vos tsu iz iberik.
Too much is superfluous.

970

Vos tsu iz umgezunt.
Excess is unhealthy.

971

Vos vainiker me ret, iz als gezunter.
The less you talk, the better off you are.

972

Vos vintsiker me fregt, iz als gezunter.
The less you ask, the healthier.

973

Vu honik, dort fligen.
Where there is honey, there flies gather.

974

Vu Toireh, dort iz chochmeh.

Where there is knowledge of the Scriptures, there is wisdom.

975

Vu me darf moyech, helft nit kain koyech.

Where you need intellect, strength will not do.

976

Vu sholom, dort iz brocheh.

Where there is peace, there is blessing.

977

Yedeh hartz hot soides.

Every heart has secrets.

978

Yeden dacht zich az bei yenem lacht zich.

One always thinks that others are happy.

979

Yeder barg-aroif hot zein barg-arop.

Every way up has its way down.

980

Yeder mentsh hot zein peckel.

Every man has his burden.

981

Yeder mentsh hot zein aigeneh meshugass.
Every person has his own idiosyncrasies.

982

Yeder mentsh iz oif zich alain blind.
Every man is blind to his own faults.

983

Yeder mentsh vaist az er vet shtarben, ober kainer vil es nisht
gloiben.
Every man knows he will die but no one wants to believe it.

984

Yeder morgen brengt zich zorgen.
Every day brings forth its own sorrows.

985

Yedeh mutter denkt ir kind iz shain.
Every mother thinks her child is beautiful.

986

Yeder vaist vu se drikt im der shuch.
Everyone knows where his shoe pinches.

987

Zai shtimen vi a katz un a hunt.
They agree like cat and dog.

988

Zicher iz men nor miten toit.
One is certain only of death.

989

Alleh shlosser ken men efenen mit a goldenem shlissel.
All locks can be opened with a golden key.

990

An einredenish iz erger vi a krenk.
An imaginary illness is worse than a real one.

991

As a laib shloft, los im shlofen!
Let sleeping lions lie!

992

Az me est chazzer, zol men essen fetten.
If you're going to eat pork, let it be good and fat.

993

Az me laight zich in klei'en, shlepen di chazzerim.
He who lies in the sty will be eaten by the pigs.

994

Besser dos besteh fun dem ergsten aider dos ergsteh fun dem besten.
Better the best of the worst than the worst of the best.

995

Fil meloches, vainik broches.
Jack of all trades, master of none.

996

Tachrichim macht men on keshenes.
Shrouds are made without pockets.

997

Fun fartrikenteh baimer kumen kain paires nit arois.
No fruit falls from withered trees.

998

Bist a botu'ach, ober shik arein m'zumonim!
I trust you, but send cash!

999

Ain mol iz geven a chochmeh.
A trick is clever only once.

1000

Ain sheitel holtz macht nit varem dem oiven.
A single log doesn't warm the fireplace.

1001

Altsding lozt zich ois mit a gevain.
Everything ends in weeping.